THE NEW CAMBRIDGE SHAKESPEARE

GENERAL EDITOR: Brian Gibbons

ASSOCIATE GENERAL EDITOR: A. R. Braunmuller

From the publication of the first volumes in 1984 the General Editor of the New Cambridge Shakespeare was Philip Brockbank and the Associate General Editors were Brian Gibbons and Robin Hood. From 1990 to 1994 the General Editor was Brian Gibbons and the Associate General Editors were A. R. Braunmuller and Robin Hood.

ALL'S WELL THAT ENDS WELL

For this updated edition, Alexander Leggatt has written a wholly new introduction to Russell Fraser's edition of one of Shakespeare's most puzzling, ambiguous and demanding plays. Leggatt's interest in performance informs his introduction and his account of the instability of the main characters. He offers a full, illustrated and thoughtful account of the play's critical and theatrical fortunes to the end of the twentieth century, and of our experience as an audience of seeing and hearing it performed. An updated reading list completes the edition.

THE NEW CAMBRIDGE SHAKESPEARE

All's Well That Ends Well, edited by Russell Fraser
Antony and Cleopatra, edited by David Bevington
The Comedy of Errors, edited by T. S. Dorsch
Hamlet, edited by Philip Edwards
Julius Caesar, edited by Marvin Spevack
King Edward III, edited by Giorgio Melchiori
The First Part of King Henry IV, edited by Herbert Weil and Judith Weil
The Second Part of King Henry IV, edited by Giorgio Melchiori
King Henry V, edited by Andrew Gurr
The First Part of King Henry VI, edited by Michael Hattaway
The Second Part of King Henry VI, edited by Michael Hattaway
The Third Part of King Henry VI, edited by Michael Hattaway
King Henry VIII, edited by John Margeson
King John, edited by L. A. Beaurline
The Tragedy of King Lear, edited by Jay L. Halio
King Richard II, edited by Andrew Gurr
Macbeth, edited by A. R. Braunmuller
Measure for Measure, edited by Brian Gibbons
The Merchant of Venice, edited by M. M. Mahood
The Merry Wives of Windsor, edited by David Crane
A Midsummer Night's Dream, edited by R. A. Foakes
Much Ado About Nothing, edited by F. H. Mares
Othello, edited by Norman Sanders
Pericles, edited by Doreen DelVecchio and Antony Hammond
The Poems, edited by John Roe
Romeo and Juliet, edited by G. Blakemore Evans
The Sonnets, edited by G. Blakemore Evans
The Taming of the Shrew, edited by Ann Thompson
The Tempest, edited by David Lindley
Titus Andronicus, edited by Alan Hughes
Troilus and Cressida, edited by Anthony B. Dawson
Twelfth Night, edited by Elizabeth Story Donno
The Two Gentlemen of Verona, edited by Kurt Schlueter

THE EARLY QUARTOS
The First Quarto of Hamlet, edited by Kathleen O. Irace
The First Quarto of King Lear, edited by Jay L. Halio
The First Quarto of King Richard III, edited by Peter Davison
The Taming of A Shrew: The 1594 Quarto, edited by Stephen Roy Miller
The First Quarto of King Henry V, edited by Andrew Gurr
The First Quarto of Othello, edited by Scott McMillin

ALL'S WELL THAT ENDS WELL

Updated edition

Edited by
RUSSELL FRASER

Austin Warren Professor of English Language and Literature,
University of Michigan

With an Introduction by
ALEXANDER LEGGATT

University of Toronto

CAMBRIDGE
UNIVERSITY PRESS

PUBLISHED BY THE PRESS SYNDICATE OF THE UNIVERSITY OF CAMBRIDGE
The Pitt Building, Trumpington Street, Cambridge, United Kingdom

CAMBRIDGE UNIVERSITY PRESS
The Edinburgh Building, Cambridge CB2 2RU, UK
40 West 20th Street, New York, NY 10011–4211, USA
477 Williamstown Road, Port Melbourne, VIC 3207, Australia
Ruiz de Alarcón 13, 28014 Madrid, Spain
Dock House, The Waterfront, Cape Town 8001, South Africa

http://www.cambridge.org

First published 1985
Reprinted 1989, 1996, 1998, 2000
Updated edition 2003

Printed in the United Kingdom at the University Press, Cambridge

Library of Congress catalogue card number: 85–4167

British Library Cataloguing in Publication data
Shakespeare, William
All's well that ends well. – (New Cambridge Shakespeare)
I. Title   II. Fraser, Russell
822.3′3   PR2801.A2

ISBN 0 521 82793 0 hardback
ISBN 0 521 53515 8 paperback

UP

For MARY AND RALPH GESUALDI

CONTENTS

ILLUSTRATIONS

PREFACE TO FIRST EDITION

This edition draws on the labour of most of Shakespeare's editors who have preceded me, beginning with Rowe in 1709. Sir Arthur Quiller-Couch and John Dover Wilson, who began *The New Shakespeare* in 1921, are conspicuous among these predecessors. The *New Cambridge Shakespeare* in which the present volume appears does not depend on their work, and is a completely new edition. Shakespeare's critics, beginning with Meres in 1598 and coming down to the present, are represented in this edition as their critical comments seem pertinent. I have often had G. K. Hunter's work in mind, and his Arden edition (1959) deserves special mention. No particular school or point of view gets primacy, however.

I have had the good fortune of being able to depend on the extraordinary resources of the University of Michigan libraries, and I am grateful for this. The Rackham School of the University and my own department helped me financially, not least by enabling me to engage Brian Foley as my assistant. He did all the typing, checked all the collations, and his help in these and other ways has been indispensable throughout.

R. F.

University of Michigan

ix

ABBREVIATIONS AND CONVENTIONS

Shakespeare's plays, when cited in this edition, are abbreviated in a style modified slightly from that used in the *Harvard Concordance to Shakespeare*. Other editions of Shakespeare are abbreviated under the editor's surname (Evans, Hunter) unless they are the work of more than one editor. In such cases, an abbreviated series name is used (NS, Var. 78). When more than one edition by the same editor is cited, later editions are discriminated with a raised figure (Rowe³). References to Abbott's *Shakespearian Grammar* are to paragraph numbers. All quotations from Shakespeare, except those from *All's Well*, use the text and lineation of *The Riverside Shakespeare*, under the general editorship of G. Blakemore Evans.

1. Shakespeare's plays

Ado	*Much Ado about Nothing*
Ant.	*Antony and Cleopatra*
AWW	*All's Well That Ends Well*
AYLI	*As You Like It*
Cor.	*Coriolanus*
Cym.	*Cymbeline*
Err.	*The Comedy of Errors*
Ham.	*Hamlet*
1H4	*The First Part of King Henry the Fourth*
2H4	*The Second Part of King Henry the Fourth*
H5	*King Henry the Fifth*
1H6	*The First Part of King Henry the Sixth*
2H6	*The Second Part of King Henry the Sixth*
3H6	*The Third Part of King Henry the Sixth*
H8	*King Henry the Eighth*
JC	*Julius Caesar*
John	*King John*
LLL	*Love's Labour's Lost*
Lear	*King Lear*
Mac.	*Macbeth*
MM	*Measure for Measure*
MND	*A Midsummer Night's Dream*
MV	*The Merchant of Venice*
Oth.	*Othello*
Per.	*Pericles*
R2	*King Richard the Second*
R3	*King Richard the Third*
Rom.	*Romeo and Juliet*
Shr.	*The Taming of the Shrew*
STM	*Sir Thomas More*
Temp.	*The Tempest*
TGV	*The Two Gentlemen of Verona*

Tim.	*Timon of Athens*
Tit.	*Titus Andronicus*
TN	*Twelfth Night*
TNK	*The Two Noble Kinsmen*
Tro.	*Troilus and Cressida*
Wiv.	*The Merry Wives of Windsor*
WT	*The Winter's Tale*

2. Other works cited and general references

Abbott	E. A. Abbott, *A Shakespearian Grammar*, 1869, reprinted 1966
Addis	John Addis, '*All's Well That Ends Well*', *N&Q* 10 (1866), 446
Alexander	Peter Alexander (ed.), *Works*, 1951
Brigstocke	W. Osborne Brigstocke (ed.), *All's Well That Ends Well* (Arden Shakespeare), 1904
Cam.	William George Clark, J. Glover and William Aldis Wright (eds.), *Works* (Cambridge Shakespeare), 1863–6
Capell	Edward Capell (ed.), *Works*, 1768
Case	Arthur E. Case (ed.), *All's Well That Ends Well* (Yale Shakespeare), 1926
Collier	John P. Collier (ed.), *Works*, 1842–4
Collier MS.	in Perkins's Second Folio, 1632 (Huntington Library)
conj.	conjecture
CQ	*Critical Quarterly*
Craig	W. J. Craig (ed.), *Works*, 1891
Daniel	Peter A. Daniel, *Notes and Conjectural Emendations of Certain Doubtful Passages in Shakespeare's Plays*, 1870
Delius	Nicholaus Delius (ed.), *Works*, 1854–60
Dyce	Alexander Dyce (ed.), *Works*, 1857
Dyce²	Alexander Dyce (ed.), *Works*, 1864
E&S	*Essays and Studies*
EIC	*Essays in Criticism*
EIT	*Essays in Theatre*
ELH	*ELH: A Journal of English Literary History*
Evans	G. Blakemore Evans (ed.), *The Riverside Shakespeare*, 1974
F	*Mr William Shakespeares Comedies, Histories, and Tragedies*, 1623 (First Folio)
F2	*Mr William Shakespeares Comedies, Histories, and Tragedies*, 1632 (Second Folio)
F3	*Mr William Shakespeares Comedies, Histories, and Tragedies*, 1664 (Third Folio)
F4	*Mr William Shakespeares Comedies, Histories, and Tragedies*, 1685 (Fourth Folio)
Globe	William George Clark and William Aldis Wright (eds.), *Works* (Globe Shakespeare), 1864
Glover	John Glover (*see* Case, *above*)
Hanmer	Thomas Hanmer (ed.), *Works*, 1743–4
Harrison	G. B. Harrison (ed.), *Works* (Penguin Shakespeare), 1937–56
Heath	Benjamin Heath, *A Revisal of Shakespeare's Text*, 1765
HLQ	*Huntington Library Quarterly*

Hunter	G. K. Hunter (ed.), *All's Well That Ends Well* (Arden Shakespeare), 1959
JEGP	*Journal of English and Germanic Philology*
Johnson	Samuel Johnson (ed.), *Works*, 1765
Kittredge	George L. Kittredge (ed.), *Works*, 1936
Knight	Charles Knight (ed.), *Works*, 1838–43
Lowes	John L. Lowes (ed.), *All's Well That Ends Well* (Tudor Shakespeare), 1912
Malone	Edmond Malone (ed.), *Works*, 1790
MLQ	*Modern Language Quarterly*
N&Q	*Notes and Queries*
Neilson	William A. Neilson (ed.), *Works*, 1906
NS	John Dover Wilson and Arthur Quiller-Couch (eds.), *All's Well That Ends Well* (New Shakespeare), 1929
OED	*Oxford English Dictionary*, 1884–1928
Onions	C. T. Onions, *Shakespeare Glossary*, 1911
PMLA	*Publications of the Modern Language Association*
Pope	Alexander Pope (ed.), *Works*, 1723–5
Pope²	Alexander Pope (ed.), *Works*, 1728
PQ	*Philological Quarterly*
Rann	Joseph Rann (ed.), *Works*, 1786–94
RES	*Review of English Studies*
Riverside	See Evans, *above*
Rowe	Nicholas Rowe (ed.), *Works*, 1709
Rowe²	Nicholas Rowe (ed.), *Works*, 1709
Rowe³	Nicholas Rowe (ed.), *Works*, 1714
RQ	*Renaissance Quarterly*
SB	*Studies in Bibliography*
SD	stage direction
SEL	*Studies in English Literature*
SH	speech heading
Singer	S. W. Singer (ed.), *Works*, 1826
Singer²	S. W. Singer (ed.), *Works*, 1856
Sisson	Charles Sisson (ed.), *Works*, 1953
SP	*Studies in Philology*
SQ	*Shakespeare Quarterly*
S.Sur.	*Shakespeare Survey*
Staunton	Howard Staunton (ed.), *Works*, 1858–60
subst.	substantively
Tannenbaum	S. A. Tannenbaum, 'Removing a scar from *All's Well* (IV.ii.38–39)', *Shakespeare Association Bulletin* 18 (1943), 133–6
Theobald	Lewis Theobald (ed.), *Works*, 1733
Theobald²	Lewis Theobald (ed.), *Works*, 1740
Thirlby	Dr Styan Thirlby (see John Nichols, *Illustrations of the Literary History of the Eighteenth Century*, 8 vols., 1817–58, pp. 189–647)
Thiselton	A. E. Thiselton, *Some Textual Notes on All's Well That Ends Well*, 1900
TLS	*Times Literary Supplement*
TSLL	*Texas Studies in Language and Literature*
Tyrwhitt	Thomas Tyrwhitt, *Observations and Conjectures upon Some Passages of Shakespeare*, 1766

UTQ	*University of Toronto Quarterly*
Var. 73	Samuel Johnson and George Steevens (eds.), *Works*, 1733
Var. 78	Samuel Johnson and George Steevens (eds.), *Works*, 1778
Var. 93	George Steevens and Isaac Reed (eds.), *Works*, 1793
Walker, W. S.	William S. Walker, *A Critical Examination of the Text of Shakespeare*, 1860
Warburton	William Warburton (ed.), *Works*, 1747
White	Richard Grant White (ed.), *Works*, 1857

All quotations from the Bible are taken from the Geneva version, 1560.

INTRODUCTION

Sources and traditions

Shakespeare's principal source for *All's Well That Ends Well* was the story of Giletta of Narbon, the ninth tale of the third day of Boccaccio's *Decameron*. Though he may have consulted the French version by Antoine le Maçon, Shakespeare is most likely to have used the English version in William Painter's *The Palace of Pleasure* (1595).[1] Giletta is the daughter of a physician who belongs to the household of the Count of Rossillion. She spends her childhood in the company of the Count's son Beltramo, and falls in love with him 'more than was meet for a maiden of her age' (p. 389). When on his father's death Beltramo goes to Paris, Giletta is determined to follow him, but being 'rich and fatherless' (p. 389) and surrounded by kinsfolk who keep foisting prospective husbands on her, she is at first at a loss about how to get away. Learning that the King of France has 'a swelling upon his breast, which by reason of ill cure was grown to be a fistula' (p. 390), she takes this as an excuse to visit Paris, with a herbal cure devised by her father. The King, after some initial scepticism, decides 'This woman peradventure is sent unto me of God' (p. 390), and puts himself in her hands. The price she specifies is a husband of her own choosing, and having cured the King she names Beltramo. Beltramo, 'knowing her not to be of a stock convenable to his nobility' (p. 391), refuses her. The King will not break his promise to Giletta, and insists on the marriage, 'for the maiden is fair and wise, and loveth you most entirely' (p. 391). Beltramo goes through the ceremony, but instead of consummating the marriage runs off to join the Florentine army at war in Tuscany. Giletta returns to Rossillion, where she wins the love of the Count's subjects by her effective management of his estate, which had fallen into disorder.

Beltramo sends a message declaring that he refuses to live with Giletta unless she can get a ring, which he guards carefully 'for a certain virtue that he knew it had' (p. 392), off his finger, and produce a son of his begetting. Giletta takes this as a challenge, and having 'assembled the noblest and chiefest of her country' (p. 392) announces she is going on a pilgrimage. Instead she journeys to Florence, where she finds that Beltramo, who enjoys the reputation of 'a courteous knight, and well beloved in the city' (p. 393), is paying court to a young impoverished gentlewoman. She tells her story to the gentlewoman's mother, and arranges that the gentlewoman will demand the ring as an assurance of Beltramo's love; on receiving it she will agree to go to bed with him. Giletta gets the ring, and takes the gentlewoman's place in bed. On

---

[1] On le Maçon, see Howard C. Cole, *The All's Well Story from Boccaccio to Shakespeare*, 1981, pp. 86–7. Painter's version is conveniently reprinted in Geoffrey Bullough (ed.), *Narrative and Dramatic Sources of Shakespeare* 2, 1968. Quotations from Painter are from Bullough, modernized.

the first encounter she conceives twin boys. Several other encounters follow, and once she is sure she is pregnant Giletta rewards the gentlewoman with a dowry of five hundred pounds, five times what her mother asked for. After she has given birth, she confronts the Count at a great feast, falling weeping at his feet and declaring, 'I am thy poor unfortunate wife' (p. 396). She then presents the ring and the twins, proving she has fulfilled his conditions. Yielding to pressure from his subjects and the ladies of his court, Beltramo accepts her, 'to the great pleasure and contentation of those that were there, and of all his other friends', and 'from that time forth he loved and honoured her as his dear spouse and wife' (p. 396).

Boccaccio's tale is one of problem-solving, of challenges overcome by determination and ingenuity. So is Shakespeare's. But while Boccaccio's characters have the basic feelings required to motivate the story, and no more, Shakespeare's are more rounded and complex, and elicit a less straightforward response. To the class pride of Beltramo Shakespeare adds in Bertram a realistic callowness and immaturity. While in Boccaccio's denouement Beltramo, who is giving the feast that forms its setting, has one thing to do – hear his wife's story and graciously accept its conclusion – Bertram, more culprit than authority figure in the last scene, is trapped, squirming, in a series of lies and evasions before the appearance of Helena rescues him. His final acceptance of her is hedged about with 'if' clauses, and Boccaccio's happy-ever-after ending is replaced by the King's cautious 'All yet seems well' (5.3.322). Giletta is a public figure, rich and well connected, a conspicuous success as a manager of her absent husband's estate. Helena is poor, withdrawn, a loner with a quality of hiddenness. The sympathy she draws is not from a large community, but from individuals who meet her one on one – the Countess, Lafew (both characters are Shakespeare's inventions) and the King. Once Giletta is married the narrator calls her the Countess; we seldom think of Helena that way. It is characteristic of Helena's hidden quality that while Giletta produces twin boys Helena's child at the end of the play is still unborn. And while Giletta follows a straight narrative line to the fulfilment of her purpose, encountering only one major bump on the road (Beltramo's refusal), Helena, while following the same line, has more local setbacks to overcome, and feelings that are more tentative and conflicted. Shakespeare compresses the bed-trick, reducing the several encounters to one, which produces only one child. Elsewhere he expands: Parolles is added as Bertram's companion (and, some characters claim, his misleader) and develops a story of his own. Boccaccio's background of nameless subjects and kinsfolk becomes a talkative supporting cast that fills out the social worlds of Rossillion, Paris and Florence. A brisk, straightforward story with minimal characterization has become a rich, complex and difficult play.

While Boccaccio was Shakespeare's principal source, there are other influences and traditions at work. The bed-trick has a long ancestry, appearing in the Bible in Genesis 29, where Jacob thinks he is marrying Rachel and finds her father has substituted her sister Leah. The Amphitryon story, told and re-told through the centuries, concerns a wife who thinks she is sleeping with her husband when she is actually sleeping with Jupiter. In Menander's *Epitrepontes* and Terence's *Hecyra* women are impregnated in anonymous encounters with men who will eventually be their husbands. Marliss C. Desens has counted forty-four plays of Shakespeare's time that use versions of the bed-trick.[1] The device is both a convenient story-telling formula, a way to create a problem and a way to solve it, and a haunting myth that touches on the impersonality of sex and the uncertainty built into the closest of relationships. In using this device Shakespeare is not just borrowing from Boccaccio but tapping into a long tradition.

Russell Fraser has suggested that in the background of the play are some historical characters, including Christine de Pisan (1385?–1430), a 'resourceful feminist' who learned philosophy, language and sciences from her father, a physician and astrologer who tried unsuccessfully to cure the French king Charles V of a fistula. He also sees a 'train of associations' with the ninth-century Burgundian count Girart of Rossillion, who bears Bertram's title, and whose proper name is close to that of Helena's father. In the epic that bears his name, Girart defies Charlemagne, who has chosen a wife for him. Repenting, he builds a church to house the relics of Mary Magdalen, who died at Marseilles (one of the play's settings), a church that later became a starting point for the pilgrimage Helena claims to be taking to Santiago de Compostella.[2] Susan Snyder finds a source for the dialogue on virginity between Helena and Parolles in Erasmus's colloquy 'Proci et puellae', where two speakers debate the relative merits of marriage and virginity.[3]

Parolles himself, like the bed-trick, has a long ancestry. The figure of the braggart soldier runs through the comedy of Greece and Rome, well into the Renaissance and beyond. The most famous classical example is Pyrgopolynices, the title character of the Miles Gloriosus of Plautus, itself based on a Greek original, Alazon (The Braggart). In Plautus, the plot against the title character hinges not on his military boasts but on his vanity about his success with women. His come-uppance is a beating and the threat of castration; he ends the play drawing a moral about the punishment of lechery. The stock pattern of ridiculous boasting ending in humiliation is clear enough in Parolles; but if Shakespeare is thinking of Plautus in particular, he has deflected the theme of the embarrassing consequences of lechery onto Bertram. Earlier English examples of the braggart soldier include the title character of Nicholas Udall's Roister Doister, Sir Topas in John Lyly's Endymion, and Bobadill in Ben Jonson's Every Man in his Humour. Shakespeare never uses the type without giving it a twist. Ancient Pistol is perhaps his most straightforward braggart, but even he has an extra dimension: spouting quotations from old plays, he is a walking metatheatrical joke, not just embodying a familiar theatrical type but poking fun at the whole idea of theatrical tradition. The braggart soldier is one ingredient, but only one, in the rich compound that makes up

---

[1] Marliss C. Desens, The Bed-Trick in English Renaissance Drama: Explorations in Gender, Sexuality and Power, 1994, p. 11. Zvi Jagendorf traces the bed-trick from Genesis to Molière in 'Strangers in the Night: Sexual Encounters in Religious and Secular Texts', UTQ 53 (1983–4), 135–48. On Menander and Terence, see Robert S. Miola, 'New Comedy in All's Well That Ends Well', RQ 46 (1993), 23–43 (pp. 35–7). Miola notes that Boccaccio copied out the whole of Terence by hand (p. 24).
[2] Introduction to the New Cambridge Shakespeare edition, 1985, pp. 5–6.
[3] World's Classics edition, 1993, pp. 6–8, 233–9.

Sir John Falstaff. Don Armado in *Love's Labour's Lost* starts as a conventional brag-gart, but by the end of the play he has acquired, as Parolles will do, a surprising dignity.

Closer to Shakespeare's immediate theatrical context is a range of plays, mostly comedies, that appeared around the turn of the century, featuring abusive prodigal husbands and long-suffering, forgiving wives. Three characteristic examples, all anonymous, are *The Fair Maid of Bristow*, *How a Man May Choose a Good Wife From a Bad* and *The London Prodigal*.[1] In *Fair Maid* and *How a Man May Choose* the hus-bands are drawn away from their wives by courtesans; in *The London Prodigal* Flowerdale, deserting his wife, tells her 'Why, turn whore, that's a good trade, / And so perhaps I'll see thee now and then' (3.3.295–6). (Something like this literally happens to Bertram, when he tries to commit fornication and ends up consummating his marriage instead; the programme note for the Chicago Shakespeare Theatre's 2000 production was titled 'The Man Who Committed Adultery with his Own Wife'.) The deserted wives all show a Griselda-like patience and self-abnegation, a manner Helena adopts in the disastrous early days of her marriage. But Helena is never quite so abject as Mistress Arthur in *How a Man May Choose*:

> Or if you think me unworthy of the name
> Of your chaste wife, I will become your maid,
> Your slave, your servant, any thing you will,
> If for that name of servant, and of slave,
> You will but smile upon me now and then. (B1v–B2r)

The loving concern Helena sends after Bertram when he goes to war finds an equiva-lent in Annabel in *The Fair Maid of Bristow* when her husband goes off with a prosti-tute: 'wheresoe'er thou art, / God send thee never a less loving heart' (C2v); and Helena's tendency to blame herself is like Annabel's 'Call him not wretch, he is wretched but by me' (C3v). In criticism and frequently in production Bertram's youth is made the excuse for his behaviour. He simply needs to grow up. Annabel takes a similar line: ''Tis incident for young men to offend, / And wives must stay their leisures to amend' (F2r). In this vein it is hard to match Dorothea, the Griselda heroine of Robert Greene's *James IV*, who does not seem particularly offended when her husband tries to have her murdered: 'Youth hath misled: tut, but a little fault'.[2]

Arthur in *How a Man May Choose* tells his wife how she can please him: 'die sud-denly, / And I'll become a lusty widower' (B2r). He hurries the process along with what he thinks is poison; it is the usual harmless sleeping drug, just enough to send Mistress Arthur, like Helena, into an apparent death from which she miraculously recovers. In the end all three husbands are as abject in their repentance as their wives are in patience. Flowerdale is typical:

---

[1] For a fuller discussion see Robert Y. Turner, 'Dramatic Conventions in *All's Well That Ends Well*', *PMLA* 75 (1960), 497–502. References are to the original editions of *The Fair Maid of Bristow* (1605) and *How A Man May Choose a Good Wife From a Bad* (1602), and the text of *The London Prodigal* in C. F. Tucker Brooke (ed.) *The Shakespeare Apocrypha*, 1908. Quotations are modernized.
[2] J. A. Lavin (ed.), New Mermaid edition, 1967, 5.6.10.

                    wonder among wives!
        Thy chastity and virtue hath infused
        Another soul in me, red with defame,
        For in my blushing cheeks is seen my shame.   (5.1.320–3)

The relationship of these plays to Shakespeare's is a matter not so much of source or
influence as of a stockpile of popular conventions that the anonymous writers used one
way and Shakespeare used another. The runaway, finally repentant husband and the
patient, forgiving wife are Helena and Bertram in outline, but only in outline. Helena
takes too much initiative to be a simple Griselda, and her moments of self-rebuke are
only moments. Shakespeare had already shown a simple, total repentance on the part
of an erring male in Proteus in *The Two Gentlemen of Verona*, and he seems determined not to do that again. Bertram's use of the word 'if' in the final scene adds a note
of caution, an acknowledgment that turning one's life around is not so easy as conventional plays make it look. As he does with Boccaccio, Shakespeare takes a story that
in other hands aims at straightforward satisfaction, and complicates it. If he is engaged
with his fellow dramatists, that engagement is adversarial.

The Shakespearean context (and the date)

Any account of Shakespeare's sources needs to include Shakespeare himself. I have
already suggested that his variation on the *miles gloriosus* tradition with Parolles owes
something to Armado. In the matter of names *All's Well That Ends Well* is an echo
chamber for the rest of the Shakespeare canon. Many of the echoes are incidental,
others less so. One of the Florentine soldiers on parade in 3.5 is Escalus (the prince in
Romeo and Juliet and the more agreeable deputy in *Measure for Measure*). In the scene
of Parolles' interrogation one of the hitherto nameless French Lords picks up the
name Dumaine from *Love's Labour's Lost*, and Parolles lists among the generals one
Corambus (the Polonius of the First Quarto *Hamlet*). Polonius has a servant called
Rinaldo; so does the Countess. Diana, the Florentine girl Bertram is trying to seduce,
is a Capilet. The woman who advises her to beware of men – and this echo seems more
pointed – is Mariana. Sometimes pregnant in production and therefore speaking from
experience, she bears the name of the woman who replaces Isabella in the bed-trick of
Measure for Measure. It seems even less coincidental that the Helena of *A Midsummer
Night's Dream* is riddled with self-doubt, and spends the early scenes of the play pursuing a man who does not want her.

     All's Well shares with *Twelfth Night* a sense of the incipient exhaustion of
comedy. Olivia warns Feste that his fooling grows old and people dislike it; Lavatch
finds that a routine he thought was reliable has let him down: 'I ne'er had worse luck
in my life in my "O Lord, sir!" I see things may serve long, but not serve ever'
(2.2.45–46). Parolles, blindfolded and set upon by a crowd of soldiers speaking gibberish, may recall Malvolio shut in darkness and enduring a nonsensical conversation with Sir Topas the curate. In both cases Shakespeare is tapping a vein of
comedy, the cruel practical joke, that is more characteristic of Ben Jonson. Even the

1 'Occasion on her wheel' (see 5.1.14, 5.3.39). From Geoffrey Whitney's *A Choice of Emblems* (Leyden, 1586), Sig. z3r, p. 181

battered Falstaff of *The Merry Wives of Windsor* is invited to rejoin the community and laugh over a country fire. Malvolio and Parolles, like Jonson's comic victims, are left alone with their humiliation, Malvolio by his own choice and Parolles by his tormentors. *Twelfth Night* is if anything darker, since Malvolio's resilience takes the form of vengeful anger, and the idea that the joke has gone too far is explicit in the play, while Parolles' resilience comes from wry self-knowledge, and for the joke against him to cross the line into excessive cruelty is more a production choice than a requirement of the text.

All's Well shares the bed-trick device with *Measure for Measure*, and critics infer the order of composition according to which play seems to them to present the more refined treatment.[1] It shares a sceptical view of war (and a character called Helen) with

---

[1] Fraser, pp. 4–5, sees *All's Well* as a more refined and sceptical treatment of the device, suggesting Shakespeare is taking a second look at it. G. K. Hunter, in the Arden edition, 1959, takes the plays in the other order, seeing 'a slight development and clarification' of the motif in *Measure* (p. xxiv).

Troilus and Cressida. Rosalind in *As You Like It* has, like Helena, lost a father at the beginning of the play, though while Helena's father is dead Rosalind's is in exile and recoverable. Both women find themselves turning to new male interests. Helena says of her father:

> What was he like?
> I have forgot him. My imagination
> Carries no favour in't but Bertram's.   (1.1.69–71)

This seems a hard-edged version of Rosalind's 'what talk we of fathers, when there is such a man as Orlando?' (3.4.38–9). Cressida joins the group when her father arranges a prisoner exchange that will take her from Troy and Troilus, and she declares, 'I have forgot my father' (4.2.96).

Among the plays, *All's Well*'s most interesting affinities are with *Hamlet*. Its unusual opening stage direction, which has four characters entering '*all in black*', recalls the conspicuous black of the mourning Prince, and through the opening minutes the note of loss is struck over and over. Helena and Bertram have lost their fathers, and the Countess is about to lose her son when he goes to Paris as ward of the King. The King himself, we learn, is virtually on his deathbed, and in 1.2 the sight of Bertram sends him into a nostalgic lament for Bertram's father, whom he idealizes as Hamlet idealizes his own lost father, saying, in effect, we shall not look upon his like again. Back in the first scene, Helena shows affinities with Hamlet. When the Countess warns her against excessive sorrow lest it be thought affected, she replies, 'I do affect a sorrow indeed, but I have it too' (1.1.42). Hamlet too distinguishes between his outer shows of mourning and 'that within which passes show' (1.2.85) – the difference being that while his outer and inner mourning are directed to the same object, his father, Helena appears to be mourning for her father but her real, inner grief is the imminent loss of Bertram. Lafew advises her, almost in the tones of Claudius, 'Moderate lamentation is the right of the dead; excessive grief the enemy to the living' (1.1.43–4). The movement of the play can be seen as an attempt to shake off grief and get on with life, though it is the first sign of a certain callowness in Bertram that he seems tactlessly eager to do just that. He interrupts the dialogue with Helena, as though impatient with the attention the Countess and Lafew are showing her (why does she matter?), telling his mother, 'Madam, I desire your holy wishes' (1.1.47). He gets in return prudent advice that might have come from Polonius to Laertes:

> Love all, trust a few,
> Do wrong to none. Be able for thine enemy
> Rather in power than use, and keep thy friend
> Under thine own life's key. Be checked for silence,
> But never taxed for speech.   (1.1.52–6)

Evidently this is the sort of thing a young man on his way to Paris needs to hear. As the play goes on the *Hamlet* echoes fade, as though the play itself, like its younger characters, is shaking off a memory.

All's Well, then, picks up echoes from other plays; but its most pervasive and fascinating affinities are with Shakespeare's Sonnets.[1] Helena in her self-abnegation is at times very like the speaker of the Sonnets in his relation to the young man: 'To leave poor me thou hast the strength of laws. / Since why to love I can allege no cause' (49.13–14); 'Farewell, thou art too dear for my possessing' (87.1). She seems at one point prepared to get out of Bertram's life by pretending to die: 'After my death, dear love, forget me quite' (72.3). Helena has forgotten her father, and the speaker in Sonnet 112 declares, 'You are so strongly in my purpose bred / That all the world besides methinks are dead' (13–14). When Bertram goes to court Helena regrets 'That wishing well had not a body in't / Which might be felt' (1.1.156–7). In the young man's absence the speaker of Sonnet 44 declares, 'If the dull substance of my flesh were thought, / Injurious distance should not stop my way' (1–2). The speaker of Sonnet 61, like Helena, feels abandoned: 'For thee watch I, whilst thou dost wake elsewhere; / From me far off, with others all too near' (13–14). Bertram is, other characters agree, all too near Parolles: 'Ah, wherefore should he with infection live, / And with his presence grace impiety' (67.1–2). Parolles himself, not knowing Bertram is listening, calls him 'a foolish idle boy, but for all that very ruttish' (4.3.178–9); Parolles is 'That tongue that tells the story of thy days / (Making lascivious comment on thy sport)' (95.5–6). If anything excuses Bertram it is his youth: 'Some say thy fault is youth, some wantonness, / Some say thy grace is youth and gentle sport' (96.1–2). But as his behaviour deteriorates towards the end of the play, we wonder if anything, including youth and good looks, can excuse him: 'For sweetest things turn sourest by their deeds; / Lilies that fester smell far worse than weeds' (94.13–14).

Bertram, who would rather go to war in male company than to bed with Helena, recalls the frigid Adonis of *Venus and Adonis*, who would rather hunt the boar with his friends than make love to Venus. He has an aristocratic position to keep up, and a noble father to live up to. He conspicuously fails to do the latter, but through the bed-trick Helena at least sees to it that the line will not die out: 'You had a father, let your son say so' (13.14). Class difference sets at times a wide gap between the speaker and the young man, as it does between Helena and Bertram; but as the speaker finds a role in the young man's life by advising him to get a child and continue the line, Helena symbolically involves herself in Bertram's class by getting his ancestral ring from him, and conceives his child. Yet Helena finds the experience itself problematic: 'so lust doth play / With what it loathes for that which is away' (4.4.24–5). Bertram's lovemaking was lust in action, with a woman he claims to hate. Its paradoxes are not unlike the paradox of lust itself, loathed and desired: 'All this the world well knows; yet none knows well / To shun the heaven that leads men to this hell' (129.13–14).

Does all this mean that *All's Well* is a personal play, with Helena embodying Shakespeare's hopeless love for a cold-hearted aristocrat? Can we even see Parolles, a social climber claiming familiar acquaintance with those above him, as a comic self-

---

[1] See Roger Warren, 'Why Does It End Well? Helena, Bertram and the Sonnets', *S.Sur* 22 (1969), 79–92; Richard P. Wheeler, *Shakespeare's Development and the Problem Comedies: Turn and Counter-Turn*, 1981, pp. 57–75; and David Schalkwyk, *Speech and Performance in Shakespeare's Sonnets and Plays*, 2002, pp. 198–237.

2   'A Gentle Astringer' (see 5.1.6 SD). From George Turberville's *Booke of Faulconrie or Hawking* (London, 1575), part 2, p. 75

image? The same kind of question can be raised about *Love's Labour's Lost*, where Berowne finds himself, to his own chagrin, in love with a dark lady with a reputation for promiscuity. The problem is that the evidence cuts two ways: it can suggest that *All's Well* and *Love's Labour's Lost* are indeed more personal than we might have thought; or that the Sonnets are more a dramatist's invented story than we might have thought. We can at least say that Shakespeare as an artist was interested in the experience of loving hopelessly, obsessively, and against one's better judgement; and what interested him as an artist is likely to have interested him as a man. It is even possible that on another issue he identified not with Helena but with Bertram: R. B. Parker has suggested a link between Bertram's resentment at being forced to marry Helena and Shakespeare's own shotgun wedding.[1] This could apply both to the King's enforcement of the match and to Helena's appearance in the last scene, which declares, in effect, I'm pregnant and that settles it. When Bertram flees 'the dark house and the

[1] In a lecture at the Festival Theatre at Stratford, Ontario in July 2002. Parker is currently preparing his argument for publication.

detested wife' (2.3.269), are we glimpsing Shakespeare's feelings as he heads for London?

These are questions that must remain as questions. The date of the play is equally elusive, and equally bound up with its relation to Shakespeare's other work. There are no references to the play earlier than the 1623 entry in the Stationer's Register that licenses its publication in the Folio. Frances Meres' tantalizing reference to *Love's Labour's Won* in *Palladis Tamia* (1598) used to be taken as a possible reference to *All's Well*, at least in an early version; not much credence is given to this suggestion now. Links to contemporary events that might help us pin down a date are more suggestive than decisive. The King's war policy – stay out of it, but let your young men fight if they want to – is not unlike Queen Elizabeth's policy for the Low Countries. Susan Snyder suggests another link with Elizabeth in Lavatch's complaint about a man being at a woman's command.[1] Both links, if they are there at all, could suggest a date just after the Queen's death. The play features a monarch dying and reborn: are we on the cusp between Elizabeth and James? We are left with the play's relation to the rest of the canon, and it is characteristic of our problem that its closest links are with the Sonnets, whose date of composition is a matter of dispute. They were first published in 1609, and the two that appeared in 1599 in *The Passionate Pilgrim* (138 and 144) are not closely linked with *All's Well*. (Sonnet 138, with its punning reference to lying together, could be seen as a kind of bed-trick, sex combined with deception, but the 1599 phrasing – 'Therefore I'll lie with love, and love with me' – blurs the effect.) In any case to establish echoes between *All's Well* and other Shakespeare texts leaves us with the chicken-or-egg problem: which came first?

Attempts at dating the play generally come down to comparisons of its style with those of works whose dates are more secure. There are outbreaks of what can seem an early manner in, for example, the gnomic rhyming couplets by which Helena persuades the King to try her skill; but there are other such outbreaks in middle-period plays. That *All's Well* is such a play is the current consensus. The convoluted prose of its first few speeches, which seems to be telling the audience they will have to listen closely, represents a manner (in both prose and verse) that can be seen in *Measure for Measure* and *Troilus and Cressida*, a manner that continues in the openings of *Cymbeline* and *The Winter's Tale* and goes right through to the Shakespeare scenes of *The Two Noble Kinsmen*. I have suggested earlier that *All's Well* picks up echoes from other plays (or are they anticipations?) in matters as important as the bed-trick and the experience of mourning, and as unimportant as the names of unseen characters. None of the plays it so echoes (or anticipates) can be confidently dated after 1604. If we see it as one of a group of plays in conversation with each other, this discourages a late date. *All's Well*, a play often regarded as peripheral, is arguably at the centre – at least the chronological centre – of Shakespeare's work, a period of stock-taking around the turn of the century when *Twelfth Night* ended the sequence of romantic comedies and *Henry V* the sequence of history plays, and the radically experimental *Troilus and*

[1] World's Classics introduction, p. 23.

Cressida suggested a clearing of the ground for new possibilities. *All's Well*'s links with the Sonnets, assuming the Sonnets are autobiographical, may also suggest a personal stock-taking. In the present state of our knowledge we do not have a secure date for *All's Well;* but if we place it in 1603, we may not be far wrong.

Critical reception and stage history

All's Well That Ends Well's first significant critic of whom we have record was King Charles I, who wrote beside the title in his copy of the Second Folio the words, 'Monsieur Parolles'. The King's sense that Parolles is the character who matters most was echoed throughout eighteenth century criticism, beginning with Nicholas Rowe, who in the preface to his 1709 edition of Shakespeare called the braggart 'as good as any thing of that kind in Plautus or Terence'.[1] Thomas Davies's appreciation in his *Dramatic Miscellanies* (1784) adds to the usual tributes a sense that the character is not just a one-note type, but has a certain complexity: 'an odd compound of cowardice, folly, ignorance, pertness, and effrontery, with certain semblances of courage, sense, knowledge, adroitness, and wit'.[2] But the eighteenth-century comment on the play that has had the greatest staying power is that of Samuel Johnson:

> I cannot reconcile my heart to Bertram; a man noble without generosity and young without truth; who marries Helena as a coward and leaves her as a profligate: when she is dead by his unkindness, sneaks home to a second marriage, is accused by a woman whom he has wronged, defends himself by falsehood and is dismissed to happiness.[3]

What Johnson sees is not just the unsatisfactory character of Bertram – though that is the point other critics have taken up time and again – but a set of disconnections, between what we expect of Bertram and what he is, between what he deserves and what he gets.

When we come to the Romantic period, we find a similar disconnection in Coleridge's view of Helena. He calls her Shakespeare's 'loveliest character', but he does so in the context of wondering whether she has been caught telling a lie; and elsewhere he raises deeper misgivings: 'Indeed, it must be confessed that her character is not very delicate, and it required all Shakespeare's consummate skill to interest us for her; and he does this chiefly by the operation of the other characters – the Countess, Lafeu, etc. We get to like Helena from their praising and commending her so much.'[4] This time the disconnection is between what we might think of Helena on her own and what we are made to think by the way other characters talk about her. Coleridge

---

[1] Quoted from Brian Vickers (ed.), *Shakespeare: The Critical Heritage* 2, 1974, p. 195. There is a full survey of the critical reception of *All's Well* to 1964 in Joseph G. Price, *The Unfortunate Comedy: A Study of All's Well That Ends Well and its Critics*, 1968, pp. 75–129, and a brief but informative survey of the critical reception to the 1980s in Sheldon P. Zitner, *Twayne's New Critical Introductions to Shakespeare: All's Well That Ends Well*, 1989, pp. xix–xxv. My summary is indebted to both.
[2] Vickers, *Critical Heritage* 6, 1981, p. 375.
[3] H. R. Woodhuysen (ed.), *Samuel Johnson on Shakespeare*, 1989, p. 191.
[4] Thomas Middleton Raysor (ed.), *Coleridge's Shakespearean Criticism*, 1930, 1. p. 113, 2. p. 357.

opposes to Johnson's reading of Bertram a sympathetic defence based on his age and class; but he resembles Johnson in sensing the play's ability to provoke a divided response. Other critics of the early nineteenth century were less divided in their admiration of Helena. Nathan Drake declared that 'Helen, the romantic, the love-dejected Helen, must excite in every feeling bosom a high degree of sympathy' for her 'patient suffering . . . united with modesty and beauty' not to mention 'the most engaging humility . . . the most bewitching tenderness of heart'.[1] If the eighteenth century found in Parolles an engaging comic type, the early nineteenth found in Helena a sentimental heroine. Anna Brownell Jameson went further: 'There never was, perhaps, a more beautiful picture of a woman's love . . . Her love is like a religion, pure, holy, and deep.'[2]

Such idealistic readings could not survive long, and from the late nineteenth century well into the twentieth the play sank in critical estimation. The inconsistency of the characters, the unpleasantness of the bed-trick and of the comedy generally, the immodesty of the heroine – all these were too much for late Victorian palates, and early twentieth-century tastes were similarly offended. Bernard Shaw's admiration of the play (he saw Helena as a Shavian heroine) did not find many echoes. By the middle of the twentieth century the prevailing tendency in criticism was to look for the organic unity of a work of art, usually in patterns of language around a theme, and *All's Well* offered slim pickings. W. W. Lawrence, in *Shakespeare's Problem Comedies* (1931), looked seriously at the play's origins in traditional stories centring on the figure of the Clever Wench, but even he found that the play filled out the story half-heartedly: Shakespeare 'never put his whole heart and soul into it' (p. 76). Subsequent critics who have traced romance elements in the play have generally found a clash between romance and awkward reality, a clash they find frustrating or interesting according to their own critical expectations. In his influential Arden edition (1959) G. K. Hunter asked, 'how are we to describe the genuine effects of this play so that readers (or audiences) can see it as a whole, or at least as a work with a centre?' He goes on, 'The play has undoubtedly a strongly individual quality, but it is difficult to start from this, since it is mainly a quality of *strain*' (p.xxix; emphasis in original). We have seen that Johnson and Coleridge felt that strain in their own ways.

In the later years of the twentieth century, however, aesthetic coherence (and aesthetic considerations generally) came to matter less in criticism. The question of whether or not *All's Well* works as a play has receded in favour of investigations of the social conditions and ideological values imbedded in it. Margaret Loftus Ranald has examined the play in the context of wardship and marriage; David Haley has re-evaluated Bertram in light of notions of honour.[3] Richard P. Wheeler gives a psychoanalytic reading linked to the Sonnets.[4] The play's treatment of gender roles has been

---

[1] Price, *Unfortunate Comedy*, p. 84.
[2] Ibid.
[3] Margaret Loftus Ranald, *Shakespeare and His Social Context*, 1987; David Haley, *Shakespeare's Courtly Mirror*, 1993.
[4] *Shakespeare's Development*, pp. 34–91.

examined by, among others, David McCandless, R. B. Parker and Carol Rutter.[1] Besides the surveys of the play's stage history offered by Joseph G. Price and J. L. Styan, Carol Rutter has provided accounts of performance with a close focus on feminist questions.[2] Throughout this work (and I have mentioned on only a few items from a wide field) episodes from which earlier critics recoiled in distaste, notably Bertram's rejection of Helena, and the bed-trick, have been examined closely for the values they embody and the questions they raise. There has been increasing attention to the play in performance. In 1950, in *Shakespeare's Problem Plays*, E. M. W. Tillyard pronounced the play a failure, as critics of that time tended to do, but added a reservation that was also a prophecy: 'Fail the play does, when read: but who of its judges have seen it acted? Not I at any rate; and I suspect that it acts far better than it reads' (p. 89). Shortly after Tillyard wrote those words, productions of the play began to accumulate; and while it has not become a standard repertory piece, critics writing on the play now have a range of productions on which to draw.

We have no record of any performance of the play before 1741. We may assume that it was performed by the King's Men at the Globe, but the closest we come to evidence that it was in their active repertory is Susan Snyder's note that stage directions for cornets (unusual in public theatres before 1609) suggest the manuscript was altered for performance after that date.[3] The reproduction of Shakespeare's Globe on the Bankside has allowed us to see how the plays of the time function on the stage for which they were designed, and one feature is of particular importance for *All's Well That Ends Well*. The pillars – massive, intrusive and controversial – effectively divide the stage into two acting areas: a central area for the main action and a U-shaped perimeter for commentary from the sidelines. This would be particularly helpful for the scene in which Helena, working up to her choice of Bertram, rejects the other young lords while Lafew, evidently at some distance from the action, thinks they are rejecting her. The drawing by C. Walter Hodges for this edition (fig. 3) shows a possible staging of this scene with Lafew and Parolles in the perimeter, and Lafew's sight of the young lords partially blocked by a pillar. Lafew has a similar role as commentator in the final scene, including some by-play with Parolles; a similar staging could be used. The fullest use of onstage commentary is in the drum sequence, with Parolles' soliloquy and his later interrogation playing off against the voluble comments of the spectators. For the soliloquy, Hodges' drawing (fig. 4) shows Parolles at the front, appealing directly to the audience. (In our theatres, the darkened auditorium works

[1] David McCandless, *Gender and Performance in Shakespeare's Problem Comedies*, 1997; R. B. Parker, 'War and Sex in "All's Well That Ends Well"', *S.Sur.* 37 (1984), 99–113; Carol Rutter, 'Helena's Choosing: Writing the Couplets in a Choreography of Discontinuity. (*All's Well That Ends Well* 2.3)', *EIT* 9 (1991), 121–39.

[2] Price, *Unfortunate Comedy*, pp. 3–72; J. L. Styan, *Shakespeare in Performance: All's Well That Ends Well*, 1984; Rutter, 'Helena's Choosing' and Carol Rutter et al., *Clamorous Voices: Shakespeare's Women Today*, 1989. The latter is a series of conversations with actors who have played Shakespeare's women, including Harriet Walter, who played Helena in Trevor Nunn's 1981 Royal Shakespeare Company production (pp. 73–96).

[3] World's Classics introduction, p. 54.

3   'Here, take her hand,
  Proud scornful boy, unworthy this good gift . . .'
A possible Elizabethan staging of Act 2, Scene 3, drawn by C. Walter Hodges

against such intimacy.) His assailants are creeping up on him in two parties; evidently each party has just been hiding behind a pillar. The centre-and-perimeter format would also work in the ensuing interrogation, where Bertram and the others lords offer an extended commentary which Parolles evidently does not hear. Throughout the play, in fact, there is a pattern of action and commentary: Coleridge, we have seen, found his liking for Helena resting more on what other characters say about her than on Helena herself. This is not always bound up with questions of staging (much of the praise of Helena occurs in her absence) but there are moments when staging comes actively into play, visually underlining the importance of commentary and making natural use of the geography of the Globe stage.

The degree of the play's popularity in its own time is moot: enough, perhaps, for a post-1609 revival, not enough to leave the trail of references we have for such hits as *Romeo and Juliet*, *Hamlet* and the Falstaff plays. The recorded stage history of *All's Well* begins in 1741 with Henry Giffard's production at Goodman's Fields. The play was billed as 'written by Shakespeare and not acted since his time'.[1] Throughout the

---

[1] Price, *Unfortunate Comedy*, p. 5. My summary of the play's pre-twentieth-century stage history is generally indebted to Price.

4   Parolles ambushed (Act 4, Scene 1); reconstruction of an early performance, by C. Walter Hodges

eighteenth century the play's popularity, in the theatre as in criticism, rested on Parolles. Giffard cast a minor actor, Joseph Peterson, in the role, and Peterson seems to have scored a personal success sufficient to give him a later career as Parolles in the provinces. In the following year Theophilus Cibber made a hit as Parolles in Drury Lane, repeating the role at Covent Garden in 1746. David Garrick's adaption for the 1756 Drury Lane revival cut the text, Helena included, to highlight Parolles as a vehicle for Harry Woodward. Woodward continued to play the role, to great acclaim, up to 1777. A three-act version at the Haymarket in 1785 was likewise trimmed to centre on Parolles. John Bannister, like his predecessors, won praise in the role. Clearly the eighteenth-century taste for flamboyant comic types was satisfied by Shakespeare's braggart, and on one point at least Charles I was vindicated. Throughout this time the play's production record, though not spectacular, was respectable. It might have done even better if it had not acquired (like *Macbeth* in the twentieth century) the reputation of an unlucky play, dogged by the illnesses, even the deaths, of some performers.

This began with the 1742 Drury Lane revival, whose Helena, Peg Woffington, was regularly ill. During one performance she fainted and had to be replaced. William Milward, who played the King, fell ill and subsequently died.

Tastes changed in the Romantic period, and Helena, sacrificed to Parolles in the later eighteenth century, was restored to prominence by John Philip Kemble in a revised version acted in 1794. But it was a bowdlerized, sentimental Helena, no longer bantering with Parolles about virginity, no longer under orders to get pregnant, and with the bed-trick to be discreetly inferred. The jinx continued: during the 1794 revival Kemble (playing Bertram) fell ill and his Helena, Mrs Jordan – ironically, in view of Kemble's efforts to desexualize the text – was undergoing a difficult pregnancy. Throughout the nineteenth century, as the play sank in critical estimation, its theatrical fortunes waned. In 1811 Charles Kemble dropped it after two performances. In 1832 an operatic version at Covent Garden met with a hostile reception, much of the hostility directed against the indecency of the play, 'the *only* play of Shakespeare that is really exceptionable in its moral tone and tendency'.[1] Shakespeare's mid-century champion Samuel Phelps managed a successful revival at Sadler's Wells in 1852, scoring a personal success as Parolles; but he too had to weather criticism of the play's indecency. An American revival contemplated by Augustin Daly in the 1880s never took place. Henry Irving, the leading Shakespearean actor of the late Victorian period, left *All's Well* alone. There were scattered productions in the first half of the twentieth century, but none succeeded in establishing the play, and in 1950, as we have noted, E. M. W. Tillyard could claim he had never seen it.

From the early 1950s the play gradually returned to the theatre, though in England the first attempts were not promising. At the Old Vic in 1953 Michael Benthall, working his way through the Folio, came to *All's Well That Ends Well*. Finding the play (by his own admission) distasteful, he decided on 'fairy-tale unreality' as the manner of the production, with backdrops designed by the cartoonist Osbert Lancaster, 'clear and bright like cut-outs from a child's picture book'. Fairy-tale led to farce: the King was 'a figure of fun, a fretful invalid . . . with crown askew', accompanied by comic doctors fussing with 'potions and basins' and a comic monk 'who burst into terrified chanting at his royal master's every spasm'. In the midst of the farce Claire Bloom was an attractive if simplified Helena, 'an April creature of quick tears and laughter in the early scenes and strangely moving in her very stillness and solemnity at the end'. Some critics were offended by Benthall's treatment of the play, but for Eric Keown in *Punch* the production worked as planned: 'laughter is the kindest anaesthetic against the increasing outrage of the plot'.[2] The other major centre of Shakespeare production in England was the Shakespeare Memorial Theatre at Stratford-upon-Avon, and there in 1955 Noel Willman, while treating the play as a sombre dark comedy, loaded it with heavy sets and elaborate late seventeenth-century costumes (Lancaster's Old Vic

[1] The *Court Journal* of 20 October 1832, quoted in Price, *Unfortunate Comedy*, p. 36; emphasis in original.
[2] Roger Wood and Mary Clarke, *Shakespeare at the Old Vic* [vol.1], 1954, pp. 58–9.

5 Court ball to celebrate the curing of the King in Tyrone Guthrie's production (designed by Tanya Moiseiwitsch) at Stratford, Ontario, 1953. Alec Guinness as the King, Irene Worth as Helena. (Peter Smith: Courtesy of Stratford Festival Archives)

setting had been storybook mediaeval). The critics were not enthusiastic, and took the occasion to attack the play as not worth reviving.[1] According to J. L. Styan, Joyce Redman played Helena 'like a Victorian miss just out of finishing school, hiding her ruthlessness behind coy smiles and adopting the playfulness of a kitten. The effect of this was so disagreeable that the audience could not help but feel that she and Bertram deserved each other.'[2]

Meanwhile, on the other side of the Atlantic, the play's vindication as a stage piece had begun. Stratford, Ontario, a small provincial city chiefly notable as a railway town, opened the first season of what was to be an annual Shakespeare Festival with *Richard III* and *All's Well That Ends Well*. Tyrone Guthrie, the Festival's founding director, picked *Richard III* as a vehicle for his star actor, Alec Guinness, and *All's Well* as an ensemble piece whose unfamiliarity would put the imported performers and production team and the local Canadian actors on equal terms. Both productions were enthusiastically received, but in the critical consensus the unfamiliar comedy, to general surprise, eclipsed the history play. Set in modern dress, light-hearted, elegant and

[1] Price, *Unfortunate Comedy*, pp. 55–7.
[2] *Shakespeare in Performance*, p. 18.

romantic, the play, for all its reputation as a bitter comedy, impressed Robertson Davies as 'filled with a sweet spirit'. (It probably helped that Lavatch was cut, though Davies, noting the cut, denies it made any difference.) In contrast to Benthall's blend of fairy-tale and farce, Guthrie delivered, according to Davies, 'high romantic comedy. The story had a superficially unreal, fairy-tale quality; underneath this it was true, convincing and satisfying.'[1] Looking back on the production in a commemorative volume for the Stratford Festival's fiftieth anniversary, Martin Hunter suggests its links to the theatrical taste of its time, in which fantasy, poetic drama, and romantic comedy with a bitter edge, had a currency they have since lost: 'It was surprising, contemporary, funny. A fairy tale with the elegance and grace of Jean Anouilh, a problem play with the wit and paradox of George Bernard Shaw, a fantasy with the rich poetic colouring of Christopher Fry.'[2] While Benthall and Willman in different ways overdecorated the play, Guthrie's staging was part of an experiment in Shakespeare without scenery. The audience (covered in Stratford's early years with a tent) sat in a semicircle around a thrust stage, designed by Tanya Moiseiwitsch as a permanent formal set with a balcony supported by pillars. In this simple but dynamic space, Guthrie and Moiseiwitsch created a court in elegant dress uniforms, a court ball with white tie and tails and 1950s gowns to mark the King's cure, war scenes recalling the North African campaign in the Second World War, and a finale in which Helena (Irene Worth), dominating the stage in a striking yellow dress, brought the romantic comedy to a triumphant conclusion.

Back in England, Guthrie returned to the play in 1959 at the Shakespeare Memorial Theatre, in a more visually elaborate production with the elegant modern dress replaced by an Edwardian–Ruritanian style and the war scenes broadened into slapstick as the Duke of Florence tried to address his troops through a recalcitrant sound system. Reports of Guthrie's two productions suggest a general coarsening in 1959, but M. St Clare Byrne's detailed, appreciative review of the later production found it a revelation. Her account suggests the ways in which Guthrie satisfied the contemporary desire for a unified experience. (G. K. Hunter's Arden edition, with its concern to find such unity in the play, was published in the same year.) The production opened, she reports, on a note of 'elegiac sadness' – broken branches, brown leaves, and a general air of autumnal melancholy as life drained out of Rossillion. The curing of the King was signalled, as in the Ontario production, by a court ball, a 're-assertion of life and hope, with all the bustle of preparation, the entry of musicians, footmen bringing in lights, the gay chatter of expectation and excitement'. In the finale life returned to Rossillion with the lighting of candles and the placing of furniture as the 'house of mourning' was restored to 'its former glories'. The total effect, in the characteristic critical language of the period, 'gave the artistic satisfaction that comes from realizing the wholeness of the dramatic pattern'. Byrne, like Davies, claimed Guthrie had dispelled the play's dark reputation: 'how anyone can describe as bitter a comedy that

---

[1] Tyrone Guthrie, Robertson Davies and Grant Macdonald, *Renown at Stratford*, 1953, p. 50.
[2] *Romancing the Bard: Stratford at Fifty*, 2001, p. 20.

6 The unmasking of Parolles in Tyrone Guthrie's production of 1959 at the Shakespeare Memorial Theatre: impression by Neil Harvey

ends on this note of life and affirmation in the reconciliation of the young husband and wife will certainly surprise those who make acquaintance with it for the first time in this production'.[1]

The next production at Stratford-upon-Avon (now the home of the Royal Shakespeare Company) was in 1967. John Barton restored the play to the seventeenth century, giving it a grave and sensitive production whose quiet manner and subdued colours were suddenly broken by drumbeats and bright red costumes for the opening of the war sequence. Barton found touches of wry humour, like the small shower of confetti that fell from Bertram's hatbrim as he entered, drooping, from his wedding. At Stratford, Ontario in 1977 David Jones followed Barton in the seventeenth-century setting, and Guthrie in an autumnal opening – Lavatch sweeping up the leaves from around a sundial – leading to a burst of springlike colour for the last scene as the play

[1] 'The Shakespeare Season at the Old Vic, 1958–59 and Stratford-upon-Avon, 1959', SQ 10 (1959), 545–67 (pp. 558–9).

came to its harmonious close.[1] Neither production aimed at the high romance and high spirits of the Guthrie versions, settling instead for a tone of low-key, bittersweet comedy moving toward a happy ending based on the tolerance of human frailty.

The early 1980s saw, in rapid succession, two of the play's most successful productions to date. The 1980 BBC television version, directed by Elijah Mojinsky, used the resources of the medium to create a distinctive visual idiom reminiscent of seventeenth-century Dutch paintings. Rossillion was in the style of Vermeer, with checkered floors, dark walls, corridors giving a strong sense of interior perspective, and light filtered through cross-hatched windows. The first glimpse of the King in bed, half-naked, with attendants grouped around him, was a direct quotation from Rembrandt's *The Anatomy Lesson of Dr. Tulip*. Colour-coding was used for emphasis: against the prevailing brown of the Florence scenes, Helena stood out in blue and Parolles in red (which he lost during his interrogation, being stripped to his shirt). The play's concern with commentary that gives a perspective on the action found a visual equivalent when characters were seen not directly but reflected in mirrors. Parolles' first appearance was preening himself in a mirror; a curved mirror reflected Helena dancing with the King. Our sense that Helena is at first hidden from us became literal: in the opening sequence she was playing a spinet, with her back to the camera, or silhouetted against a window, her face unseen. On 'Not my virginity, yet . . .' we saw her face in close-up for the first time. In general, the medium was used to stress the intimacy and privacy of the drama. Lavatch, as he bantered with the Countess, was sitting at a table eating. There was no military spectacle, as there sometimes is on stage. The Duke of Florence was cut altogether, and while we saw the women watching the military parade, all we saw of the parade itself was a tight close-up of Parolles muttering about the lost drum. This was a low-key, domestic, realistic *All's Well*, stressing not romance or public actions but personal relations observed in close-up.

Trevor Nunn's 1981 Royal Shakespeare production set the play in an 'Edwardian twilight', with an all-purpose glass set variously suggesting Kew Gardens and Paddington Station. 'This world was elegant but evidently doomed, the shadows across the stage like the shadows over the dying King's court.'[2] A recurring waltz tune added to the air of nostalgia,[3] as a recurring tune on the spinet in the BBC version (a kind of seventeenth-century 'As Time Goes By') conveyed Helena's romantic longing. Rossillion was 'a haven of stillness and calm, of Chekhovian grace, presided over by the quiet dignity and love of the Countess [Peggy Ashcroft], haunted by the songs of birds and the sound of wistful piano music'. In the world outside Rossillion, by contrast, characters were 'restlessly, tiringly, on the move, often seen carrying suitcases', accompanied by 'the rush of trains and the roar of primitive motor cars'. The war was realistic, 'dominated by the flash and bang of exploding shells', and it was evident that Bertram achieved his command because he

[1] Styan, *Shakespeare in Performance*, p. 35; Roger Warren, 'Comedies and Histories at Two Stratfords, 1977', *S.Sur.* 31 (1978), 141–53 (pp. 145–6).
[2] Rutter, 'Helena's Choosing', p. 130.
[3] Styan, *Shakespeare in Performance*, p. 9.

7   Act 2, Scene 3. Helena (Harriet Walter) choosing Bertram (Philip Franks) in Trevor Nunn's production of 1982 at the Barbican Theatre. Set designed by John Gunter

was the only suitable officer who had survived.[1] The period setting allowed class distinctions to be equally realistic: 'Helena wore the house keys at her waist while Bertram spent time at the officers' club in Paris'.[2] The ending was less straightforwardly romantic than in previous productions, though Harriet Walter (who played Helena) reports that this was not so much a director's decision as a compromise among competing views. Trevor Nunn saw Helena as Bertram's 'redeemer', and wanted an 'optimistic ending'; Mike Gwilym, playing Bertram, resisted, thinking the ending should be 'bitter for Bertram'; Walter herself saw realistic characters making the best of a bad job in a situation in which both had been compromised. In the end, she reports, Bertram and Helena did not kiss, but walked out 'side by side, just our fingertips touching'.[3]

Nunn's production was warmly received. The Royal Shakespeare Company's 1989 production, directed by Barry Kyle in a mix of Renaissance and nineteenth-century costuming, was more controversial. Peter Holland found it a mish-mash of pointless inventions (including an attempt, which other reviewers also found confusing and meaningless, to identify the Countess with Queen Elizabeth and the King with James I). The final three-way embrace of Helena, Bertram and the Countess, very unlike the tentative ending of the Nunn production, seemed for Holland too glib, failing to take

[1] R. L. Smallwood, '*All's Well That Ends Well* at the Royal Shakespeare Theatre', *CQ* 24.1 (1982), 25–31 (pp. 25–6).
[2] Styan, *Shakespeare in Performance*, p. 15.
[3] Rutter, *Clamorous Voices*, p. 88.

account of what the characters had been through.[1] Barbara Everett, on the other hand, though complaining that the production's court and war scenes lacked the male 'social tonality' they needed, and reporting that Rossillion this time was a bleak northern setting of 'chill winds' and 'autumn bonfires' with Lavatch as 'an odd, sour and Calvinistical clown', found the production as a whole 'subtle, touching and funny'.[2] The production opened, Robert Smallwood reports, with a little boy and a little girl playing with toy soldiers. 'The boy won the game, moved away from the table, leaving the girl weeping, and climbed into the tree house.' This suggests a childhood relationship between Bertram and Helena, to be mirrored in their adult lives. Benedict Nightingale saw the production's Bertram (Paul Venables) as 'not bad, not good, just going through a callow, narcissistic, toy-soldier phase', while Smallwood found in him a 'slight goofiness'. Naive and thoughtless, he was 'ultimately forgivable at the play's end', the three-way embrace suggesting his 'final escape from boyhood'. Smallwood's final judgement was that the production was 'coherent and engaging'.[3]

That any production of *All's Well* should produce a divided response seems appropriate, given the self-divisions of the text. Even the Nunn production, one of the most successful in the play's history, embodied the contrary views of its director and two of its leading actors. Two more recent productions, Peter Hall's for the Royal Shakespeare Company at the Swan in 1992 and Richard Monette's at Stratford, Ontario in 2002, showed how the play can take its interpreters in opposite directions. Both returned the play to its seventeenth-century setting. Both were characterized by a clear, unfussy approach to the text, with a close concentration on the language, no elaborate staging gimmicks, and a minimum of interpretative slanting. Both, in other words, were what is sometimes called 'straight'. The result in Hall's production was a dark, disturbing and challenging *All's Well*, while Richard Monette delivered a romantic comedy on the order of *Much Ado About Nothing*, passing through a period of darkness but moving confidently to a happy ending. To begin with the Hall production: the Countess, played with grace and sympathy by Edith Evans (1959) and Peggy Ashcroft (1981), became in Barbara Jefford's performance fierce and proud, unsympathetic to Helena's love, sternly critical of Bertram, and humiliated to the point of tears by his conduct in the last scene. The gulling of Parolles was not funny but cruel and painful. Lavatch (Anthony O'Donnell) was a 'running sore', his fool's bauble a phallus used for aggression, not comedy, his eyes sunken, his face covered in sores. Sophie Thompson's Helena, 'short, dour and very weepy, was a figure one could well appreciate Bertram trying to avoid'.[4] She was 'not the passionate handsome Helena of tradition, but an intense girl who sometimes seems awkward to the point of being gawky, and ingenuous to the brink of gormlessness'. Toby Stephens' Bertram was 'a supercilious,

[1] 'Shakespeare Performances in England, 1989–90', *S.Sur.* 44 (1992), 157–90 (pp. 158–61).
[2] 'The love of a good woman', *TLS*, 27 October–2 November 1989, 1185.
[3] Robert Smallwood, 'Shakespeare at Stratford-upon-Avon, 1989 (Part II)', *SQ* 41 (1990), 491–9 (pp. 493–5); Benedict Nightingale, 'Common-sense coward', *The Times*, 2 April 1990, 20. Nightingale's review is of the production's London transfer at the Barbican.
[4] Peter Holland, 'Shakespeare Peformances in England, 1992', *S.Sur.* 46 (1994), 159–89 (pp. 165–8).

8 Sophie Thompson as Helena in Peter Hall's production at the Swan Theatre, 1992 (Malcolm Davies)

pouting cub, as lacking in charm as maturity'.[1] Robert Smallwood summarized the production as 'a hard, clear-sighted, unsentimental look at a tough play, never letting the audience off the hook'.[2]

In Richard Monette's production, Helena (Lucy Peacock) was very much the passionate, handsome Helena of tradition, noticeably older than her Bertram (David Snelgrove), who was not supercilious but young and vulnerable. Ordered to marry Helena, he burst into tears as he watched the youth he never had slipping away. The gulling of Parolles was not nasty but straightforwardly funny. Lavatch (Benedict Campbell) was not a running sore but a quiet, phlegmatic figure, looking more like a gardener than a clown, speaking his lines not as conscious jokes but as wry observations. In this he resembled Paul Brooke in the BBC version; but while Brooke had no live audience on which to test his delivery, Campbell's simple, unfussy readings produced laugh after laugh. The production moved from early scenes in black, grey and silver to warm orange for the scenes in Florence, with the soldiers in red. Its general movement from austerity to new life was captured in Helena's curing of the King. The King (William Hutt, a Stratford veteran who had walked on as a courtier in the 1953 Guthrie production, and had played the King once before in 1977) had been carried everywhere in a chair. His voice was feeble, his manner querulous. After he agreed to let Helena try her chances, he called, 'Give me some help here ho!', clearly expecting his attendants to appear and carry him off. Taking his hand, Helena made him stand and walk. His surprise and delight that he could actually do it ended the production's first act on a note of restorative comedy, signalling that whatever troubles the characters had to pass through, this was a play about healing. While (in Peter Holland's account) the characters in Hall's production, 'vulnerable and hurt, . . . stumbled towards the end',[3] Monette guided the play to a largely untroubled romantic conclusion.

Tillyard's sense that the play needs to be seen, and justifies itself in performance, is borne out by the fifty-year stage history that begins with Guthrie's first production. Though it seems unlikely ever to be one of the warhorses of the Shakespeare canon, it continues to be performed around the world in many languages, wherever Shakespeare is regularly acted, and a critical interpretation of the play needs to take account of the choices its stage interpreters have made in the face of the challenges it raises.

The play

The mainspring of the action is Helena's love of Bertram, and the play raises in particularly acute form a question raised throughout Shakespearean comedy (not to mention life): what on earth does she see in him? But if Proteus is unworthy of Julia, Claudio of Hero, Bassanio of Portia and even Orlando of Rosalind, at least one can say in those cases that the couple has a love-relationship that, however damaged or unbal-

---

[1] Benedict Nightingale, 'Hall thrives on moral ambiguity', *The Times*, 2 July 1992, Arts 2.
[2] 'Shakespeare at Stratford-upon-Avon, 1992', *SQ* 44 (1993), 343–62 (p. 358).
[3] 'Shakespeare Performances . . . 1992', p. 168.

anced, gives something to build on at the end. *All's Well That Ends Well* opens with Helena pining hopelessly for Bertram, her feelings known only to the audience. His farewell to her as he leaves for Paris, 'Be comfortable to my mother, your mistress, / And make much of her' (1.1.64–5), suggests that at the most he respects her and trusts her to perform well in the subservient role to which her station in life has assigned her. There is no reference to a shared childhood, nothing on which to build speculation about a boy and girl growing up together; only a present distance that is agonizing for her and a matter of course for him. There is in fact no relationship between them, and when Helena wins him as a husband he is shocked.

From that point on, Bertram's conduct seems to justify Samuel Johnson's view of him. Far from reconciling us to Bertram, Shakespeare seems to go out of his way to make such reconciliation difficult. That he should be uneasy at marrying Helena, even reject her, is understandable. But his rejection is cold, focused only on his own interests, showing no concern for her feelings and no curiosity about why she might have wanted him in the first place. The ceremony completed, he runs away, covering his departure with deception. By letter, he sets what he clearly intends to be impossible conditions for accepting her as his wife. In the war sequence his valour is a matter of report; the play foregrounds instead his attempted seduction of Diana. The news of Helena's death leaves him seemingly unmoved, and in the final scene he is ready for a new wife. Called on to explain the ring he got from Helena during the bed-trick, he twists and lies. (Bassanio, similarly embarrassed over Portia's ring, is quite frank about how and why he gave it away.) Arguably, Bertram's part in what looks like their reconciliation at the end is a shamefaced acknowledgment that she has caught him fair and square.

There are hints of other ways the story could have been handled that might have made Bertram a less difficult character. When he calls himself, on his arrival in the war, a 'hater of love' (3.3.11), he is taking the opening position of many a man in many a traditional love story, from Chaucer's Troilus to Shakespeare's Valentine and Benedick. But no love story follows, other than what may be seen compressed into a couple of lines in the last scene. He may call what he feels for Diana love, but he lets his actual feelings slip out when he begs her, 'give thyself unto my sick desires, / Who then recovers' (4.2.35–6). Other characters, the Countess in particular, think he has been misled by Parolles: 'My son corrupts a well-derivèd nature / With his inducement' (3.2.80–1). This appears to set up a convention of the prodigal play: the young man falls into bad company and will learn the error of his ways when his seducers turn against him. But this turns out to be a blind alley. Bertram's disillusionment with the braggart produces no change in his character, and in their earlier relationship Parolles seems to be not so much misleading Bertram as marshalling him the way that he was going. We are left to make what we can of his youth, and productions have done just that. Trevor Nunn had him choke on a cigarette.[1] M. St Clare Byrne describes Guthrie's 1959 Bertram, Edward de Souza, as 'very, very young, stiff with

[1] Rutter, *Clamorous Voices*, p. 82.

undergraduate-level masculine and aristocratic self-conceit . . . one simply has to wait for him to grow up'.[1] The BBC Bertram, Ian Charleson, at least made a stab at growing up by producing a beard and moustache for the war. That all we need from Bertram is a final maturity is suggested by Robertson Davies: 'At last, when he is ready for the kind of woman that Helena is, Helena is waiting for him'.[2] But 'waiting for him' hardly accounts for what Helena has been up to in the play's final movement, and in the compression of the play's conclusion the most we can say of Bertram's maturity is that he may be on the threshold of it. As for showing its actual development, as Berowne puts it near the end of *Love's Labour's Lost*, 'That's too long for a play' (5.2.878).

We can at least muster sympathy for his frustration at being held back from the war (in the BBC production he was glimpsed carrying a flask of the King's urine, suggesting his employment at court was unglamourous), and his understandable chagrin at having a wife foisted on him. We may even feel for him as he makes an embarrassing spectacle of himself in the last scene. In the brusque manner of his rejection he subjected Helena to public humiliation. The riddling tricks by which Helena's final entrance is prepared trap him in a similar if more ingeniously plotted ordeal. But on the whole Shakespeare has gone out of his way to block sympathy for Bertram. If we are dissatisfied with the play's hero this is not the result of sloppy playwriting but of the playwright's intention, quite deliberately carried out, to challenge us. We are made to confront as honestly as possible the fact that Helena is obsessively in love with a man who has no obvious qualifications as a love object apart from (presumably) his good looks – and to ask, is this really so strange? This is the experience of the Sonnets. The beautiful young man turns cold and sour and the speaker, hurt and complaining, remains obsessed with him. In a similar way, the speaker faces the dark lady's promiscuity with a volatile mix of anger, cynical wit, pain and acceptance. What he cannot do is get his mind off her. Anyone who finds such irrational feelings unrecognizable may be congratulated on a lucky escape.

It is only a slight exaggeration to say that everyone is down on Bertram but Helena. His mother disowns him, and what credit he wins in the war evaporates in the last scene. Lafew, who intends at first to marry his daughter to him, goes from 'I long to talk with the young noble soldier' (4.5.82–3) to 'I will buy me a son-in-law at a fair, and toll for this. I'll none of him' (5.3.146–7). Samuel Johnson is not the only one who cannot reconcile his heart to Bertram. Virtually no one in the play can – except Helena. By the same token, everyone in the play sees through Parolles and mocks him – except Bertram. And everyone admires and praises Helena – except Bertram. In Helena's choice of Bertram, Bertram's choice of Parolles, and Bertram's rejection of Helena, there is the same pattern of perverse but recognizable psychology: the need to make, at whatever cost to common sense or general approval, a decision that is stubbornly one's own. To say that the heart has its reasons of which the reason knows nothing, to

---

[1] 'Shakespeare Season', p. 562.
[2] *Renown at Stratford*, p. 75.

say that one loves without counting the cost – all this may sound romantic. Shakespeare makes us confront what such commitments can be like, how much humiliation can be involved.

The puzzle of Helena is more than just the puzzle of someone with an inexplicable attachment. As Barbara Everett puts it, 'Helena is *inward*. There is nothing which we do not know about the earlier heroines, in so far as we need to know anything; and the fact is that we do not need to know much. There is a good deal we need to know about Helena, and we never know it all'. In fact, she adds, 'we cannot "know" her; we can only watch, with a greater or lesser degree of sympathetic involvement, a dynamic process of change called Helena'.[1] It is symptomatic of our problem in reading her that one of her most eloquent speeches, beginning 'There shall your master have a thousand loves' (1.1.141), can have totally different meanings according to whether 'There' means Helena's virginity, or the court to which Bertram is going. Harriet Walter, who played Helena in Trevor Nunn's production, finds her 'very tentative' and says of the soliloquy that ends the first scene, 'Every line is split half way so that the sense of the sentence is in the first half of the next line. You get the feeling of an impulse to keep explaining, as if she herself doesn't know quite what she's doing. She isn't declarative.'[2] Angela Down, who played her in the BBC production, speaks of a division between what Helena says – and genuinely means – and what she actually does.[3] In the play's opening Helena is quiet and withdrawn; in the BBC production, quite literally hard to see. The Countess's praise of her, early in the scene in which she uncovers what she calls 'The mystery of your loneliness' (1.3.143), notes a quality of self-effacement: 'There is more owing her than is paid, and more shall be paid her than she'll demand' (1.3.81–2). She does not yet know that Helena will demand nothing less than her son.

When Helena is left alone for her first soliloquy, the note she strikes is one of absolute hopelessness:

> I am undone! There is no living, none,
> If Bertram be away. 'Twere all one
> That I should love a bright particular star
> And think to wed it, he is so above me.
> . . .
> The hind that would be mated by the lion
> Must die for love.   (1.1.72–80)

She goes on to describe the maddening pleasure, 'pretty, though a plague' (80), of simply looking at him, and concludes, 'he's gone, and my idolatrous fancy / Must sanctify his relics' (85–6). It is love for a star, for another species, for a dead saint; it is idolatry. It is a love she can neither fulfil nor justify.

Then Parolles enters. What follows is the first of a number of scenes in which

[1] Introduction to the New Penguin edition, 1970, pp. 16, 17; emphasis in original.
[2] Rutter, *Clamorous Voices*, p. 77.
[3] Styan, *Shakespeare in Performance*, p. 20. Styan surveys the great variety of ways in which Helena has been played (pp. 16–20).

Helena, through contact with another character, is virtually re-made before our eyes. She takes a moment to introduce Parolles, in an aside, as one she loves for Bertram's sake but knows to be a liar, a fool and a coward. That might prepåre us for a scene in which she mocks him, as Lafew will do. What happens is rather different. Their first encounter is brisk, snapping us out of the reflective, discursive manner of the play so far:

> PAROLLES 'Save you, fair queen!
> HELENA And you, monarch!
> PAROLLES No.
> HELENA And no. (1.1.94–7)

Immediately a bargain is struck: don't play games with me and I won't play games with you. If in Parolles' greeting there is a pun on 'quean' then Helena is brushing off a sexual insult. But the basic effect is that these are two self-aware people who, whatever faces they may show to the world, insist on being with each other simply the things they are.

Bantering with Parolles on the subject of virginity, Helena goes from 'Man is enemy to virginity; how may we barricado it against him?' (1.1.100–1) to 'Is there no military policy how virgins might blow up men?' (107–8) (with the innuendo, how can I get a man sexually excited?), to 'How might one do, sir, to lose it to her own liking?' (129). If Bertram is in her thoughts (and it is safe to assume he is) she goes from a conventional resistance, to the thought of arousing him, to the thought of consummation. In thought and manner, she is a different character from the one whose hopeless, longing soliloquy we have just heard. And it is Helena, not Parolles, who introduces the comic equation of sex and war that dominates the first part of their dialogue. She uses Parolles' military pose (in its own way as far from reality as her love) to get her mind going, and she matches his frank bawdry with her own. As Harriet Walter notes, the dialogue 'shows her as someone not weepy but someone witty, *sexy*. And it shows one of Helena's best traits, the way she can speak the right language for the right person – apart from the fact that she can't open her mouth when she's with Bertram.'[1] It seems to be a new Helena who speaks the soliloquy at the end of the scene, the earlier hopelessness replaced by confidence and determination, looking no longer to a remote heaven but to her own resources – 'Our remedies oft in ourselves do lie, / Which we ascribe to heaven' (1.1.187–8) – with the impossible suddenly transformed into the certain: 'Who ever strove / To show her merit that did miss her love?' (1.1.197–8). She even has a plan: the King's disease will take her to Paris, and the rest (what it is she does not say; though determined, she is still a bit hidden) will follow. It is as though Parolles, a social climber who has succeeded against the odds, a plain speaker who jokes about sex as an inevitable part of life, has charged her batteries.

It is a different Helena again who meets with the Countess in 1.3. We have seen her go from straightforward hopelessness to equally straightforward determination. With

---

[1] Rutter, *Clamorous Voices*, p. 80; emphasis in original.

the Countess she is subtle and riddling, at once hiding her feelings about Bertram and making the Countess (whose approval she needs) draw them out. When the Countess calls herself a mother to Helena, Helena objects that this cannot be, because Bertram cannot be her brother:

> My master, my dear lord he is, and I
> His servant live, and will his vassal die.
> He must not be my brother.   (1.3.130–2)

Her sense of the class gulf, once painfully real, is now a tactical role she plays, leading the conversation around to Bertram. After a suitable period of resistance she lets the Countess draw out her secret; but she still insists, 'I know I love in vain, strive against hope' (1.3.173). She is the idolater of her first soliloquy, adoring the sun (1.3.176–9). Yet we know that her plans are already laid; the hopelessness, like the humility, is a role to play until she has the Countess's full approval. Her next move is to appeal to the Countess's own memories of youthful love:

>   if yourself,
> Whose agèd honor cites a virtuous youth,
> Did ever in so true a flame of liking
> Wish chastely, and love dearly . . .   (1.3.181–4)

She has struck a chord. As Helena entered for this meeting the Countess, watching her, declared, 'Even so it was with me when I was young' (1.3.100). That was not for Helena's ears, and presumably she did not hear it; but something tells her that when she speaks of love the Countess will know what she is talking about. The women finally bond, however, not just in a shared experience of love but in mutual frankness. Knowing Helena wants to go to Paris, the Countess gets her, this time with no difficulty at all, to confess that her motive is not to cure the King but to see Bertram. She and Parolles were frank with each other at the start of their scene, and then relaxed into banter. The mutual frankness she and the Countess achieve comes after a good deal of skilled probing on both sides, and forms the basis for the fullest, most sympathetic relationship Helena has with another character. Yet it is part of the achievement of the scene that the hesitations and evasions I have seen as tactical can equally well be read as genuine uncertainty, a series of fumbles that lead Helena, by sheer luck, in the right direction.

She heads for Paris with an air of confidence, and she enters the King's presence with, it seems, no confidence at all. Lafew has to tell her twice, 'Nay, come your ways' as though she balks at coming on stage (2.1.89–90), and his comment, 'A traitor you do look like' (2.1.92) tells us that she looks afraid. Trying to persuade the King that she can cure him, she appeals to her father's skill (2.1.96–110). His refusal sends her packing, the humble, self-effacing Helena who knew her love for Bertram was hopeless: 'I will no more enforce mine office on you' (2.1.122). But as she heads for the door he holds her for a moment with a last expression of gratitude, leading to a final dismissal: 'But what at full I know, thou know'st no part, / I knowing all my peril, thou no art' (2.1.128–9). The insult is not to her father but to her, a mere ignorant girl, and she takes it as a challenge, turning back to confront him: 'What I can do can do no hurt to try' (2.1.130). What *I* can do: from this point it is not her father's skill but her own that is on trial; and not just her skill but her whole being. Her next few speeches appeal to heaven, and catch the King's interest; but what clinches the matter for him is the price she offers to pay if she fails:

> Tax of impudence,
> A strumpet's boldness, a divulgèd shame,
> Traduced by odious ballads; my maiden's name
> Seared otherwise; ne worse of worst – extended
> With vilest torture, let my life be ended. (2.1.166–70)

She began the scene afraid to enter the room; she ends it willing to risk her life. She began the play pining in secret over a hopeless love; now she is willing to be shamed in public as a strumpet. This offer – on which she dwells longer than she does on death by torture – has no logical connection with the business at hand, and might be written off as one of those mysteries about Helena that we will never solve. Yet it has its own logic, as the most extreme risk she can take. Secretive, she is willing to be cruelly exposed; longing to be a wife, she is ready to endure a slander that would end such hopes forever. After this, death would be merely a way of ending a life that was not worth having. The King has drawn all this out of her, by questioning her art. She takes this as a challenge to her very being, and raises the stakes as high as they can go.

Helena is created for us by her soliloquies, and by her interaction with other characters. It is a volatile mix. She seems always ready to sink into self-effacement and despair. She needs to be teased, as she is by Parolles ('Are you meditating on virginity?') (1.1.98); challenged, as she is by the Countess; insulted, as she is by the King. Her responses re-make her before our eyes. She is also the centre of a set of conversations that go on throughout the play, about the mix of ingredients that go to make up a human being. In the first scene, as she stands silent, the Countess analyses her: 'I have those hopes of her good that her education promises. Her dispositions she inherits, which makes fair gifts fairer . . . She derives her honesty and achieves her goodness' (1.1.30–35). She is made up of education, heredity, and her own achievements. In the Countess's later claim to be her mother, even the notion of her parentage can be re-negotiated: 'Adoption strives with nature, and choice breeds / A native slip to us from foreign seeds' (1.3.116–17). The King re-defines honour as the term applies to her:

> The property by what it is should go,
> Not by the title. She is young, wise, fair,
> In these to nature she's immediate heir;
> And these breed honour. (2.3.122–5)

As the Countess claims the right to be Helena's mother, re-defining motherhood in the process, the King, shifting ground, goes on to claim that Helena's honour can be his own doing, not hers: 'Virtue and she / Is her own dower; honour and wealth from me' (2.3.135–6). There is a discursiveness in passages like these that recalls *Measure for Measure* and *Troilus and Cressida*, where questions of justice and value, arising from the immediate dramatic situation, lead to general debates. In the opening scene the Countess sees Bertram as she sees Helena, a mix of what he inherits and what he naturally is:

> Thy blood and virtue
> Contend for empire in thee, and thy goodness
> Share with thy birthright.   (1.1.50–2)

In the event, Bertram's virtue is little in evidence and his birthright, in the form of his ancestral ring, he gives away to bed Diana.[1] In the last scene Helena has the ring. Does she return it to him? The text does not specify. Symbolically, whatever dignity he can recover rests on her decision. What are we in ourselves, and what do we owe to others? How far can the seemingly inevitable bonds of parentage and ancestry be re-negotiated? Such questions, which begin with Helena, do not end with her.

The high-life characters may talk of virtue and inheritance as the ingredients that make a human being. It takes Parolles and Lavatch to insist that sex is an important part of the mix. Parolles gets Helena to talk about it; and it forms the centre of much of Lavatch's fooling. The Countess finds Lavatch out of place, breaking off a conversation about Helena to ask, 'What does this knave here? Get you gone, sirrah' (1.3.6). But he stays, bantering with her as Parolles does with Helena, and his desire to marry Isbel forms a bawdy counterpoint to Helena's desire for Bertram. It is God's will: 'I shall never have the blessing of God till I have issue a'my body; for they say barnes are blessings' (1.3.19–20). Helena too will need to produce a child, though for reasons that have little to do with God. Lavatch goes on to admit that there are other, lower forces at work: 'My poor body, madam, requires it. I am driven on by the flesh, and he needs must go that the devil drives' (1.3.22–3). For some critics that is the answer to the puzzle of Helena's attraction to Bertram: it is 'merely physical'.[2]

Even if we agree with that, we may question the word 'merely'. Shakespeare adds to Boccaccio a surprising, seemingly irrelevant, undercurrent of sexuality in Helena's curing of the King. Besides her offer to be traduced as a strumpet, there are suggestions in the language that Helena is restoring not just the King's general health but his potency. Lafew tells the King that Helena's 'simple touch / Is powerful to araise King Pippen' (2.1.71–2). In Richard Monette's production, Lafew (Bernard Hopkins) illustrated the line with a quick upward thrust of his staff of office. Leaving doctor and patient alone together, Lafew calls himself 'Cressid's uncle' (2.1.93). The time between the King's agreement and the King's cure is taken up with Lavatch's routine about his answer that fits all questions, a kind of verbal copulation, 'as Tib's rush [ring] for Tom's forefinger . . . as the nail to his hole . . . as the nun's lip to the friar's mouth, nay, as the pudding to his skin' (2.2.17–21). This element in the King's cure was

---

[1] In the BBC production the Countess gave Bertram the ring on the word 'birthright', in the speech just quoted.
[2] Robert Ornstein, *Shakespeare's Comedies: From Roman Farce to Romantic Mystery*, 1986, p. 175. R. B. Parker calls Helena's initial feeling for Bertram 'wholly sexual . . . and totally visual': 'War and Sex', p. 107.

heavily emphasized in the BBC production. When Lafew said that Helena could make Charlemagne 'write to her a love-line' the King (Donald Sinden) reacted with sudden interest to the word 'her'. Contemplating the youth and beauty Helena is willing to surrender with her life, he ran his hands over her face. By the end of the scene they were sharing a long kiss, which Helena herself initiated. Later, when telling Bertram what he owed Helena, the King declared 'she has raised me [heavy pause] from my sickly bed'. This performance may be accused of over-emphasizing the sex, turning the King in particular into a dirty old man. But the bawdy comedy alerts us to an important element in the King's cure. Helena has to do more than restore his health; she has to give him a reason for going on living. He has been tired and dispirited, merely waiting to die. When she puts her life on the line he is made to think about the value of life itself, embodied (literally) in the young, attractive woman he sees in front of him:

> Thy life is dear, for all that life can rate
> Worth name of life in thee hath estimate:
> Youth, beauty, wisdom, courage, all
> That happiness and prime can happy call.   (2.1.175–8)

Lavatch has seen procreation as the will of God and sexuality as the work of the flesh and the devil. His later cuckold-jokes suggest a weariness with the whole business. But the King sees in Helena's youth and physical attraction a reason why the world is worth living in after all. The bawdy suggestions in the language, like Parolles' banter about virginity, are the surface hints of a deeper, more powerful and serious force at work. We do not need to imagine improprieties in the consulting room to say that it is Helena's body that cures the King. In the bed-trick she uses her body again, more practically and literally, and it is not so clear that the result is to cure Bertram. But the same force is at work, and her final entrance, not just back from the dead but pregnant, embodies for the play as a whole what she embodied for the King, the power of life itself.

Another element in Helena's cure of the King, and in the mix of ingredients that makes up human life, is the power of heaven. She presents herself not just as a skilled physician, but as the instrument of that power: 'Of heaven, not me, make an experiment' (2.1.150). This is in a long speech in rhyming couplets, which in performance has sometimes been given a mystical quality: in Guthrie's 1959 production, by incantatory delivery; in Peter Hall's production, by the mechanical aids of music and an echo on the sound system.[1] Through Helena's youth and beauty the King sees a higher power at work: 'Methinks in thee some blessed spirit doth speak / His powerful sound within an organ weak' (2.1.171–2). The final emphasis falls, I think, on Helena herself. But the forces that go to make her up include not just her own skill and virtue, her physical attraction, her inheritance from her father, her adoption by the Countess, and the honour the King bestows, but something from beyond this world.

[1] Byrne, 'Shakespeare Season', p. 563; Holland, 'Shakespeare Performances . . . 1992', p. 165.

Helena, who at the beginning of the play seemed (to herself at least) to have nothing going for her, now has everything going for her. Except Bertram. I have said that in his rejection of her he takes no account of her feelings. But has she ever taken account of his? Her question has been simply, how can I win him? In the BBC production, when the King bestowed Helena on him, Ian Charleson's Bertram began with a long pause, glancing back and forth between the King and Helena, then a laugh of incredulity. When he objected to Helena's class, he fingered the ring that was the sign of his family honour. So far he was not petulant but making what seemed to him a reasonable argument; only on 'I cannot love her' did he become angry and stubborn. Critics who have defended Bertram at this point see him as resisting, as he has every right to do, an unwarranted assertion of royal power, opposing to it 'the heroic resolution of an aristocrat'.[1] As many of Shakespeare's contemporaries would have understood the matter, the King is abusing his authority: his right to dispose of a ward in marriage is 'subject to two limitations: equality of rank, and consentual freedom of the ward'.[2] The King raises Helena's rank by arbitrary fiat, and gets Bertram's consent by bullying. Audience reactions to this moment can be complex. In a production directed by Martin Hunter at Hart House Theatre, University of Toronto, in 1976, Bertram's first response to Helena's choice of him was to look around in a panic, getting a laugh. On 'A poor physician's daughter my wife? Disdain / Rather corrupt me ever!' there were gasps of shock. (On stage as Lafew, I noted that this double reaction was consistent, night after night.) There was a similar turn from laughter to shock in Richard Monette's production. The modern audience, it might be said, does not appreciate Bertram's viewpoint, not having read the right books. But the play has set up the audience's shock by Helena's dialogues with the nameless young lords that precede her choice of Bertram. She declines each of them, professing her unworthiness, seeing herself as Bertram will see her; they politely demur, seemingly ready to accept her. Only one young lord sees her as unworthy, and that is the one she picks. However we may debate the rights and wrongs of Bertram's refusal (and they are debatable) Helena's plan founders on one simple fact: Bertram does not want her. It is the answer to a question she has never asked.

What looked like her triumph has become a disaster. Once again the hopeless, despairing Helena of the first scene, she tells the King, 'That you are well restored, my lord, I'm glad. / Let the rest go' (2.3.139–40). Echoing her action on the King's first rebuff, Harriet Walter at this point tried to leave, and had to be dragged back.[3] In the BBC production, when Bertram took her hand on the King's orders, Helena looked down and away, her face registering failure. Re-made before our eyes as a positive, determined woman by her interaction with other characters in earlier scenes, Helena is now broken before our eyes by the man on whom she has centred her life. 'Let the rest go' are her last words in the scene, which becomes a power struggle between the two men while she stands mute. Bertram addresses not a word to her during the entire

[1] Haley, *Courtly Mirror*, p. 44. See also Cole, *All's Well Story*, pp. 98–9.
[2] Ranald, *Social Context*, p. 38.
[3] Rutter, *Clamorous Voices*, pp. 83–4.

scene; he speaks only to the King. And from the moment of Helena's choice the King speaks only to Bertram. When he declares, 'Mine honour's at the stake, which to defeat, / I must produce my power' (2.3.141–2) he shifts from Helena's interests to his own. Actors playing the King (including Sebastian Shaw for the Royal Shakespeare Company in 1967 and William Hutt at Stratford, Ontario in 1977), have taken a sharp turn at this point from reasonable argument to angry tirade. Shaw's outburst triggered a slamming of doors as though the attendants recognized that when he was in this sort of mood it had better be kept private; the effect was also to trap Bertram. And not just Bertram; Helena's last words show that the King is forcing two people into a marriage neither of them now wants.

From this point the play breaks into a series of short scenes, with characters represented by letters and reports, and action shuttling rapidly between different locations. Bertram gives instructions to Helena through Parolles, speaking guardedly to her in his own person, and sets out the conditions about the child and the ring, which he intends as a final dismissal, by letter. Helena dwindles into a self-deprecating Griselda figure, like the submissive wives of popular drama: 'Sir, I can nothing say, / But that I am your most obedient servant' (2.5.65–6). The marriage solemnized but not consummated, the couple are in a legal twilight zone; should they continue in this state for a period of time, Bertram could have the marriage dissolved.[1] Helena is torn about her right even to ask for a kiss:

> I am not worthy of the wealth I owe,
> Nor dare I say 'tis mine; and yet it is;
> But like a timorous thief, most fain would steal
> What law does vouch mine own. (2.5.73–6)

The self-deprecating Helena and the assertive Helena are simultaneously present, at war with each other. The first Helena seems to win out (and the word 'thief' returns) in the soliloquy that ends 3.2, as she blames herself for the danger Bertram faces in the war and creeps away, not the Countess of Rossillion but a thief in the night: 'with the dark, poor thief, I'll steal away' (3.2.121). She is far as she could be from Boccaccio's Giletta, who at this point has had a triumphant public career as manager of her husband's estate. She goes to an unknown destination, withdrawn not just from our view but from our knowledge. From this point, R. L. Smallwood has noted, she appears in fewer scenes (five out of thirteen, as opposed to seven out of ten) and speaks half the number of lines she did before.[2] Like Bertram, she communicates by letter, announcing she is on a pilgrimage to Santiago de Compostella, for a period of self-chastisement even more severe than the discipline assigned to the men at the end of *Love's Labour's Lost*:

> Ambitious love hath so in me offended,
> That barefoot plod I the cold ground upon
> With sainted vow my faults to have amended. (3.4.5–7)

[1] Ranald, *Social Context*, p. 43.
[2] 'The Design of "All's Well That Ends Well"', *S.Sur.* 25 (1972), 45–61 (p. 54).

From this point, so far as the characters who have known her are concerned, she disappears into rumors and reports, in the last of which she dies.

Love's Labour's Lost is about to become *Love's Labour's Won*, but the means are not straightforward. Florence is not exactly on the route to Santiago de Compostella, and Helena's appearance there is neither anticipated nor explained; it just happens. We are less in her confidence than ever. Her identity concealed, she hears the women of Florence report Parolles' insulting view of her, and apparently agrees: 'she is too mean / To have her name repeated' (3.5.53–4). Is this in a straight line from the abject view of herself she took on her last appearance, or is it (as the hopelessness she adopted with the Countess might have been) a role to play until her plans are ripe? Again, we cannot be sure. One thing we can say is that, having been argued over by two angry men in a room full of other men, she now surrounds herself with women, among whom she finds sympathy. Before she even knows her, Diana takes her side:

> Alas, poor lady,
> 'Tis a hard bondage to become the wife
> Of a detesting lord.   (3.5.56–8)

When they know who she is, Diana and her mother are almost fulsome in their willingness to serve her (4.4.15–6, 28–30). We are now very far from the court; the BBC version showed Diana shaping bread and the Widow cutting up vegetables. This is also a world in which money matters; the Widow is short of it, and while she initially hesitates over the bed-trick, Helena's offer of 3,000 crowns for Diana's dowry produces a quick 'I have yielded' (3.7.36). In the BBC version (whose evocation of Dutch paintings of bourgeois life came fully into play here) Helena's persuasion of the widow began with a close-up of coins in her hand.

If her body had a figurative role in the curing of the King, it has a literal role in the bed-trick. There is still some play with the figurative, however. War, sex and death have already been connected in the punning of Lavatch: 'The danger is in standing to't; that's the loss of men, though it be the getting of children' (3.2.34–6). Helena undergoes the 'death' of orgasm with Bertram (without which, according to contemporary medical theory, she would not have got pregnant) at the same time as the false report of her literal death arrives in the camp. Bertram's attempted conquest of Diana is figuratively a siege: as Sheldon P. Zitner puts it, 'seduction as the continuation of war by other means'.[1] Sex is paradoxical as well as figurative. Helena presents the bed-trick not as the straightforward completion of a task, the answer to a riddle, but as a riddle in itself:

> Why then tonight
> Let us assay our plot, which if it speed,
> Is wicked meaning in a lawful deed,
> And lawful meaning in a lawful act,
> Where both not sin, and yet a sinful fact.
> But let's about it.   (3.7.43–8)

[1] *New Critical Introductions*, p. 120. See also Parker, 'War and Sex', p. 105.

The speech begins and ends with the practical, assertive Helena, determined to get on with it. In between, beginning with 'if' (the word that will provide a drag on the comic momentum of the finale), there is the hesitant Helena who apologised for begging a kiss to which she was entitled and not entitled. What Helena is about to do is ensnared in riddling language that produces a temporary stasis.

Both Helena and Bertram are involved in the riddle: while she is doing something technically proper (having sex, knowingly, with her husband) he is doing is something more paradoxical (fornicating with his wife) and she is enabling it. When they have done the deed Helena has another riddling speech, this time not about the legalities but about the personal feelings involved, and now the paradoxes centre on Bertram:

> But O, strange men,
> That can such sweet use make of what they hate,
> When saucy trusting of the cozened thoughts
> Defiles the pitchy night; so lust doth play
> With what it loathes for that which is away –
> But more of this hereafter. (4.4.21–6)

In the first part of the play they were physically apart, and while worshipping him from afar she thought nothing of his feelings about her. Now she looks back on physical intimacy, and it is as though what she has felt in Bertram's lovemaking was his hate. As in the early discussions of the mix that makes up a human being, 'O, strange men' turns her problem with Bertram into a generalization, a woman's feeling that the lust men direct to them is a form of hatred. She has been played with, used, by lust. Yet it was 'sweet' use, and at a greater distance, in the last scene, moving toward what she hopes will be reconciliation, she pays him a wry compliment: 'O my good lord, when I was like this maid, / I found you wondrous kind' (5.3.299–300). 'Kind' is a shifty word. She may be saying only that he did what comes by nature, and we may think back on Lavatch's cynical 'Your marriage comes by destiny, / Your cuckoo sings by kind' (1.3.48–9). Or she may be saying that he was after all a gentle, understanding lover – because he thought she was someone else.

Being offstage, their encounter can be hidden from us by Helena's riddles and paradoxes. But some productions have brought the bed-trick on stage, so far as it is possible to do so. Revealingly, the effect was pure comedy. In Elias Zarou's unusually light-hearted production for Tempest Theatre at the Annex Theatre in Toronto (1996), Diana, in a white nightdress, led Bertram to bed in a dim light; she then beckoned to Helena, who came on in an identical nightdress, climbing into bed with Bertram as Diana withdrew and the lights went out. Throughout the exchange both women were smiling. The effect was to turn the episode into an amusing, bawdy trick; we were in Boccaccio country. In Richard Monette's production Diana blindfolded Bertram; Helena then appeared, kissed him (getting the kiss she had been denied earlier) and led him off. Bertram later emerged on the balcony with a smug grin and a sigh of satisfaction. The audience's laugh was at once complicit and ironic: mission accomplished, but it was not the mission he thought it was. In the play as written, where we have only

the riddling language and disturbed feelings that surround the bed-trick, the easy satisfaction such comedy brings is denied.

Monette's staging of course drew out the parallel between the tricking of Bertram
and the tricking of Parolles. Bertram's blindfold was orange, the dominant colour of
the Florentine scenes; he was being led off for sex. Parolles' blindfold was black; he was
threatened with death. Even without such staging, the parallel is there in the text. In
the gulling of Parolles, though this time we see everything, Parolles is as much in the
dark as Bertram. Master and man are fooled together. As identities dissolve in the
darkness of the bedroom and the impersonality of sex, language for Parolles (the man
of words) dissolves in the gibberish spoken by his assailants. The parallels may prevent
us from getting too solemn about the bed-trick, reminding us that whatever else can
be said about it, it is, after all, a trick.

Shakespeare cuts back and forth between the two tricks, teasing us with similarities
and differences. (In the one, Bertram is hoodwinked; in the other, his eyes are opened.)
But the most remarkable thing about the fooling of Parolles is the way it ends, and this,
we shall see, has a bearing on the final movement of the play. Up to a point the gulling
of Parolles is a holiday for the audience, drawing on easy responses. The braggart
boasts of being able to recover a drum captured by the enemy; trying to carry out his
boast, he is set upon and interrogated by his fellow soldiers, who pretend to be the
enemy. The eagerness with which he betrays his own side to save his life reveals his
cowardly nature. The drum is an appropriate symbol for Parolles himself as he has
appeared up to this point in the play: it is an image of the externals of soldiership, loud
and empty.[1] But as he broods on his folly in offering to recover the drum, we learn that,
however he may lie to others, Parolles does not lie to himself:

> What the devil should move me to undertake the recovery of this drum, being not ignorant
> of the impossibility, and knowing I had no such purpose? I must give myself some hurts,
> and say I got them in exploit. Yet slight ones will not carry it . . . And great ones I dare not
> give.   (4.1.27–31)

The Second Lord, overhearing, asks, 'Is it possible he should know what he is, and be
that he is?' (4.1.35–6). As we saw in his first exchange with Helena, Parolles does
indeed know what he is. This gives the character an underlying firmness and clarity,
even as, under arrest, he collapses in humiliating panic. And in describing the
Florentine officers he scores points off his tormentors with a set of insults so extrava-
gant that one of his victims declares, 'I begin to love him for this'. Bertram, who has
no discernible sense of humour, is puzzled: 'For this description of thine honesty?'
(4.3.221–2). But his colleague has begun to relish Parolles, as the audience has all
along, for being the thing he is.

Threatened with death – a threat that seemed quite serious in the BBC production,
as his assailants forced his forehead down on to the table, lifted his back hair, and laid
a sword blade across the back of his neck – Parolles cries out, 'O Lord, sir, let me live,
or let me see my death!' (4.3.259). The quick echo of Lavatch's routine ('O Lord, sir')

[1] Parker, 'War and Sex', pp. 103–4; Zitner, *New Critical Introductions*, p. 74.

reminds us this is still comedy. But the real surprise is that the cowardly braggart who has built his career on lies wants to look his death in the face. The soldier who has been acting as interpreter takes this as his cue to remove Parolles' blindfold: 'That shall you, and take your leave of all your friends' (4.3.260). Parolles faces not his death, but his life. The shock he gets on seeing Bertram and his fellow officers, and on knowing he has revealed himself to them, anticipates the shock Bertram will get when Helena appears and reveals that she was the woman he slept with in Florence. But while Bertram will have only two very short speeches in which to react, Parolles, left alone, gets a soliloquy in which he comes to terms with his disgrace and plans not just to rise above it but to exploit it as a survival strategy:

> Captain I'll be no more,
> But I will eat, and drink, and sleep as soft
> As captain shall. Simply the thing I am
> Shall make me live . . .
> Rust sword, cool blushes, and, Parolles, live
> Safest in shame! Being fool'd, by fool'ry thrive!
> There's place and means for every man alive.
> I'll after them.   (4.3.278–87)

The last three words have the brisk determination of Helena's 'But let's about it' (3.7.48). In each case a scene ends on an incomplete line, suggesting both unfinished business and a decision to get on with it.

Parolles survives by latching himself on to Lafew, not despite but because of the fact that it was Lafew who first exposed him: 'O my good lord, you were the first that found me!' (5.2.35). And Lafew accepts him, exactly as Parolles predicted, for what he is: 'though you are a fool and a knave, you shall eat' (5.2.43–4). In the BBC version Peter Jeffrey's Parolles was transformed, unrecognizable, his hair clipped short, his beard and moustache gone, his red costume succeeded by slate-grey, his obsequious manner suggesting Uriah Heep. By one interpretation, we were seeing the inner, original man who was underneath the braggart (just as we learn at the end of *Tartuffe* that the impostor has another name, known only to the all-seeing King). There was also a suggestion here of a new Parolles, and this would explain why, when he first encounters him in 5.2, Lafew does not recognize him. Yet what Lafew wants is the old Parolles: 'How does your drum?' (5.2.34). In the 1967 Royal Shakespeare production this was backed by a simple, telling detail: Parolles had a begging-box in the shape of a small drum.

Parolles' decision to seek out the man who once despised him, and Lafew's acceptance of him, not transformed but as he is, may provide some underpinning for the mutual acceptance of Helena and Bertram in the last scene. But the relatively simple route Parolles takes to recovery and acceptance also plays off against the more difficult route taken by the characters of the main plot, highlighting the difficulties by contrast. Now that Helena has made the King mobile she has trouble tracking him down. The finale is delayed when she arrives late at Marseilles, only to find he has left for Rossillion – though that delay might suggest a greater sense of fulfilment at the end,

9   Act 4, Scene 3. Clive Swift as Parolles, Patrick O'Connell as Morgan, Ian Richardson as Bertram and David Moynihan as Dumaine the Elder, in John Barton's production of 1967 at the Royal Shakespeare Theatre (Zoë Dominic)

as the story returns to its starting point. Helena herself, in the minds of the other characters, has disappeared into nostalgic, idealized memories, as though she has joined the dead, idealized fathers of the play's opening. The last scene, whose apparent opening business is a new wife for Bertram, is at first held back by memories of the old one, beginning with the King's 'We lost a jewel of her' (5.3.1). The word 'jewel' recalls the exchange of rings in the bed-trick, and that trick looks like being oddly duplicated when, as Helena substitutes for Diana, Lafew's daughter Maudlin seems about to substitute for Helena. Maudlin never appears, and Lafew's first reference to her, well into a conversation in which he has been recalling Helena and bantering with Lavatch, begins with the words, 'I was about to tell you' (4.5.54). It is as though he himself is a bit absent-minded about her, as the play certainly is. Once introduced, she disrupts our reading of Bertram, giving him a past of which we previously had no inkling. He recalls that Maudlin was his first love, and his devotion to her made him despise any other woman, including Helena – whom he now claims to love since he lost her (5.3.44–55). This is a new Bertram, re-written before our eyes as Helena has been, with new feelings and motives. Two literal-minded questions arise: why didn't he say all this before? We would have understood his rejection of Helena much better. But that presupposes that this is a play by Ibsen, in which the revelation of a suppressed truth about the past really can transform the drama. The second literal-minded question is

10 The finale of Tyrone Guthrie's production (designed by Tanya Moiseiwitsch) at the Shakespeare Memorial Theatre, 1959. Zoe Caldwell as Helena, Edward de Souza as Bertram (Angus McBean)

perhaps more apposite: do we take any of this seriously, or is Bertram (or the play) making it up on the spot? The King's response, 'Well excused' (5.3.55), suggests we can read Bertram's account as just that, an excuse. It belongs to the Bertram of the present scene, trying to ingratiate himself with the people he has offended; it is not a new way of seeing the Bertram of the earlier action but another false clue. Maudlin – in effect, a non-character – is also doing a job for the play, providing an ersatz new wife for Bertram as part of the protracted riddling that brings his true wife back on to the stage. The ring Bertram gives Lafew as a love-token for Maudlin is Helena's ring, and it starts the chain reaction that leads to her return.

Throughout the play Helena has presented different faces to us. As a character she is not a beam of white light but a range of colours, light broken as it passes through the prism of the drama. Her final entrance is preceded by false images and substitutions: memories of her as someone dead, mourned and soon to be forgotten as life goes on; Maudlin as her predecessor in Bertram's affections, and her successor; Diana as the woman he slept with and should marry. False versions of the story proliferate: Bertram is accused of killing Helena; he accuses Diana of being the camp prostitute. Diana's riddling gets reckless and crazy: she claims that if she ever slept with a man it was the King, and if she is not a maid she is Lafew's wife (5.3.277, 283). Her climactic riddle is the riddle of Helena herself:

> Dead though she be, she feels her young one kick.
> So there's my riddle: one that's dead is quick –
> And now behold the meaning.   (5.3.292–4)

Through the play Helena has been the question; now it seems she is the answer.

In the process Bertram, who has if anything been all too clear, breaks in two. One Bertram submits to Helena with the simplicity of a reformed prodigal. When Helena calls herself 'the shadow of a wife . . . / The name, and not the thing', Bertram replies, 'Both, both. O, pardon!' (5.3.297–8). His focus is on her: what she is for him, and how he has wronged her. He tries to integrate her into a single being, shadow and substance fused. Moments later there is another, more cautious Bertram: 'If she, my liege, can make me know this clearly, / I'll love her dearly, ever, ever dearly'. He is speaking once more to the King, not to her. Helena takes up the challenge, speaking to him, forcing his attention back to her: 'If it appear not plain and prove untrue, / Deadly divorce step between me and you!' (5.3.305–8). Rosalind set up the finale of *As You Like It* with a series of 'if'-clauses, telling Phoebe, 'I will marry you, if ever I marry woman' and Orlando, 'I will satisfy you, if ever I satisfied man' (5.2.13–15), and so on. The ending of the play answers the question behind each 'if'-clause. *All's Well That Ends Well* ends before that happens, the resolution held off even in the King's final couplet: 'All yet seems well, and if it end so meet, / The bitter past, more welcome is the sweet' (5.3.321–2). He also promises to find a husband for Diana if she is a virgin, and she is (5.3.316). Do we take this as a clue for reading the 'if's of Helena and Bertram? The condition seems to be that Helena can prove her story. Surely she can; she is, after all, pregnant, and she has the ring. But is the child Bertram's? Of course; but lacking the resources of modern science, can she prove it? That paternity can never be proved is a classic male anxiety. The King's first greeting to Bertram was, 'Youth, thou bear'st thy father's face' (1.2.19). Will Bertram say this to Helena's child? Set against these doubts, if they are at all serious, is the fact that Helena and Bertram are talking to each other. As Barbara Hodgdon points out, the bargaining may not be romantic, but it 'articulates – in this text, for these characters – a startling mutuality'.[1]

The Epilogue, spoken not by the King but by the actor who played the King, leaves the final decision to us: 'All is well ended, if this suit be won, / That you express content' (2–3). Having wondered how to read the characters, we are now made to wonder how to read the title. Is it straight or ironic? Is our content to come from a satisfying romantic ending, or from the honest openness that holds off such an ending? In staging the ending, productions have made a variety of choices. We have already noted the difference between the three-way embrace of Barry Kyle's production and the barely touching fingertips of Trevor Nunn's. In the BBC version, and in Richard Monette's production, Bertram's 'if' was underplayed, while the 'seems' and 'if' of the King's final speech were stressed more heavily. In the television version the selectivity of the camera came into play. The King was seen in close-up, looking into the fire. Was he looking into the past, or into the future? In any case he was detached from the main action which had just come to a seemingly confident conclusion. His doubts were private. Bertram had taken Helena's face in his hands (as the King did earlier) and

[1] 'The Making of Virgins and Mothers: Sexual Signs, Substitute Scenes and Doubled Presences in *All's Well That Ends Well*', *PQ* 66 (1987), 47–71 (p. 67).

Drum and Colours

Antonio

Escalus

Bertram

Parolles

"Lose our drum! Well...."

Diana

Helena

Violenta

Mariana

C.W.H.

11 'Drum and Colours. Enter Bertram, Parolles and the whole army.' A reconstruction with Elizabethan costumes for Act 3, Scene 5, by C. Walter Hodges

kissed her, their placing in the frame recalling an earlier close-up of Bertram and Diana. We were seeing the birth of a love of which earlier relationships had been shadows. For the characters at that moment there was no doubt; for the King, and perhaps the viewer, thinking over the whole action, there was some. In Guthrie's 1959 production, Bertram knelt to Helena, clinging to her, and M. St Clare Byrne claimed that though he spoke his 'if'-couplet it did not register as a reservation.[1] In Peter Hall's production, on 'This is done', Helena tore up Bertram's letter. Different audience members read the moment differently: as offering a fresh start and the possibility of love, as leaving Bertram free to reject her again, as suggesting that their relations were damaged beyond repair.[2]

In our doubt-ridden age we are no longer inclined to seek the inner unity of a work of art, to look for total patterns and satisfying conclusions. In *All's Well That Ends Well* we have a comedy that questions its own procedures, divided, like its heroine, between certainty and doubt, between a determination to produce an ending and a need to question that ending. It deals in riddles and paradoxes, and it leaves its questions with us. Helena surprises us with her instability, Parolles with his integrity. It is a love story that does not just mock at love in the manner of earlier Shakespearean comedies but takes a frank, tough-minded view of romantic obsession. Entertaining and disturbing, it leaves its interpreters, whether performers or readers, to strike the final balance – or to decide that the truth of the play lies in its instability. In Russell Fraser's words, it is 'a great play whose time has come round'.[3]

Alexander Leggatt

[1] 'Shakespeare Season', pp. 557–8.
[2] Holland, 'Shakespeare Performances . . . 1992', p. 167; Smallwood, 'Shakespeare Performed', p. 358.
[3] Cambridge introduction, p. 8.

NOTE ON THE TEXT

The Folio is the only authoritative text of the play and all later texts derive from it. It is probable that the text was first set from Shakespeare's manuscript, with a number of confusions and anomalies owed to authorial slips or changes of mind. Stage directions have been clarified (but rarely amplified or supplemented) and speech headings made consistent. Spellings have been modernised in accordance with the conventions of the series, old forms being retained only when they are judged to have an expressive significance. The collation records only those variants and emendations which seem likely to correct or illuminate the Folio text. The authority for the reading in the text follows immediately upon the square bracket after the lemma; other readings, if any, follow in chronological order. Where the authority is in a form differing from that of the text, the old form is quoted first in the gloss (e.g. vilest] vildest F). Readings that differ substantially are divided by a semi-colon (;), those that differ only formally, by a comma (e.g. lose] F4, loose F). Where syllables require an emphasis not usual in modern speech they are marked with a *grave* accent (`). Significant additions to the Folio stage directions, and occasionally to the text, are enclosed in square brackets. An asterisk in the lemma of a note in the Commentary is used to call attention to a word or phrase that has been emended in the text. References and abbreviations are listed under Abbreviations and Conventions (pp. x–xiii above), and a fuller account of the text is given in the Textual Analysis (pp. 155–8 below).

All's Well That Ends Well

LIST OF CHARACTERS

KING OF FRANCE
DUKE OF FLORENCE
BERTRAM, *Count of Rossillion*
LAFEW, *an old lord*
PAROLLES, *a follower of Bertram*
The brothers DUMAINE, *two French lords in the Florentine service*
RINALDO, *steward of the Countess*
LAVATCH, *a Clown, servant of the Countess*
A PAGE
A MESSENGER
COUNTESS OF ROSSILLION, *mother of Bertram*
HELENA, *a gentlewoman protected by the Countess*
WIDOW CAPILET *of Florence*
DIANA, *her daughter*
VIOLENTA ⎫
MARIANA ⎭ *neighbours and friends of the Widow*
A GENTLE ASTRINGER
French and Florentine LORDS, ATTENDANTS, SOLDIERS, CITIZENS

SCENE: *Rossillion, Paris, Florence, Marseilles*
Notes
The list of characters was first supplied by Rowe; not in F.
brothers DUMAINE The Lords Dumaine are named for the first and last times in Act 4, Scene 3 (176–283), where Parolles is tormented by his captors. Otherwise they appear in stage directions as *Lords, French Lords, French Gentlemen, Frenchmen, Gentleman,* and *French Captaines*. The Folio speech headings include the use of letters *G* and *E*, apparently to distinguish the FIRST and SECOND LORDS (*Lord. G.,* 1.*Lo.G., L.G.,* 2.*Lo.E., Cap.E.,* etc.). The present text usually interprets *G* as FIRST LORD and *E* as SECOND LORD, but a few emendations are necessary (see notes on SHS 3.6.2, 87, 89; 4.1.1) to maintain consistency. It is often assumed for production purposes that one brother is the elder, and some editors have emended in an attempt to give the initiatives to the FIRST LORD; there is no reason for supposing them twins, but it seems likely that Shakespeare gave little thought to precedence.
RINALDO So named for the first time at 3.4.19. In Folio stage directions he is *Steward* and in speech headings *Stew.* or *Ste.*
LAVATCH So named for the first and only time by Parolles in 5.2.1. Otherwise he appears as *Clown* throughout the Folio.
HELENA So named and spelt in the Folio at 1.1.0 SD and at 1.1.52; but Parolles calls her 'Little Hellen' (1.1.188 F) and in 1.3 the forms Helen and Hellen are used exclusively. The present text retains the forms 'Helen' and 'Helena' in the dialogue but regularises all stage directions as HELENA, without collation.
GENTLE ASTRINGER Noble falconer. See 5.1.6 SD n. and 5.3.127 SD n.
SOLDIERS Including an important role for the INTERPRETER in 4.1 and 4.3 – perhaps the 'Morgan' named at 4.3.91.

ALL'S WELL THAT ENDS WELL

1.1 *Enter young* BERTRAM, *Count of Rossillion, his Mother* [*the* COUNTESS], *and* HELENA, *Lord* LAFEW, *all in black*

COUNTESS In delivering my son from me, I bury a second husband.

BERTRAM And I in going, madam, weep o'er my father's death anew; but I must attend his majesty's command, to whom I am now in ward, evermore in subjection.

LAFEW You shall find of the king a husband, madam; you, sir, a father. 5
He that so generally is at all times good must of necessity hold his virtue to you, whose worthiness would stir it up where it wanted, rather than lack it where there is such abundance.

COUNTESS What hope is there of his majesty's amendment?

LAFEW He hath abandoned his physicians, madam, under whose 10
practices he hath persecuted time with hope, and finds no other advantage in the process but only the losing of hope by time.

COUNTESS This young gentlewoman had a father – O, that 'had', how sad a passage 'tis – whose skill was almost as great as his honesty; had it stretched so far, would have made nature immortal, and death 15

Act 1, Scene 1 1.1] *Actus primus. Scaena Prima.* F   0 SD *Enter*] *Eneer* F   1 SH COUNTESS] *Rowe; Mother* F
(Mo./hereafter through scene)   2 SH BERTRAM] *Rowe; Ros.* F *(through scene)*

Act 1, Scene 1

1.1 F marks act and scene here, and act divisions hereafter. Editors, following Theobald or Capell, locate the scene in the Count's palace at Rossillion.

0 SD *Rossillion* The English form of French 'Rousillon', an ancient province separated from Spain by the Pyrenees.

1 **delivering** sending away. With a residual sense of 'childbirth', opposing or complementing the death of Bertram's father; and hence opening immediately one of the principal themes of the play, the intimate connection between birth and death.

3 **attend** obey.

3–4 **in ward** This fatherless heir is still a minor and hence under the protection of the King, who acts as trustee for the estate.

5 **of** in.

6 **generally** Probably 'to all people'; also 'usually'.

6–7 **hold his virtue** continue his virtuous behaviour.

7–8 **whose...abundance** worthiness in you would stir up his virtue towards you, even were he lacking in virtue, rather than fail to stir it where it is so abundant.

8 **lack** Theobald's 'slack' is often preferred but requires that the King be understood as subject of this clause.

9 **amendment** recovery.

11 **practices** medical treatment. Some editors (e.g. Thiselton) detect a legal metaphor in the conjunction of 'practices', 'persecuted' and 'process' (11–12).

14 **passage** (1) occurrence (with the sense of time passing away), (2) word.

14 **honesty** integrity, honour.

15 **had...far** had his skill been equal to his absolute integrity.

47

should have play for lack of work. Would for the king's sake he were living! I think it would be the death of the king's disease.

LAFEW How called you the man you speak of, madam?

COUNTESS He was famous, sir, in his profession, and it was his great right to be so – Gerard de Narbon. 20

LAFEW He was excellent indeed, madam. The king very lately spoke of him admiringly and mourningly. He was skilful enough to have lived still, if knowledge could be set up against mortality.

BERTRAM What is it, my good lord, the king languishes of?

LAFEW A fistula, my lord. 25

BERTRAM I heard not of it before.

LAFEW I would it were not notorious. Was this gentlewoman the daughter of Gerard de Narbon?

COUNTESS His sole child, my lord, and bequeathed to my overlooking. I have those hopes of her good that her education promises. Her 30 dispositions she inherits, which makes fair gifts fairer; for where an unclean mind carries virtuous qualities, their commendations go with pity – they are virtues and traitors too. In her they are the better for their simpleness. She derives her honesty and achieves her goodness. 35

LAFEW Your commendations, madam, get from her tears.

COUNTESS 'Tis the best brine a maiden can season her praise in. The remembrance of her father never approaches her heart but the tyranny of her sorrows takes all livelihood from her cheek. No more of this, Helena. Go to, no more, lest it be rather thought you affect 40 a sorrow than to have.

30 promises. Her] *Rowe (subst.)*; promises her F; promises her; *Theobald*   41 than to have.] *Var. 73*; then to haue – F; than have it. *Capell*

16 **should have** would have had.
22 **admiringly and mourningly** with wonder for his skill and with sorrow for his death.
23 **still** forever.
25 **fistula** Strictly, a long, flute-shaped abscess, but the word is used by Painter in the source-story to describe a painful swelling on the King's breast.
27 **notorious** known to everyone.
29 **overlooking** supervision.
30 **education** upbringing.
31 **dispositions** natural tendencies.
31 **gifts** i.e. those conferred by her upbringing.
32 **unclean mind** bad nature.
32–3 **their...pity** praises of them are mingled with regret.
33 **traitors** i.e. to their bad nature as they misrepresent that nature by the virtue that denotes them. Warburton glosses: 'the advantages of education enable an ill mind to go further than it would have done without them'.
34 **simpleness** singleness, not mixed with evil.
34 **derives** inherits.
34 **achieves** acquires by her own efforts.
36 **get** beget; as at 113.
37 **season** preserve (as in brine). The word suggests the recurrent theme of seasoning, i.e. preserving or improving with experience.
39 **tyranny...cheek** i.e. her sorrows, as they tyrannically exact their tribute of blood, turn her cheek pale.
39 **livelihood** animation.
40 **Go to** Interjection in mild reproof.
40 **affect** (1) assume the character of, (2) love.
41 **have** have it. F's reading, 'have –', suggests that the compositor failed to recognise that the sense was complete.

HELENA I do affect a sorrow indeed, but I have it too.

LAFEW Moderate lamentation is the right of the dead; excessive grief
    the enemy to the living.

COUNTESS If the living be enemy to the grief, the excess makes it soon   45
    mortal.

BERTRAM Madam, I desire your holy wishes.

LAFEW How understand we that?

COUNTESS Be thou blest, Bertram, and succeed thy father
    In manners as in shape. Thy blood and virtue   50
    Contend for empire in thee, and thy goodness
    Share with thy birthright. Love all, trust a few,
    Do wrong to none. Be able for thine enemy
    Rather in power than use, and keep thy friend
    Under thy own life's key. Be checked for silence,   55
    But never taxed for speech. What heaven more will,
    That thee may furnish, and my prayers pluck down,
    Fall on thy head. – Farewell, my lord.
    'Tis an unseasoned courtier; good my lord,
    Advise him.

LAFEW   He cannot want the best   60
    That shall attend his love.

COUNTESS   Heaven bless him!
    Farewell, Bertram.   [*Exit*]

61–6 Heaven...father.] *As verse, Cam.; as prose,* F   62 SD] F2; *not in* F

42 As we learn in her next soliloquy, Helena's
sorrow is occasioned by her love for Bertram. The
line may be spoken as an aside.

43–4 **Moderate...living** Richmond Noble
(*Shakespeare's Biblical Knowledge*, 1935) compares
Ecclus. 38.17 and 20–2. Hunter, citing Seneca and
Plutarch, points to the classical *topos* behind the
passage.

45 **be enemy to** resist.

45–6 **excess...mortal** grief dies quickly of its
own excess.

47–8 **Madam...that?** Theobald, who transposes these two lines, is frequently followed by later
editors.

48 **How...that?** Lafew's question, which has
puzzled editors, refers presumably to 'wishes' and
is answered in the speech that follows.

50 **manners** moral behaviour.

50 **Thy...virtue** (May) your inherited and
acquired qualities.

51 **Contend for empire** Strive for sovereignty.

52 **Share...birthright** Divide the sovereignty
with your nobility of birth.

52 **Love** Behave kindly to; as again at 87.

53 **able for** capable of dealing with.

54 **in power** potentially.

54–5 **keep...key** guard your friend's life as you
would your own.

55 **checked** reproved.

56 **taxed for speech** censured for talking too
much.

57 **furnish** endow.

57 **pluck** draw.

59 **unseasoned** inexperienced; with a reminiscence of 'brine' and 'season' at 37. (The Countess
turns to Lafew.)

60–1 **He...love** A cryptic thought; it may mean
that Bertram cannot lack the best rewards in return
for devoted service to the court. But 'best' could
signify either moral or material benefits, and 'love'
could mean amiable or well-disposed behaviour, as
in 52 and 87.

BERTRAM   The best wishes that can
          Be forged in your thoughts be servants to you.
          [*To Helena*] Be comfortable to my mother, your mistress,
          And make much of her.
LAFEW   Farewell, pretty lady.   65
          You must hold the credit of your father.
                              [*Exeunt Bertram and Lafew*]
HELENA O, were that all! I think not on my father,
          And these great tears grace his remembrance more
          Than those I shed for him. What was he like?
          I have forgot him. My imagination   70
          Carries no favour in't but Bertram's.
          I am undone! There is no living, none,
          If Bertram be away. 'Twere all one
          That I should love a bright particular star
          And think to wed it, he is so above me.   75
          In his bright radiance and collateral light
          Must I be comforted, not in his sphere.
          Th'ambition in my love thus plagues itself.
          The hind that would be mated by the lion
          Must die for love. 'Twas pretty, though a plague,   80
          To see him every hour; to sit and draw
          His archèd brows, his hawking eye, his curls,
          In our heart's table – heart too capable
          Of every line and trick of his sweet favour.
          But now he's gone, and my idolatrous fancy   85
          Must sanctify his relics. Who comes here?

66 SD] *Rowe; not in* F   75 me.] *After Rowe* (me:)*; me* F   81 hour;] *Theobald; houre* F

63 forgèd shaped. Compare *H5* 1 Chorus 25: 'In
the quick forge and working-house of thought'.
   64 comfortable comforting, helpful.
   65 make much of attend sedulously on.
   66 hold the credit keep up the reputation.
   68–9 his...him Helena thinks at once of
Bertram ('his') and of her father ('him'); compare
the shift of pronouns in 87.
   71 favour (1) face (as generally, e.g. 84 below),
(2) love-token.
   73–4 'Twere...That It would be the same thing
if.
   76 collateral reflected, as from a different
sphere. In the geocentric (Ptolemaic) scheme, the
motion of the spheres was parallel or collateral.
Hence the heavenly bodies were visible to one
another but never made physical contact.

78 ambition i.e. which aims beyond my sphere.
   79 hind female deer.
   80 pretty pleasing to the fancy.
   82 hawking piercing.
   83 table Usually taken to be 'the board or flat
surface on which a picture is painted' (Onions). But
since Helena has been drawing surreptitiously, it
may be a table-book, meant for private notes (see
OED Table *sb* 2b).
   83 capable (1) susceptible, (2) easily drawn
upon.
   84 trick characteristic expression.
   85 fancy (1) love, (2) imagination.
   86 sanctify his relics worship his remains (as
they exist in her imagination).

Enter PAROLLES

One that goes with him. I love him for his sake;
And yet I know him a notorious liar,
Think him a great way fool, solely a coward.
Yet these fixed evils sit so fit in him   90
That they take place when virtue's steely bones
Looks bleak i'th'cold wind. Withal, full oft we see
Cold wisdom waiting on superfluous folly.

PAROLLES 'Save you, fair queen!

HELENA And you, monarch!   95

PAROLLES No.

HELENA And no.

PAROLLES Are you meditating on virginity?

HELENA Ay. You have some stain of soldier in you: let me ask you a
question. Man is enemy to virginity; how may we barricado it   100
against him?

PAROLLES Keep him out.

HELENA But he assails, and our virginity, though valiant, in the defence
yet is weak. Unfold to us some warlike resistance.

PAROLLES There is none. Man, setting down before you, will undermine   105
you and blow you up.

HELENA Bless our poor virginity from underminers and blowers-up! Is
there no military policy how virgins might blow up men?

PAROLLES Virginity being blown down, man will quicklier be blown
up. Marry, in blowing him down again, with the breach yourselves 110
made, you lose your city. It is not politic in the commonwealth of

---

100 barricado] *Rowe*; barracado F   103 valiant,...defence] F; valiant...defence, *Var. 73*   105 setting] F; sitting *Johnson*

---

86 SD PAROLLES From French *paroles*, meaning 'words'.

89 a great way mostly a.

90 fixed evils strongly seated vices.

90 sit...him fit him so well (i.e. denote him naturally).

91–2 take place...wind i.e. take precedence in society, while virtue is left out in the cold.

91 steely bones The hard and bare quality of virtue, making an unattractive antithesis to the becoming or natural vice of Parolles.

92 Looks Abbott (333) notes Shakespeare's common use of a singular verb with a plural subject.

92 Withal With this.

93 Cold Naked, unprovided.

93 superfluous (1) excessively provided, (2) overclothed.

94 'Save God save.

94 queen With a quibble on 'quean' = hussy.

96–7 No. And no I am no monarch. And I am no queen.

99 stain trace.

105 setting down before laying siege to.

106 blow you up explode you; make you pregnant.

107 Bless God preserve.

108 policy stratagem.

108 how to indicate how.

108 blow up With a pun here and what follows on tumescence.

110 Marry A mild interjection: 'By the Virgin Mary' (as at 130).

111 city i.e. virginity.

111 politic expedient.

nature to preserve virginity. Loss of virginity is rational increase, and there was never virgin got till virginity was first lost. That you were made of, is metal to make virgins. Virginity by being once lost may be ten times found; by being ever kept it is ever lost. 'Tis too 115 cold a companion. Away with't!

HELENA I will stand for't a little, though therefore I die a virgin.

PAROLLES There's little can be said in't; 'tis against the rule of nature. To speak on the part of virginity is to accuse your mothers, which is most infallible disobedience. He that hangs himself is a virgin: 120 virginity murders itself, and should be buried in highways out of all sanctified limit, as a desperate offendress against nature. Virginity breeds mites, much like a cheese; consumes itself to the very paring, and so dies with feeding his own stomach. Besides, virginity is peevish, proud, idle, made of self-love, which is the most inhibited 125 sin in the canon. Keep it not; you cannot choose but lose by't. Out with't! Within ten year it will make itself two, which is a goodly increase, and the principal itself not much the worse. Away with't!

HELENA How might one do, sir, to lose it to her own liking?

PAROLLES Let me see. Marry, ill, to like him that ne'er it likes. 'Tis 130

---

113 got] F2; goe F   123 paring] *Rowe*, payring F   127 ten] F; the *Harrison*; t'one *Evans*   127 two] F; ten *Hanmer*

---

112 rational increase reasonable increase; increase of reasonable beings.

113 That That which.

114 metal mettle. The words are indistinguishable in Elizabethan usage, and hence the ideas of 'substance' and more specifically 'coin' are both present here. The same double sense recurs at 2.1.40.

115 ten times found i.e. by creating ten new virgins.

117 stand for't defend it; with a quibble on tumescence.

117 die With the common secondary sense of sexual intercourse. See, for example, *Sonnets* 151.

118 in't in its defence.

119 on the part in defence.

120 infallible certain.

120 He...virgin Since virgins, by declining to propagate, are suicides..

121 buried in highways i.e. at the crossroads, where Elizabethan suicides were buried.

121–2 out...limit away from consecrated ground.

123 mites These tiny spiders carry disease and are therefore inimical to the host. (As mites are also paltry coins, this residual sense continues the monetary image begun at 112.)

123 paring last particle (with residual sense of 'pairing' or 'coupling', as in *WT* 4.2.154). Parolles's comparison of virginity to 'withered pears' (137) is anticipated.

124 his its (as generally in Shakespeare).

124 stomach With residual sense of 'pride'.

125 idle worthless.

125 inhibited prohibited.

126 canon Generically 'law' or 'rule', in particular, 'Church law'. Noble compares Deut. 6.4–5, Lev. 19.18 and Mark 12.29–33.

126–7 Out with't! (1) away with it! (as at 128), (2) put it out at interest!

127 ten...two If we admit the first reading above (126–7) this line is comprehensible only if meant sardonically; if we admit the second, the line explains itself. Ten per cent per year, the allowed rate of interest, would double the capital in ten years. Editors who are disinclined to see this as a 'goodly increase' frequently emend 'ten' to 'the' or 'two' to 'ten'. Reading 'the' for 'ten' could mean 'get a second virgin', which would emphasise the 'goodly increase' of virgins, as distinct from return on capital.

129 How What.

130 ill...likes i.e. to do ill by preferring a man who does not like virginity.

a commodity will lose the gloss with lying; the longer kept, the less worth. Off with't while 'tis vendible. Answer the time of request. Virginity, like an old courtier, wears her cap out of fashion; richly suited, but unsuitable: just like the brooch and the toothpick, which wear not now. Your date is better in your pie and your porridge   135 than in your cheek; and your virginity, your old virginity, is like one of our French withered pears: it looks ill, it eats drily. Marry, 'tis a withered pear; it was formerly better; marry, yet 'tis a withered pear! Will you anything with it?

HELENA Not my virginity yet: 140
    There shall your master have a thousand loves,
    A mother, and a mistress, and a friend,
    A phoenix, captain, and an enemy,
    A guide, a goddess, and a sovereign,
    A counsellor, a traitress, and a dear;   145

---

135 wear] *Capell;* were F   140 virginity yet:] F; virginity; yet...*Hunter*   145 traitress] F2, Traitoresse F

131 **will** that will.
131 **gloss** appearance of newness.
131 **lying** remaining unused.
132 **Off with't** Get rid of it.
132 **Answer...request** Sell it while it is marketable.
133–4 **richly...unsuitable** dressed richly but unfashionably.
134 **brooch...toothpick** Each worn in the hat, the latter denoting a travelled man, and evidently no longer in fashion ('wear not now', as at 178) when the play was written. Perhaps an obscene quibble is intended, remembering 'breach' at 110.
135–6 **Your...your** An impersonal use of the possessive to indicate people or things of a certain type. Thus 'your pie' is equivalent to 'a pie', and 'your virginity' to 'this virginity we are talking about'. The idiom was common in Shakespeare's time. See Abbott 221 and *OED* Your 5b.
135 **date** (1) fruit, (2) age. The Elizabethans often used dates rather than sugar for sweetening.
137 **ill** unappetising.
137 **eats drily** tastes dry.
139 **Will you** Will you do.
140 **Not...yet:** Presumably 'my' is emphasised, as against the aspersions of Parolles. Editors conjecture that something has dropped out here, but a moment of meditative silence is often found appropriate in performance.
141 **There** This adverb is supposed by most editors to refer to the court (152). In grammatical propriety it could refer also to 'my virginity', and

that is the reading proposed here. For a corroborative view, see G. Wilson Knight, 'The third eye', in *The Sovereign Flower*, 1958, p. 137.
141–50 **There...gossips** Editors generally suppose that Helena is recapitulating the stock business of Elizabethan love poetry, and that it is this business which will engross Bertram at court. Her paradoxes and oxymorons seem, however, to be descriptive of herself, and to anticipate the riddle on which the resolution of the play depends. Like Rosalind (in *AYLI* 3.2.141–8), she includes all women in herself, not only Lucrece but Helen of Troy, Cleopatra and Atalanta.
142 **A...friend** i.e. every kind of love, enumerated in the four lines that follow. Editors have been troubled by the bizarre-seeming collocation of 'mother' and 'mistress' and have tried to get round it by making 'mother' mean something else, e.g. 'mauther', dialect for 'maiden'. It is quite possible, however, to hold that the collocation is deliberate and emphatic: Helena presents a range of possible emotional relationships.
142–5 **mother...dear** Helena lists, in the language of courtly love, the titles of the lady that Parolles's 'master' will serve.
143 **phoenix** one of a kind, the unique thing.
143 **enemy** By convention, the lady was foe as well as friend.
145 **traitress** Like 'enemy' (143) 'traitress' perhaps anticipates Helena's frustration of Bertram's later determination to put her away.

His humble ambition, proud humility,
His jarring, concord, and his discord, dulcet,
His faith, his sweet disaster; with a world
Of pretty, fond, adoptious christendoms
That blinking Cupid gossips. Now shall he – 150
I know not what he shall. God send him well!
The court's a learning-place, and he is one –
PAROLLES What one, i'faith?
HELENA That I wish well. 'Tis pity –
PAROLLES What's pity? 155
HELENA That wishing well had not a body in't
Which might be felt; that we, the poorer born,
Whose baser stars do shut us up in wishes,
Might with effects of them follow our friends
And show what we alone must think, which never 160
Returns us thanks.

Enter PAGE

PAGE Monsieur Parolles, my lord calls for you. [*Exit*]
PAROLLES Little Helen, farewell. If I can remember thee, I will think
of thee at court.
HELENA Monsieur Parolles, you were born under a charitable star. 165
PAROLLES Under Mars I.
HELENA I especially think, under Mars.
PAROLLES Why under Mars?
HELENA The wars hath so kept you under that you must needs be born
under Mars. 170

147 jarring, concord...discord, dulcet] F, jarring concord...discord dulcet F4   152 one –] *Rowe*; one. F   162 SD]
Theobald; not in F   166 Under Mars I] F; Under Mars, ay *conj. Hunter*

146 humble...humility These ostensible disjunctions define the foolishly ambitious hero who craves only the 'help of mine own eyes' (2.3.100), but cannot estimate the riches that are his for the taking.

147 jarring A substantive, and making an unexpected complement with 'concord'.

147 dulcet soothing (of sounds).

148 disaster calamity (literally 'an unfavourable aspect of a star or planet'). And compare 5.3.112.

149 fond foolish.

149–50 adoptious...gossips christenings of adopted children for which blind ('blinking') Cupid stands godfather. Here 'gossips' is a verb. 'Christendoms' means Christians or Christian

countries, and also nicknames or Christian names which will continue the litany of 142–8.

151 send him well! give him good fortune!

152 learning-place school.

157 felt apprehended by the senses.

157 poorer of lowly station.

158 baser stars lowly fortunes.

158 shut. .wishes confine us to mere wishing.

159 effects of them our actualised wishes.

160 show...think manifest what we can only think about or purpose.

161 Returns us thanks Brings us gratitude.

169 hath The singular verb following a plural subject is common Elizabethan usage.

169 under down.

PAROLLES When he was predominant.

HELENA When he was retrograde, I think rather.

PAROLLES Why think you so?

HELENA You go so much backward when you fight.

PAROLLES That's for advantage.   175

HELENA So is running away when fear proposes the safety. But the
composition that your valour and fear makes in you is a virtue of
a good wing, and I like the wear well.

PAROLLES I am so full of businesses I cannot answer thee acutely. I
will return perfect courtier, in the which my instruction shall serve   180
to naturalise thee, so thou wilt be capable of a courtier's counsel
and understand what advice shall thrust upon thee; else thou diest
in thine unthankfulness, and thine ignorance makes thee away.
Farewell. When thou hast leisure, say thy prayers; when thou hast
none, remember thy friends. Get thee a good husband, and use him   185
as he uses thee. So, farewell.   [*Exit*]

HELENA Our remedies oft in ourselves do lie,
Which we ascribe to heaven. The fated sky
Gives us free scope; only doth backward pull
Our slow designs when we ourselves are dull.   190
What power is it which mounts my love so high?
That makes me see, and cannot feed mine eye?
The mightiest space in fortune nature brings
To join like likes, and kiss like native things.

---

186 SD] F2; *not in* F   194 like likes] F4; like, likes F

171 **predominant** in the ascendant, and therefore most influential.

172 **retrograde** moving backwards from east to west, and therefore in an unfavourable direction and exerting a malignant influence.

175 **advantage** strategic reasons.

177 **composition** make-up of your character (with a quibble on 'truce').

177–8 **virtue...wing** i.e. the ability to fly, to run away rapidly; with a quibble on the ostentatious flaps or wings which presumably – as the next line suggests – distinguish Parolles's costume. 'Virtue' means characteristic excellence or property.

178 **wear** fashion (of your clothes).

180 **perfect** complete.

180 **which** i.e. which role.

181 **naturalise** familiarise.

181 **so** if.

181 **capable** of receptive to. 'Capable' also means 'sexually capable' and begins a train of obscene quibbles continuing with 'understand',

'thrust' and 'diest', all of which gloss a 'courtier's counsel'.

183 **makes thee away** destroys you.

184 **leisure** opportunity.

184–5 **when ... friends** unclear: perhaps an insulting suggestion that since Helena has no friends, no leisure is needed to remember them. [L]

187–200 The transition to rhyme suggests the intervention of miraculous power.

188 **fated** fateful, determining our destiny.

190 **dull** inactive.

191 **mounts...high** makes my love aspire so far beyond itself.

192 **see** i.e. my love's object (which occupies a higher sphere, as at 77.

192 **feed** satisfy the longing of.

193–4 **The...things** Persons separated by the greatest disparity in worldly fortune are united by the agency of nature as if they were alike in fortune and inherently alike.

Impossible be strange attempts to those   195
That weigh their pains in sense, and do suppose
What hath been cannot be. Who ever strove
To show her merit that did miss her love?
The king's disease – my project may deceive me,
But my intents are fixed and will not leave me.   *Exit*   200

[1.2] *Flourish cornets. Enter the* KING OF FRANCE *with letters,* [*the* FIRST
and SECOND LORDS DUMAINE] *and divers* ATTENDANTS

KING The Florentines and Senoys are by th'ears,
      Have fought with equal fortune, and continue
      A braving war.
FIRST LORD   So 'tis reported, sir.
KING Nay, 'tis most credible. We here receive it
      A certainty, vouched from our cousin Austria,   5
      With caution, that the Florentine will move us
      For speedy aid; wherein our dearest friend
      Prejudicates the business, and would seem
      To have us make denial.
FIRST LORD   His love and wisdom,
      Approved so to your majesty, may plead   10
      For amplest credence.
KING   He hath armed our answer,

199 The king's disease –] *Rowe;* (The King's disease) F   Act 1, Scene 2   1.2] *Capell; not in* F   3, 9 SH FIRST LORD]
Rowe (subst.); 1. *Lo.G.* F   4–5 it A] *Capell;* it, A F

195 **strange** extraordinary.

196 **That…sense** Who estimate rationally the
arduous nature of the undertaking.

196–7 **do…be** think those feats impossible
which have been accomplished before.

198 **miss** fail to win.

200 **fixed** This play is notable for suggesting
unlikely associations through the recurrence of words
and phrases. Helena's 'fixed intents' recall the
'fixed evils' (90) that sit so becomingly on Parolles.

Act 1, Scene 2

1.2 Editors, following Capell, locate the scene in
the King's palace in Paris.

0 SD *Flourish cornets* Sound a fanfare of horns.
In modern productions the King often enters on a
litter or in a wheel-chair.

1 Senoys People of Siena.

1 by th'ears quarrelling.

3 **braving** full of mutual defiance.

3 **SH FIRST LORD** The speech heading in F
reads: 1. Lo.G., leading to the conjecture (e.g. by
Evans) that 'G' is perhaps an actor's initial, as also
'E' at 15.

4 **We** The royal plural.

5 **from** by.

5 **our cousin Austria** my fellow sovereign the
Duke of Austria.

6 **Florentine** The Duke of Florence, or possibly
the Florentines of 1.

6 **move** importune.

7 **our dearest friend** Presumably (but for no
apparent reason) the Duke of Austria.

8 **Prejudicates** Prejudges.

10 **Approved** Fully attested.

11 **credence** belief.

11 **armed** armoured; i.e. the King will be
obdurate in his denial of Florence.

And Florence is denied before he comes.
Yet for our gentlemen that mean to see
The Tuscan service, freely have they leave
To stand on either part.

SECOND LORD   It well may serve   15
A nursery to our gentry, who are sick
For breathing and exploit.

KING   What's he comes here?

Enter BERTRAM, LAFEW, *and* PAROLLES

FIRST LORD It is the Count Rossillion, my good lord,
Young Bertram.

KING   Youth, thou bear'st thy father's face;
Frank nature, rather curious than in haste,   20
Hath well composed thee. Thy father's moral parts
Mayst thou inherit too! Welcome to Paris.

BERTRAM My thanks and duty are your majesty's.

KING I would I had that corporal soundness now
As when thy father and myself in friendship   25
First tried our soldiership! He did look far
Into the service of the time, and was
Discipled of the bravest. He lasted long,
But on us both did haggish age steal on,
And wore us out of act. It much repairs me   30
To talk of your good father. In his youth
He had the wit which I can well observe
Today in our young lords; but they may jest
Till their own scorn return to them unnoted

---

15 SH SECOND LORD] *Rowe (subst.);* 2 Lo.E. F   18 SH FIRST LORD] *Rowe (subst.);* 1. Lor.G. F   18 Rossillion] F2
(Rossillion); Rosignoll F

---

13 **for** with respect to.
13 **see** participate in.
15 **stand...part** Remarkably, the King is
inviting his nobles to fight on either side.
15–16 **serve A nursery** do duty as a training
school.
16–17 **sick For** desirous of.
17 **breathing** military exercise.
18 **Rossillion** The F reading 'Rosignoll' recalls
French *rossignol*, variously a nightingale or a
picklock – or, in the compound *rossignol d'Arcadie*,
a braying jackass.
20 **Frank** Liberal, bountiful.
20 **curious** (1) fastidious, (2) working carefully.

21 **parts** qualities.
25 **As** That I had.
26 **look far** see deeply.
27 **service** military service.
27–8 **was Discipled of** (1) had as his pupils, or
possibly (2) was apprenticed to.
29 **haggish** repulsive (as of a hag); that makes
one haggard.
30 **act** fitness for action.
30 **repairs** restores.
34 **scorn...unnoted** Perhaps 'scornful taunts or
jests are made so habitual by repetition as to be
unremarked even by themselves'. Scornful and
disdainful manners were the less attractive aspects

Ere they can hide their levity in honour.   35
So like a courtier, contempt nor bitterness
Were in his pride or sharpness; if they were,
His equal had awaked them, and his honour,
Clock to itself, knew the true minute when
Exception bid him speak, and at this time   40
His tongue obeyed his hand. Who were below him
He used as creatures of another place,
And bowed his eminent top to their low ranks,
Making them proud of his humility,
In their poor praise he humbled. Such a man   45
Might be a copy to these younger times;
Which followed well, would demonstrate them now
But goers backward.

BERTRAM   His good remembrance, sir,
Lies richer in your thoughts than on his tomb.
So in approof lives not his epitaph   50
As in your royal speech.

KING Would I were with him. He would always say –
Methinks I hear him now; his plausive words
He scattered not in ears, but grafted them,
To grow there and to bear – 'Let me not live' –   55
This his good melancholy oft began,
On the catastrophe and heel of pastime,
When it was out – 'Let me not live', quoth he,

of *sprezzatura*, the courtly self-possession much cultivated in Renaissance Italy and imitated elsewhere in Europe.

35 hide...honour mark their ignoble jesting by honourable activity.

36 courtier The epitome of courtesy, as illustrated, for example, in Castiglione's *Courtier* or in Spenser's *Faerie Queene*, VI.

36 contempt neither contempt.

36 bitterness asperity.

37 sharpness i.e. of wit.

38 equal i.e. in rank.

39 Clock to itself i.e. requiring no prompter but itself to tell him when to respond.

39 true minute exact moment.

40 Exception Taking exception.

41 obeyed his hand said no more than his hand was willing to answer for.

41 Who Those who.

41 below him i.e. in rank.

42 of another place i.e. as if they were from another country rather than of another social rank.

43 top head.

45 In...humbled Perhaps 'before whose poor praises he humbled himself'. Otherwise the words may repeat the effect of the previous line: 'he humbled himself to praise the poor'.

46 copy example.

47 Which Can refer to 'copy' or 'times'. The former seems preferable.

48 goers backward If 'Which' refers to 'copy' and 'them' to 'times' (i.e. men of these 'younger times'), this will mean 'followers of the past'.

50 So...epitaph The truth of his epitaph is nowhere so fully confirmed.

53 plausive pleasing.

54 ears With a quibble on the spike or head of corn.

54 grafted planted deeply.

55 bear bear fruit.

57 catastrophe latter end.

58 out (1) finished, but also (2) out at heel. The word refers proleptically to the snuffed candle in 59.

'After my flame lacks oil, to be the snuff
Of younger spirits, whose apprehensive senses   60
All but new things disdain; whose judgements are
Mere fathers of their garments; whose constancies
Expire before their fashions.' This he wished.
I, after him, do after him wish too,
Since I nor wax nor honey can bring home,   65
I quickly were dissolvèd from my hive,
To give some labourers room.
SECOND LORD   You're loved, sir;
They that least lend it you shall lack you first.
KING I fill a place, I know't. How long is't, count,
Since the physician at your father's died?   70
He was much famed.
BERTRAM   Some six months since, my lord.
KING If he were living, I would try him yet –
Lend me an arm – the rest have worn me out
With several applications. Nature and sickness
Debate it at their leisure. Welcome, count,   75
My son's no dearer.
BERTRAM   Thank your majesty.

                                        [Exeunt] Flourish

[1.3] *Enter* COUNTESS, [RINALDO, *the*] *Steward, and* [LAVATCH, *the*]
Clown

COUNTESS I will now hear. What say you of this gentlewoman?
RINALDO Madam, the care I have had to even your content, I wish

67 SH SECOND LORD] *Rowe (subst.)*; *L.2.E.* F   76 SD *Exeunt*] *Rowe*; *Exit* F   Act 1, Scene 3   1.3] *Capell; not in* F

59 **snuff** The burnt-out part of the wick which, if not trimmed off, prevents the lower part of the wick (analogically 'younger spirits') from burning properly.

60 **apprehensive** quick perceiving. Here pejorative: 'too quick perceiving' and therefore inconstant.

62 **Mere...garments** i.e. productive of nothing but new fashions.

63 **before their fashions** even before the fashions change.

64 **after...him** following him (in time), and agreeing with his views.

66 **dissolvèd** separated.

67 **labourers** i.e. as opposed to drones.

68 **it** The reference is ambiguous. It may mean 'room' (67), anticipating 'place' (69); or it may mean 'love', from 'loved' (67).

68 **lack** feel the want of.

73 **rest** i.e. of the physicians.

74 **several applications** separate treatments (peculiar to each physician).

75 **it** i.e. the question of his survival.

Act 1, Scene 3
1.3 Editors, following Capell, locate the scene in the Count's palace at Rossillion.

2 **even** make even, satisfy.

might be found in the calendar of my past endeavours, for then we
wound our modesty, and make foul the clearness of our deservings,
when of ourselves we publish them. 5

COUNTESS What does this knave here? Get you gone, sirrah. The
complaints I have heard of you I do not all believe; 'tis my slowness
that I do not, for I know you lack not folly to commit them, and
have ability enough to make such knaveries yours.

LAVATCH 'Tis not unknown to you, madam, I am a poor fellow. 10

COUNTESS Well, sir.

LAVATCH No, madam, 'tis not so well that I am poor, though many
of the rich are damned, but if I may have your ladyship's good will
to go to the world, Isbel the woman and I will do as we may.

COUNTESS Wilt thou needs be a beggar? 15

LAVATCH I do beg your good will in this case.

COUNTESS In what case?

LAVATCH In Isbel's case and mine own. Service is no heritage, and I
think I shall never have the blessing of God till I have issue a'my
body; for they say barnes are blessings. 20

COUNTESS Tell me thy reason why thou wilt marry.

LAVATCH My poor body, madam, requires it. I am driven on by the
flesh, and he must needs go that the devil drives.

COUNTESS Is this all your worship's reason?

LAVATCH Faith, madam, I have other holy reasons, such as they are. 25

COUNTESS May the world know them?

LAVATCH I have been, madam, a wicked creature, as you and all flesh
and blood are, and indeed I do marry that I may repent.

COUNTESS Thy marriage, sooner than thy wickedness.

---

12 'tis...many] *As prose, Capell; as verse,* F   14 I] F2; w F

---

3 **calendar** record.
4 **make...clearness** sully the lustre.
6 **sirrah** Form of address used to an inferior.
7 **all** altogether.
14 **go...world** i.e. accept the ways of the world and the flesh, by marrying. Compare *Ado* 2.1.218–19.
14 **woman** servingwoman.
14 **do...may** do as well as we can; with an obscene quibble on 'do' = 'have sexual intercourse'.
16 **case** With a quibble on 'vagina'.
18 **Service...heritage** i.e. because servants do not inherit estate. The expression is proverbial (see Tilley s253).

19 **issue** children.
19 **a'** of (as again at 30).
20 **they say** i.e. the expression being proverbial.
20 **barnes** bairns, children.
23 **he...drives** More proverbial wisdom. See Tilley D278.
25 **other holy reasons** 'other' because procreation is commended in the marriage-service; but 'other' also because Lavatch puns obscenely on 'holy' and 'reasons' = 'raisings' (these two words being nearly identical in Shakespeare's pronunciation).
28 **marry...repent** Alluding to the proverb 'Marry in haste and repent at leisure', as the Countess's rejoinder makes clear.

LAVATCH I am out a'friends, madam, and I hope to have friends for my   30
    wife's sake.

COUNTESS Such friends are thine enemies, knave.

LAVATCH Y'are shallow, madam, in great friends, for the knaves come
    to do that for me which I am a-weary of. He that ears my land spares
    my team, and gives me leave to in the crop. If I be his cuckold,   35
    he's my drudge. He that comforts my wife is the cherisher of my
    flesh and blood; he that cherishes my flesh and blood loves my flesh
    and blood; he that loves my flesh and blood is my friend: *ergo*, he
    that kisses my wife is my friend. If men could be contented to be
    what they are, there were no fear in marriage, for young Charbon   40
    the puritan and old Poysam the papist, howsome'er their hearts are
    severed in religion, their heads are both one: they may jowl horns
    together like any deer i'th'herd.

COUNTESS Wilt thou ever be a foul-mouthed and calumnious knave?

LAVATCH A prophet I, madam, and I speak the truth the next way: 45
        For I the ballad will repeat,
            Which men full true shall find:
        Your marriage comes by destiny,
            Your cuckoo sings by kind.

COUNTESS Get you gone, sir, I'll talk with you more anon.   50

RINALDO May it please you, madam, that he bid Helen come to you.
    Of her I am to speak.

COUNTESS Sirrah, tell my gentlewoman I would speak with her – Helen,
    I mean.

LAVATCH   'Was this fair face the cause', quoth she,   55

---

31 wife's] wives F   33 madam,] F3; Madam F   33 in] F; e'en *Hanmer*   46–9] *As verse, Rowe³ (subst.); as prose,* F

---

33 shallow superficial (i.e. your understanding of real friendship is slight).

34 ears ploughs (resuming the King's image from husbandry in the preceding scene, 54–5).

35 in harvest, bring in.

35–6 If...drudge Another proverb.

38 *ergo* therefore, Lavatch uses the Latin word to conclude his comic version of a *Sorites*, a device in logic by which a series of linked propositions is used (often with an ingenious trick) to lead to a conclusion which refers back to the original proposition.

40 what they are i.e. cuckolds.

40 Charbon Good flesh (*chair bonne*).

41 Poysam Fish (French, *poisson*). Appropriate to the papist or Catholic who practised fasting as opposed to the puritan who contemned it.

41 howsome'er howsoever.

42 both one i.e. in bearing horns, the mark of the cuckold. Hunter sees this as a comic inversion of the proverb 'Hearts may agree though heads differ' (Tilley H341).

42 jowl knock.

44 ever always.

45 next nearest, most direct (the prophet being divinely inspired).

48 Your...destiny i.e. the married man is a cuckold by destiny.

49 kind nature.

55 this fair face i.e. Helen of Troy's, suggested to Lavatch by the Countess's summoning of Helena at 53.

55 she Perhaps Helen is the speaker, perhaps Hecuba, wife of King Priam of Troy and the mother of Paris.

> 'Why the Grecians sackèd Troy?
> Fond done, done fond,
>   Was this King Priam's joy?'
> With that she sighèd as she stood,
> With that she sighèd as she stood,   60
>   And gave this sentence then:
> 'Among nine bad if one be good,
> Among nine bad if one be good,
>   There's yet one good in ten.'

COUNTESS What, one good in ten? You corrupt the song, sirrah.   65

LAVATCH One good woman in ten, madam, which is a purifying
a'th'song. Would God would serve the world so all the year! we'd
find no fault with the tithe-woman if I were the parson. One in ten,
quoth'a? And we might have a good woman born but ore every
blazing star or at an earthquake, 'twould mend the lottery well; a   70
man may draw his heart out ere 'a pluck one.

COUNTESS You'll be gone, sir knave, and do as I command you?

LAVATCH That man should be at woman's command, and yet no hurt
done! Though honesty be no puritan, yet it will do no hurt; it will
wear the surplice of humility over the black gown of a big heart.   75
I am going, forsooth. The business is for Helen to come hither.

                                                     Exit

COUNTESS Well, now.

---

57 done fond] *Rowe;* done, fond F   59 stood,] *Var. 73;* stood, *bis* F   60] *After Var. 73;* not in F   61–4] *As verse,*
Rowe; as prose, F   69 ore] F; o'er *Rowe;* or *Capell;* for *Craig*   72 be gone] F2; begone F

57 Fond Foolishly.

58 this Helen, or possibly the rape of Helen by
Paris which assured the destruction of Troy.

60 With...stood The Folio omits this line and
follows the preceding line with *bis* (Latin, 'twice'),
indicating that the verses were set to music.

61 sentence judgement.

65 corrupt the song Possibly by inverting the
optimistic sense of the original ballad which editors
suppose to lie behind these lines. In the original they
may have read: 'Among nine good if one be
bad...There's yet nine good in ten', where the ten
refers to the sons of Priam and the one to Paris.

66 One...purifying i.e. since the original
song, which makes no mention of women, has now
been amended to include one good woman.

67–8 we'd...parson i.e. if the proportion of
good women were as high as a tithe or one in ten,
the parson (who was entitled to the tenth part of
farm produce) would be as satisfied as with his
tithe-pig.

69 quoth'a did he say.

69 And If.

69 ore ere (i.e. in conjunction with).

70 blazing star comet or nova (the type of a
prodigious event, like 'earthquake').

70 mend the lottery improve the odds (of
finding a good woman).

71 pluck one draw a good woman.

73 at woman's command As opposed to the
Pauline notion that the man is head of the woman.

74–5 Though...heart i.e. no matter that I am
not over-strict in moral matters; I will conceal my
pride under the appearance of humility. Analogically,
the puritan minister hides his unlawful black
Genevan gown, the garb of the Calvinist, beneath
the canonical surplice or loose-fitting white gown of
the Church of England. Perhaps a bawdy quibble
is intended, 'honesty' meaning 'chastity', 'hurt'
the loss of chastity, and 'no puritan' suggesting the
Catholic espousal of celibacy, which the puritans
condemned.

RINALDO I know, madam, you love your gentlewoman entirely.

COUNTESS Faith, I do. Her father bequeathed her to me, and she
    herself, without other advantage, may lawfully make title to as much   80
    love as she finds. There is more owing her than is paid, and more
    shall be paid her than she'll demand.

RINALDO Madam, I was very late more near her than I think she wished
    me. Alone she was, and did communicate to herself her own words
    to her own ears; she thought, I dare vow for her, they touched not   85
    any stranger sense. Her matter was, she loved your son. Fortune,
    she said, was no goddess, that had put such difference betwixt their
    two estates; Love no god, that would not extend his might only
    where qualities were level; [Diana no] queen of virgins, that would
    suffer her poor knight surprised without rescue in the first assault   90
    or ransom afterward. This she delivered in the most bitter touch
    of sorrow that e'er I heard virgin exclaim in, which I held my duty
    speedily to acquaint you withal, sithence in the loss that may
    happen, it concerns you something to know it.

COUNTESS You have discharged this honestly, keep it to yourself. Many   95
    likelihoods informed me of this before, which hung so tottering in
    the balance that I could neither believe nor misdoubt. Pray you
    leave me. Stall this in your bosom, and I thank you for your honest
    care. I will speak with you further anon.

                       Exit [Rinaldo, the] Steward

                 Enter HELENA

    Even so it was with me when I was young.   100

---

89 level; Diana no queen] *Theobald;* leuell, Queene F   99 SD *Exit Steward*] *Placed as* F; *following 108, Singer*
100 Even] *Singer; Old Cou.* Even F

80 **herself** in herself.
80 **advantage** interest (as on money, and
pursuing the figure begun with 'bequeathed' (79)).
80 **make title to** claim.
82 **demand** ask; not peremptorily as in the
modern sense of 'demand' (used again at 2.1.21).
83 **late** lately.
86 **any stranger sense** anyone else's ears.
86 **matter** subject.
87 **no goddess** i.e. because the difference in
social station between Helena and Bertram is not
divinely ordained but turns on chance. For
reflections on Fortune, see pp. 18–21 above.
88 **extend his might** employ his power.
88 **only** except.
89 **qualities were level** the social positions
were the same.

89 **Diana no** This interpolation is Theobald's
and clarifies the F reading, which otherwise makes
no sense. Hunter compares *Ado* 5.3.12–13.
90 **suffer** allow.
90 **knight** i.e. servant of the goddess of chastity.
90 **surprised** i.e. surprised to be taken captive.
91 **touch** note (as in music).
92 **exclaim** complain.
92 **which** which thing.
93 **withal** with.
93 **sithence** since.
94 **something** to some extent.
96 **tottering** waveringly.
97 **misdoubt** doubt.
98 **Stall** Enclose.
100 **Even so** The Countess is observing Helena's
melancholy entrance.

If ever we are nature's, these are ours. This thorn
Doth to our rose of youth rightly belong;
Our blood to us, this to our blood is born.
It is the show and seal of nature's truth,
Where love's strong passion is impressed in youth.   105
By our remembrances of days foregone,
Such were our faults, or then we thought them none.
Her eye is sick on't; I observe her now.

HELENA What is your pleasure, madam?

COUNTESS   You know, Helen,
I am a mother to you.   110

HELENA Mine honourable mistress.

COUNTESS   Nay, a mother,
Why not a mother? When I said 'a mother',
Methought you saw a serpent. What's in 'mother',
That you start at it? I say I am your mother,
And put you in the catalogue of those   115
That were enwombèd mine. 'Tis often seen
Adoption strives with nature, and choice breeds
A native slip to us from foreign seeds.
You ne'er oppressed me with a mother's groan,
Yet I express to you a mother's care.   120
God's mercy, maiden! does it curd thy blood
To say I am thy mother? What's the matter,
That this distempered messenger of wet,
The many-coloured Iris, rounds thine eye?
— Why, that you are my daughter?

102 rightly] *Rowe;* righlie F   102 belong;] *Theobald;* belong F   105 youth.] *After Rowe;* youth, F   109, 111, 126, 132, 139 SH COUNTESS] *Old.Cou.* F   109–10 You...you] *As Capell; as one line* F   111–12 Nay...'a mother'] *After Pope; as one line* F

101 A hexameter line.

101 **these** i.e. tokens of love.

103 **blood** i.e. as we are born with blood a passionate disposition is born in our blood. There may be a pun on 'borne' = carried in.

104 **show** sign.

105 **impressed** As by a seal.

107 **then...none** at the time we did not consider them faults.

108 **on't** with it.

108 **observe** see through.

116 **enwombèd mine** born as my children.

117 **strives** competes.

117–18 **choice...seeds** we choose a scion or slip grown from someone else's seeds and graft it to our own stock, where our affectionate choice makes it appear to have grown there naturally.

119 **a mother's groan** i.e. childbirth.

123 **distempered** sick, afflicted (as when the weather is bad or the eyes tearstained). Compare *Lucrece* 1586–7.

123 **messenger of wet** tear.

124 **Iris** (1) rainbow, (2) Iris, goddess of the rainbow.

124 **rounds** encircles. Helena has tearful rings about her eyes through crying.

HELENA   That I am not.   125
COUNTESS I say I am your mother.
HELENA   Pardon, madam;
    The Count Rossillion cannot be my brother;
    I am from humble, he from honoured name;
    No note upon my parents, his all noble.
    My master, my dear lord he is, and I   130
    His servant live, and will his vassal die.
    He must not be my brother.
COUNTESS   Nor I your mother?
HELENA You are my mother, madam; would you were –
    So that my lord your son were not my brother –
    Indeed my mother! Or were you both our mothers,   135
    I care no more for than I do for heaven,
    So I were not his sister. Can 't no other,
    But, I your daughter, he must be my brother?
COUNTESS Yes, Helen, you might be my daughter-in-law.
    God shield you mean it not! 'Daughter' and 'mother'   140
    So strive upon your pulse. What, pale again?
    My fear hath catched your fondness! Now I see
    The mystery of your loneliness, and find
    Your salt tears' head. Now to all sense 'tis gross:
    You love my son. Invention is ashamed,   145
    Against the proclamation of thy passion,
    To say thou dost not: therefore tell me true,
    But tell me then 'tis so; for look, thy cheeks
    Confess it, t'one to th'other, and thine eyes

---

133 mother, madam; would you were –] *Rowe³ (subst.)*; mother Madam, would you were F   143 loneliness] *Theobald*; louelinesse F   149 t'one to th'other] F2 ; 'ton tooth to th'other F

125 That...not Meaning both 'That I am not your daughter' and (since the terms were interchangeable in Elizabethan usage) 'That I am not your daughter-in-law'.

129 note distinguishing mark.

129 parents antecedents.

135 both our mothers mother of us both.

136 An understated way of saying how very much Helena would wish to be daughter to the Countess – but with the reservation expressed in the next line.

137 Can 't no other Can it not be otherwise.

138 But, I But that I being.

140 shield forbid. (The Countess is playing with Helena.)

141 So strive upon Equally agitate.

142 fear...fondness suspicion has found out your foolishness and your love ('fondness' had both meanings).

143 *loneliness keeping apart. The Folio reading 'louelinesse' is no doubt occasioned by the transposing of 'n' and 'u' – i.e. 'v' – one of the commonest errors.

144 head source.

144 sense perception.

144 gross obvious (as at 150).

145 Invention The ability to fabricate lies.

146 Against In the face of.

148 then in such case (i.e. if you are going to speak the truth).

149 t'one the one. F2 corrects a manifest slip in F.

See it so grossly shown in thy behaviours   150
That in their kind they speak it. Only sin
And hellish obstinacy tie thy tongue,
That truth should be suspected. Speak, is't so?
If it be so, you have wound a goodly clew;
If it be not, forswear't; howe'er, I charge thee,   155
As heaven shall work in me for thine avail,
To tell me truly.

HELENA   Good madam, pardon me!

COUNTESS Do you love my son?

HELENA   Your pardon, noble mistress!

COUNTESS Love you my son?

HELENA   Do not you love him, madam?

COUNTESS Go not about; my love hath in't a bond   160
Whereof the world takes note. Come, come, disclose
The state of your affection, for your passions
Have to the full appeached.

HELENA   Then I confess
Here on my knee, before high heaven and you,
That before you, and next unto high heaven,   165
I love your son.
My friends were poor but honest, so's my love.
Be not offended, for it hurts not him
That he is loved of me; I follow him not
By any token of presumptuous suit,   170
Nor would I have him till I do deserve him,
Yet never know how that desert should be.
I know I love in vain, strive against hope;

---

155 forswear't; howe'er, I] *Theobald;* forsweare't how ere I F; forswear't: how ere I F3   161 disclose] F3; disclose: F

151 **in their kind** according to their nature (i.e. by weeping).

151–3 **Only...That** i.e. the only reason...is that.

153 **suspected** (1) confounded, (2) called in question.

154 **goodly clew** fine ball of twine (i.e. you have made a mess of things). Proverbial, and anticipating the 'mingled yarn' of 4.3.60.

155 **forswear't** deny it.

155 **howe'er** but whatever you do.

156 **thine avail** your benefit.

160 **Go not about** Don't quibble (by talking evasively).

160 **bond** maternal bond.

161 **Whereof...note** Which society recognises.

162 **affection** feeling.

163 **appeached** informed (against you).

165 **before you** more than you.

167 **friends** relatives.

167 **honest** honourable.

169 **follow him not** i.e. as by sending letters after him – or, alternatively, by pursuing him before he left Rossillion.

170 **By** With.

172 **never know** i.e. never can know.

Yet in this captious and intenible sieve
I still pour in the waters of my love   175
And lack not to lose still. Thus Indian-like,
Religious in mine error, I adore
The sun, that looks upon his worshipper,
But knows of him no more. My dearest madam,
Let not your hate encounter with my love   180
For loving where you do; but if yourself,
Whose agèd honour cites a virtuous youth,
Did ever in so true a flame of liking
Wish chastely, and love dearly, that your Dian
Was both herself and Love, O then give pity   185
To her whose state is such that cannot choose
But lend and give where she is sure to lose;
That seeks not to find that her search implies,
But riddle-like lives sweetly where she dies.

COUNTESS Had you not lately an intent – speak truly –   190
          To go to Paris?
HELENA   Madam, I had.
COUNTESS   Wherefore? tell true.
HELENA I will tell truth, by grace itself I swear.
        You know my father left me some prescriptions
        Of rare and proved effects, such as his reading

---

174 intenible] F2; intemihle F   174 sieve] F3, Siue F, Sive F2   176 lose] F4, loose F   187 lose] F4, loose F

---

174 captious Shakespeare apparently plays upon the usual sense 'deceitful' and 'capacious'. *OED* gives only this instance of 'captious' = capacious.

174 *intenible F2's reading, meaning 'unretentive, not holding'. F's reading 'intemible' is sometimes retained and taken to mean 'incapable of being poured out'.

175 still continually.

176 lack...still (1) fail not to continue losing (as the sieve is unretentive), (2) lack not reserves to continue squandering love.

176 Indian-like Shakespeare imagined the people of India as sun-worshippers. Compare *LLL* 4.3.217–21. [L]

179 no more i.e. than to look on him.

180 encounter with oppose in combat.

182 agèd honour honourable old age.

182 cites gives evidence of.

183 liking love. Compare *Ado* 1.1.298–300.

184 Wish...dearly Desire to be both sexually passionate and chaste (faithful) at the same time. A recurring to the oxymorons of 1.1.141–8.

184–5 your...Love i.e. the Diana you worshipped was both the goddess of chastity and the goddess of love. ('Love' is without a capital in F.)

186 state Helena may refer both to her state as lover and to her status in society.

186 that as.

186–7 cannot...lose has no choice but to render her affections with no hope of return.

188–9 i.e. Helena has no prospect of finding the object of her search (Bertram's love), but will live in the sweetness of disappointed expectation. There may be a suggestion of the Phoenix riddle of love's dying into life – Helena finds solace even in the death of her aspirations. Later in the play Helena's renewed quest takes a different riddling form (3.2.50–3).

188 that what.

192 grace the grace of God.

And manifest experience had collected   195
For general sovereignty; and that he willed me
In heedfull'st reservation to bestow them,
As notes whose faculties inclusive were
More than they were in note. Amongst the rest,
There is a remedy, approved, set down,   200
To cure the desperate languishings whereof
The king is rendered lost.

COUNTESS   This was your motive
    For Paris, was it? Speak.

HELENA My lord your son made me to think of this;
    Else Paris, and the medicine, and the king,   205
    Had from the conversation of my thoughts
    Haply been absent then.

COUNTESS   But think you, Helen,
    If you should tender your supposèd aid,
    He would receive it? He and his physicians
    Are of a mind; he, that they cannot help him,   210
    They, that they cannot help. How shall they credit
    A poor unlearnèd virgin, when the schools,
    Embowelled of their doctrine, have left off
    The danger to itself?

HELENA   There's something in't
    More than my father's skill, which was the great'st   215
    Of his profession, that his good receipt
    Shall for my legacy be sanctified
    By th'luckiest stars in heaven, and would your honour
    But give me leave to try success, I'd venture

202–3 This…Speak] *As Capell; as one line,* F   203 it? Speak.] *Var. 73;* it, speake? F   207 Haply] Happily F

195 **manifest** (1) open to the eye, (2) empirical (i.e. deriving from a knowledge of manifestations or symptoms, and contrasting with 'reading').

196 **general sovereignty** universal panaceas, remedies for every disease.

196 **willed** desired.

197 Most carefully to reserve them for use.

198 **notes** prescriptions.

198 **faculties inclusive** comprehensive powers.

199 **in note** recognised to be.

200 **approved** tested.

202 **rendered lost** said to be dying.

203 **For** i.e. for going to.

206 **conversation** back-and-forth movement.

208 **tender** offer.

208 **supposèd** supposedly efficacious.

210 **of a mind** agreed.

211 **credit** believe.

213 **Embowelled** Disembowelled, emptied.

213 **left off** abandoned.

214 **danger to itself** disease to its own course.

216 **that** so that (i.e. by virtue of the 'something in't').

216 **receipt** prescription.

217 **sanctified** blessed.

218 **luckiest** beneficent (i.e. those conferring luck).

219 **try success** test the outcome.

The well-lost life of mine on his grace's cure   220
By such a day, an hour.
COUNTESS   Dost thou believe't?
HELENA Ay, madam, knowingly.
COUNTESS Why, Helen, thou shalt have my leave and love,
Means and attendants, and my loving greetings
To those of mine in court. I'll stay at home   225
And pray God's blessing into thy attempt.
Be gone tomorrow, and be sure of this,
What I can help thee to thou shalt not miss.

Exeunt

2.[1] *Enter the* KING *with divers young* LORDS *[with the* FIRST *and* SECOND LORDS DUMAINE*] taking leave for the Florentine war;* [BERTRAM] *Count Rossillion, and* PAROLLES. *Flourish cornets*

KING Farewell, young lords, these warlike principles
Do not throw from you; and you, my lords, farewell.
Share the advice betwixt you; if both gain all,
The gift doth stretch itself as 'tis received,
And is enough for both.
FIRST LORD   'Tis our hope, sir,   5
After well-entered soldiers, to return
And find your grace in health.
KING No, no, it cannot be; and yet my heart
Will not confess he owes the malady
That doth my life besiege. Farewell, young lords,   10
Whether I live or die, be you the sons

---

221 an] F; and F2   227 Be gone] F3; Begon F   Act 2, Scene 1   2.1] Rowe; Actus Secundus. F   3 you;] Rowe; you, F
3 gain all,] Johnson; gaine, all F   5 SH FIRST LORD] After Rowe; Lord.G. F

220 **well-lost** i.e. worth losing in such a cause.
221 **such a** a specified.
222 **knowingly** knowing what I am doing.
225 **those of mine** my friends (or relations).
226 **into** upon.
228 **miss** lack.

Act 2, Scene 1
2.1 Editors, following Capell, locate the scene in the King's palace in Paris.
0 SD The King takes leave of two parties, who may leave by different stage-doors.

1 **warlike principles** military maxims.
2 **and you** The King turns from the first group of lords, bound perhaps for Florence, to a second group, bound for Siena.
3 **gain all** profit fully from (my advice).
4 **gift...received** advice will expand to the degree that it is accepted.
6 **well-entered** having become experienced as. Abbott (418) cites as a foreign (Latin) idiom.
9 **owes** possesses.

Of worthy Frenchmen. Let higher Italy
(Those bated that inherit but the fall
Of the last monarchy) see that you come
Not to woo honour, but to wed it, when 15
The bravest questant shrinks. Find what you seek,
That fame may cry you loud. I say farewell.
FIRST LORD Health, at your bidding, serve your majesty!
KING Those girls of Italy, take heed of them.
They say our French lack language to deny 20
If they demand. Beware of being captives
Before you serve.
BOTH LORDS Our hearts receive your warnings.
KING Farewell. – Come hither to me.
FIRST LORD O my sweet lord, that you will stay behind us!
PAROLLES 'Tis not his fault, the spark.
SECOND LORD O, 'tis brave wars! 25
PAROLLES Most admirable! I have seen those wars.
BERTRAM I am commanded here, and kept a coil with,
'Too young' and 'the next year' and ''tis too early'.
PAROLLES And thy mind stand to't, boy, steal away bravely.

13 bated] F; bastards *Hanmer*   15 it, when] F; it; when *Pope*   18 SH FIRST LORD] *Rowe; L.G.* F; *Second Lord / Rowe³*
22 SH BOTH LORDS] *After Capell; Bo.* F   23] *As* F; SD *Exit / Pope;* SD *To Attendants / Theobald;* SD *retires to a couch
/ Capell*   24, 34, 37 SH FIRST LORD] *Rowe; Lo.G.* F.   25, 35, 38 SH SECOND LORD] *Rowe; 2.Lo.E.* F

12 **worthy** i.e. be you worthy sons.
12 **higher** Referring either to social class (as perhaps in *Lear* 3.6.111: 'high noises') or geographical location – mountainous Tuscany where both Florence and Siena are located.
13–14 **Those...monarchy** This often-discussed passage turns partly on the sense of 'bated'. (1) Those dejected ones ('bated' being understood as a substantive) who possess only the poor remains of (?) the Holy Roman Empire (the last of the canonical four monarchies or empires familiar to Shakespeare's time from Dan. 2.40). (2) Those of higher Italy 'excepted' who inherit only (but do not earn) their places. The second reading has the merit of enforcing the antithesis, familiar from the opening scene, of acquired and inherited virtue. See e.g. 1.1.34–5. However, line 13 is partly autonomous when spoken, and suggests the reproving of those who inherit only our fallen condition.
15 **woo** flirt with.
15 **wed** it make it your own.
16 **questant** seeker after honour.
16 **shrinks** With a pun on detumescence. Here, as often, achieving is commended, and the sexual

suggestion associates the King with Parolles, 2.3.256–60.
17 **cry you loud** proclaim you loudly.
19 **girls of Italy** Proverbial for their importunate charms.
21 **captives** slaves to love.
22 **Before you serve** i.e. before you are 'well-entered' (6). The King mingles the language of war and the language of love.
23 **Come hither** The King presumably retires to a corner of the stage with some of the lords, leaving others to converse with Bertram and Parolles.
24 **sweet** dear. Used impartially of either sex – as again at 38.
25 **spark** spirited youth. As again at 39. [L]
25 **brave** splendid.
26 **seen** experienced.
27 **commanded** ordered to remain.
27 **kept...with** made a fuss about.
29 **And** If.
29 **stand to't** be resolute.
29 **bravely** becomingly. But perhaps with play upon 'courageously' and 'showily'.

BERTRAM I shall stay here the forehorse to a smock,   30
    Creaking my shoes on the plain masonry,
    Till honour·be bought up, and no sword worn
    But one to dance with! By heaven, I'll steal away.
FIRST LORD There's honour in the theft.
PAROLLES   Commit it, count.
SECOND LORD I am your accessory, and so farewell.   35
BERTRAM I grow to you, and our parting is a tortured body.
FIRST LORD Farewell, captain.
SECOND LORD Sweet Monsieur Parolles!
PAROLLES Noble heroes! my sword and yours are kin. Good sparks and
    lustrous, a word, good metals: you shall find in the regiment of the   40
    Spinii one Captain Spurio, with his cicatrice, an emblem of war,
    here on his sinister cheek; it was this very sword entrenched it. Say
    to him I live, and observe his reports for me.
FIRST LORD We shall, noble captain.
PAROLLES Mars dote on you for his novices!   45
                               [Exeunt Lords]
    What will ye do?
BERTRAM Stay: the king.
PAROLLES Use a more spacious ceremony to the noble lords; you have
    restrained yourself within the list of too cold an adieu. Be more

---

41 with his cicatrice, an] *Theobald;* his sicatrice, with an F   44 SH FIRST LORD] *Rowe; Lo.G.* F   45 SD] *Theobald (after*
49); Capell (after 47); not in F   47 Stay:] F2; Stay F

30 **forehorse...smock** leading horse of a team
driven by a woman.
31 **plain masonry** i.e. the smooth, paved floors
of the court, as opposed to the field of battle.
32 **bought up** (1) sold out, (2) engrossed by
others.
33 **to dance with** for fashion only. Hunter
compares *Ant.* 3.11.35–6, where Octavius is said to
have worn his sword 'e'en like a dancer'.
34 **theft** Picking up Bertram's 'steal' (33) and
anticipating 'Commit' and 'accessory' (34–5).
35 **accessory** Trisyllabic, with accent on first
syllable.
36 **I...body** I am becoming so attached to you
that separation is like being torn apart on the rack.
39, 42 **sword** It is likely that Parolles flourishes
his sword at these points.
40 **metals** (1) swordsmen, (2) mettlesome
fellows.
41 **Spurio** Italian for 'counterfeit'.
41 **cicatrice** scar.
42 **sinister** left.

43 **reports for me** (1) replies for me, (2) reports
of me.
45 **novices** youthful followers.
47 **Stay** Stop talking; i.e. the King is within
earshot. This reading depends on F2, where the
colon following 'Stay' makes the verb an imperative.
F omits punctuation and might be glossed: '(I will)
Attend the King'. This reading, however, contradicts
Bertram's expressed intention to 'steal away' (33).
'Business' is sometimes interpolated here, as if
Bertram is vacillating – with a shrug of the
shoulders he decides to stay because the King
requires him to.
48 **spacious ceremony** ample courtesy.
49 **list** In the primary sense of 'boundary' or
'limit'. The literal meaning of 'list' as the selvage
of cloth continues to function residually, even
subliminally, as it points to 'wear themselves in the
cap of the time' (50). Walter Whiter, *A Specimen
of a Commentary on Shakespeare* (1794), ed. Alan
Overand and Mary Bell, London, 1967, shows how
this 'associative' habit of mind forms clusters of

expressive to them, for they wear themselves in the cap of the time,   50
there do muster true gait; eat, speak, and move under the influence
of the most received star, and though the devil lead the measure,
such are to be followed. After them, and take a more dilated
farewell.

BERTRAM And I will do so.   55

PAROLLES Worthy fellows, and like to prove most sinewy swordmen.

Exeunt

Enter LAFEW. [*The* KING *comes forward*]

LAFEW [*Kneeling*] Pardon, my lord, for me and for my tidings.
KING I'll see thee to stand up.
LAFEW Then here's a man stands that has brought his pardon.
　　　　I would you had kneeled, my lord, to ask me mercy,   60
　　　　And that at my bidding you could so stand up.
KING I would I had, so I had broke thy pate,
　　　　And asked thee mercy for't.
LAFEW　　　　　　　　　　　　Good faith, across!
　　　　But, my good lord, 'tis thus: you will be cured
　　　　Of your infirmity?
KING　　　　　　　　　　No.
LAFEW　　　　　　　　　　　　O, will you eat   65
　　　　No grapes, my royal fox? Yes, but you will
　　　　My noble grapes, and if my royal fox
　　　　Could reach them. I have seen a medicine

---

56 SD *The...forward*] *Collier MS.; not in* F   57 SD] *After Johnson; not in* F   58 see] F; fee *Theobald; sue conj. Staunton*
63–8] *Divided as Capell; And...for't. / Goodfaith...thus, / Will...infirmitie? / No. / O...foxe? / Yes...if /*
My...medicine F   66 will] *Knight; will,* F

related imagery in Shakespeare's verse. Helena's
tears are 'the best brine a maiden can season her
praise in' (1.1.37). Twenty lines or so later, the
Countess, bidding Bertram goodbye, calls him 'an
unseasoned courtier'. See 4.5.59 n.

50 wear...time are leaders in the fashionable
world. (This recalls the brooch worn in the hat,
1.1.134–5.)

51 there...gait i.e. in the world of fashion
they manifest the approved courtly behaviour.

51–2 influence...star Parolles plays upon the
idea of following the latest fashion and coming
under the astrological influence (flowing-in) from
a dominant planet.

52 measure dance.

53 dilated (1) expansive, (2) circumstantial.

56 like likely.

56 SD *comes forward* In a number of productions

it has been found appropriate to have the King enter
in a wheel-chair; this gives added point to Lafew's
kneeling and to the King's apparent incapacity to
stand (61).

58 Let me see you rise.

59 his pardon i.e. Helena, and the prospect of
his cure.

62 pate head.

63 across i.e. clumsily, and so without doing
harm (as when in tilting a clumsily handled lance
strikes its object athwart rather than with the point).

65–6 eat No grapes Like the fox in Aesop's fable
who rejected the grapes as sour because they were
out of reach.

66 you will i.e. you will eat.

67 and if if.

68 medicine physician (as well as physic).

That's able to breathe life into a stone,
Quicken a rock, and make you dance canary   70
With spritely fire and motion, whose simple touch
Is powerful to araise King Pippen, nay,
To give great Charlemain a pen in's hand
And write to her a love-line.
KING   What her is this?
LAFEW Why, Doctor She! My lord, there's one arrived,   75
If you will see her. Now by my faith and honour,
If seriously I may convey my thoughts
In this my light deliverance, I have spoke
With one, that in her sex, her years, profession,
Wisdom, and constancy, hath amazed me more   80
Than I dare blame my weakness. Will you see her –
For that is her demand – and know her business?
That done, laugh well at me.
KING   Now, good Lafew,
Bring in the admiration, that we with thee
May spend our wonder too, or take off thine   85
By wondering how thou took'st it.
LAFEW   Nay, I'll fit you,
And not be all day neither.
                        [*Goes to the door*]
KING Thus he his special nothing ever prologues.
LAFEW Nay, come your ways.

                    Enter HELENA

KING   This haste hath wings indeed.
LAFEW Nay, come your ways;   90

75 Doctor She] *White;* doctor she F   87 SD] *Sisson; not in* F

70 **Quicken** Give life to.
70 **canary** A lively Spanish dance.
71 **simple** mere; with the residual sense of 'simples' or medicinal herbs.
72 **araise** raise from the dead.
72 **Pippen** The Frankish king Pepin, father of Charlemagne, died in 768.
78 **light deliverance** joking manner of speaking.
79 **profession** i.e. what she professes herself able to do.
81 **dare...weakness** would venture to attribute to the susceptibility of an old man.
84 **admiration** object of wonder.

85 **spend** expend.
85–6 **take...took'st it** take the edge off your wonder by wondering how you came to be so mistaken.
86 **fit** satisfy.
87 SD It would appear from the dialogue that Lafew has Helena waiting at the door, perhaps for his signal.
88 **special nothing** particular trifles.
88 **prologues** introduces.
89 **come your ways** come along (spoken to Helena).

This is his majesty, say your mind to him.
A traitor you do look like, but such traitors
His majesty seldom fears. I am Cressid's uncle,
That dare leave two together; fare you well.   *Exit*
KING Now, fair one, does your business follow us?   95
HELENA Ay, my good lord.
Gerard de Narbon was my father,
In what he did profess, well found.
KING   I knew him.
HELENA The rather will I spare my praises towards him,
Knowing him is enough. On's bed of death   100
Many receipts he gave me; chiefly one,
Which as the dearest issue of his practice,
And of his old experience th'only darling,
He bade me store up, as a triple eye,
Safer than mine own two, more dear. I have so,   105
And hearing your high majesty is touched
With that malignant cause wherein the honour
Of my dear father's gift stands chief in power,
I come to tender it, and my appliance,
With all bound humbleness.
KING   We thank you, maiden,   110
But may not be so credulous of cure,
When our most learnèd doctors leave us, and
The congregated college have concluded

---

105 two, more dear] *Var. 78;* two: more deare F

92 traitor...like Alluding perhaps to Helena's apprehensive appearance.
93 Cressid's uncle Pandarus, the type of the go-between.
95 follow concern.
98 well found found to be good.
100 On's On his.
101 receipts medical prescriptions.
102 dearest issue (1) favourite child, (2) most valuable product.
103 old experience many years' experience.
103 only chief.
104 triple eye i.e. third eye. The odd notion of a third eye probably comes to Shakespeare from Chaucer, who represents Prudence with three eyes in *Troilus and Criseyde*, v, 744–9. F. N. Robinson in his edition of Chaucer (*Works*, 1933) derives the underlying idea, that Prudence regards past,

present and future, from Dante, *Purgatorio*, xx, 130–2. See also C. S. Singleton's note on Dante's lines in his Commentary on the *Purgatorio* (1973), p. 723.
105 Safer i.e. in safer keeping.
106 touched afflicted.
107 cause disease.
107 wherein i.e. for the cure of which.
107 honour Essentially, 'medicinal quality'.
108 chief particularly.
109 appliance skill (in treatment).
110 bound dutiful.
111 credulous of willing to believe in the possibility of.
112 leave abandon hope for.
113 congregated college assembled society of physicians, like the Royal College of Physicians in Shakespeare's London.

That labouring art can never ransom nature
From her inaidable estate; I say we must not   115
So stain our judgement, or corrupt our hope,
To prostitute our past-cure malady
To èmpirics, or to dissever so
Our great self and our credit, to esteem
A senseless help when help past sense we deem.   120

HELENA My duty then shall pay me for my pains.
I will no more enforce mine office on you,
Humbly entreating from your royal thoughts
A modest one, to bear me back again.

KING I cannot give thee less, to be called grateful.   125
Thou thought'st to help me, and such thanks I give
As one near death to those that wish him live.
But what at full I know, thou know'st no part,
I knowing all my peril, thou no art.

HELENA What I can do can do no hurt to try,   130
Since you set up your rest 'gainst remedy.
He that of greatest works is finisher
Oft does them by the weakest minister:
So holy writ in babes hath judgement shown,
When judges have been babes; great floods have flown   135
From simple sources; and great seas have dried

---

115 inaidable] inaidible F

114 **labouring art** the endeavours of medical skill.

115 **inaidable estate** incurable condition.

116 **stain** sully.

116 **corrupt our hope** i.e. by willing it to expect the impossible.

117–18 **prostitute...èmpirics** basely give over our incurable disease to the ministrations of quacks.

118 **dissever** separate.

119 **credit** integrity.

119–20 **esteem...deem** think worthwhile a remedy which has no support in reason when we judge any remedy beyond reason. (The adverbial phrase is not simply tautologous but suggests implicitly that only what is beyond reason can effect a cure.)

121 **duty** discharging of my duty as a subject.

122 **enforce mine office** press my services.

124 **modest one** (1) slight thought, (2) thought recognising the maidenly modesty with which I have acted (Helena supposing that her forward behaviour has called this modesty in question).

124 **to...again** to take back with me.

126–206 The shift to rhyming couplets suggests the intervention of divine power, as at 1.1.187–200.

127 **live** to live.

128 **no part** not at all.

131 **set...rest** stake everything. A metaphor derived from the card game of primero. Compare *Rom.* 5.3.109–10.

134–5 **So...babes** Recalling e.g. Matt. 11.25: 'thou has hid these things from the wise and men of understanding, and has opened them unto babes'; and 1 Cor. 1.27: 'God hath chosen the weak things of the world, to confound the things which are mighty.' Perhaps there is also a reminiscence here of the judgement of Daniel in the Apocryphal story of Susannah and the Elders.

135–6 **great...sources** Shakespeare is perhaps remembering Moses' striking water from the rock in Horeb, Exod. 17.6.

136 **great...dried** Like the Red Sea when the Israelites escaped from Egypt, Exod. 14.21.

When miracles have by the great'st been denied.
Oft expectation fails, and most oft there
Where most it promises; and oft it hits
Where hope is coldest, and despair most shifts.   140

KING I must not hear thee; fare thee well, kind maid,
Thy pains not used must by thyself be paid.
Proffers not took reap thanks for their reward.

HELENA Inspired merit so by breath is barred.
It is not so with Him that all things knows   145
As 'tis with us that square our guess by shows;
But most it is presumption in us when
The help of heaven we count the act of men.
Dear sir, to my endeavours give consent,
Of heaven, not me, make an experiment.   150
I am not an impostor that proclaim
Myself against the level of mine aim,
But know I think, and think I know most sure,
My art is not past power, nor you past cure.

KING Art thou so confident? Within what space   155
Hop'st thou my cure?

HELENA   The greatest grace lending grace,
Ere twice the horses of the sun shall bring
Their fiery torcher his diurnal ring,
Ere twice in murk and occidental damp
Moist Hesperus hath quenched her sleepy lamp,   160

---

140 shifts] F; sits *Pope;* fits *Evans, conj. Theobald*   151 impostor] F3; Impostrue F; imposture *Capell*

137 **the great'st** Presumably Pharaoh.
138 **fails** is disappointed.
139 **hits** is gratified.
140 **shifts** (1) blows hot and cold, (2) contrives (i.e. governs). Some editors read 'fits' or 'sits', to rhyme with 'hits', but as Johnson points out, 'there' (138) is also unrhymed.
142 Your troubles, taken to no purpose, must be their own reward.
143 **Proffers not took** Offers not accepted.
144 **Inspired** Divinely inspired, breathed in from God.
144 **breath** i.e. words, breathed out by man.
146 **square...shows** adjust or shape our conjectures by outward appearance.
148 **count** account.
150 **an experiment** trial.
151-2 **that...aim** who promises more than she can pay.

153 Helena's certainty is expressed with philosophic ambiguity.
154 **My...power** What I profess is not beyond my power to perform.
155 **space** period of time.
156 **greatest grace** God.
157-8 **horses...torcher** Horses were supposed to draw the fiery chariot of the sun-god. This is the only use of 'torcher', meaning torch-bearer, recorded in *OED*. Hunter's reading 'coacher' is, however, a needless improvement.
158 **diurnal ring** daily circuit.
159 **murk...damp** The gloom and fog that accompanies the setting of the sun in the west.
160 **Hesperus** The evening star, referred to as 'her' because Hesperus is also the planet Venus.

Or four and twenty times the pilot's glass
Hath told the thievish minutes how they pass,
What is infirm from your sound parts shall fly,
Health shall live free, and sickness freely die.

KING Upon thy certainty and confidence   165
    What dar'st thou venter?

HELENA   Tax of impudence,
    A strumpet's boldness, a divulgèd shame,
    Traduced by odious ballads; my maiden's name
    Seared otherwise; ne worse of worst – extended
    With vilest torture, let my life be ended.   170

KING Methinks in thee some blessed spirit doth speak
    His powerful sound within an organ weak;
    And what impossibility would slay
    In common sense, sense saves another way.
    Thy life is dear, for all that life can rate   175
    Worth name of life in thee hath estimate:
    Youth, beauty, wisdom, courage, all
    That happiness and prime can happy call.
    Thou this to hazard needs must intimate
    Skill infinite, or monstrous desperate.   180
    Sweet practiser, thy physic I will try,
    That ministers thine own death if I die.

HELENA If I break time, or flinch in property
    Of what I spoke, unpitied let me die,
    And well deserved. Not helping, death's my fee,   185
    But if I help, what do you promise me?

---

167 shame,] *Capell;* shame F   169 otherwise; ne] *Singer;* otherwise, ne F; otherwise, no F2; otherwise; nay *Singer²*
169 worst –] *Alexander;* worst F   170 vilest] vildest F

---

161 **glass** hour glass.
164 **freely** of its own accord.
166 **venter** venture.
166 **Tax of impudence** Accusation of shamelessness.
167 **divulgèd** laid open.
169 **Seared otherwise** Branded as the opposite. [L]
169 **ne . . . worst** Perhaps 'nay, the worst of all possible evils'.
172 **organ** (1) voice, (2) instrument.
173–4 **what...way** that which common sense calls impossible, some other kind of sense declares possible.
175–6 **rate...life** value with the name of life.

176 **in thee...estimate** is to be found and esteemed in you.
178 **prime** youth.
179 **hazard** venture.
179 **intimate** argue.
180 **monstrous desperate** (that you are) monstrously reckless.
181 **practiser** practitioner (with the residual and opposed sense of 'cozener', 'impostor').
181 **physic** medicine.
182 **ministers** administers.
183 **break time** fail to keep the time limit assigned.
183 **flinch in property** come short in respect.
185 **Not helping** If I fail to help (cure you).

KING Make thy demand.

HELENA   But will you make it even?

KING Ay, by my sceptre and my hopes of help.

HELENA Then shalt thou give me with thy kingly hand
      What husband in thy power I will command.   190
      Exempted be from me the arrogance
      To choose from forth the royal blood of France,
      My low and humble name to propagate
      With any branch or image of thy state;
      But such a one thy vassal, whom I know   195
      Is free for me to ask, thee to bestow.

KING Here is my hand, the premises observed,
      Thy will by my performance shall be served.
      So make the choice of thy own time, for I,
      Thy resolved patient, on theé still rely.   200
      More should I question thee, and more I must –
      Though more to know could not be more to trust –
      From whence thou cam'st, how tended on, but rest
      Unquestioned welcome and undoubted blest. –
      Give me some help here ho! – If thou proceed   205
      As high as word, my deed shall match thy deed.

Flourish. Exeunt

[2.2] *Enter* COUNTESS *and* [LAVATCH, *the*] *Clown*

COUNTESS Come on, sir, I shall now put you to the height of your
    breeding.

---

188 help] F; *heaven Theobald, conj. Thirlby* 206 SD *Exeunt*] F2; *Exit.* F *Act 2 Scene 2* 2.2] *Capell; not in* F
1 SH COUNTESS] *Rowe; Lady* F *(and subst. through scene)*

187 **make it even** fulfil it.

188 **help** Theobald and most subsequent editors avoid a break in the rhyme scheme here by emending to 'heaven'. But the break from rhyme makes the King's word expressive of his need for help rather than his prospects of heaven.

190 **in thy power** i.e. whom you have power to dispose of.

191 **Exempted** Far removed.

194 **branch or image** As in a genealogical tree, from whose branches hung likenesses of members of the family.

197 **premises observed** conditions of the agreement fulfilled.

200 **resolved** determined in mind.

200 **still** ever.

203 **tended on** attended (as with a retinue or train).

204 **Unquestioned** (1) before being questioned, (2) without question.

206 **high as word** amply as you have promised.

Act 2, Scene 2

2.2 Editors, following Capell, locate the scene in Rossillion, the Count's palace.

1 **put you to the height** make a thorough test.

2 **breeding** upbringing (as at 2.3.106).

LAVATCH I will show myself highly fed and lowly taught. I know my
business is but to the court.

COUNTESS To the court! Why, what place make you special, when you   5
put off that with such contempt? But to the court!

LAVATCH Truly, madam, if God have lent a man any manners, he may
easily put it off at court. He that cannot make a leg, put off's cap,
kiss his hand, and say nothing, has neither leg, hands, lip, nor cap;
and indeed such a fellow, to say precisely, were not for the court;   10
but for me, I have an answer will serve all men.

COUNTESS Marry, that's a bountiful answer that fits all questions.

LAVATCH It is like a barber's chair that fits all buttocks: the pin-buttock,
the quatch-buttock, the brawn-buttock, or any buttock.

COUNTESS Will your answer serve fit to all questions?   15

LAVATCH As fit as ten groats is for the hand of an attorney, as your
French crown for your taffety punk, as Tib's rush for Tom's
forefinger, as a pancake for Shrove Tuesday, a morris for May-day,
as the nail to his hole, the cuckold to his horn, as a scolding quean
to a wrangling knave, as the nun's lip to the friar's mouth, nay, as   20
the pudding to his skin.

COUNTESS Have you, I say, an answer of such fitness for all questions?

10 court;] *Rowe*; Court, F

3 **highly...taught** over-fed and inadequately
educated (like the children of the rich). Hunter cites
as proverbial: 'Better fed than taught', and sees in
this interchange a comic version of the distinction
between birth and breeding on which the play
insists.

4 **but to the court** i.e. where gentle nurture is
disvalued. The negligent tone begets the Countess's
surprise and is justified in the rejoinder at 7–8.

5 **make you** do you consider.

6 **put off** dismiss.

7 **lent...manners** i.e. as superficial accoutre-
ment.

8 **put it off** carry it off, make a success. Lavatch
seems to mean that any fool can pass himself off
as a courtier, whose manners are exhausted in mere
bowing and scraping.

8 **make a leg** bend his knee in obeisance.

8 **put off's** take off his.

11 **for me** as for me.

13 **like...chair** Proverbial comparison for what
is endlessly accommodating.

13 **pin** narrow.

14 **quatch** Probably 'squat' (otherwise unre-
corded).

14 **brawn** fleshy.

16 **ten groats** ten fourpenny pieces. The usual
fee for an attorney.

17 **French crown** Syphilis, the so-called 'French
disease', induced baldness. A crown = (1) top of the
head, (2) five shillings. Thus the French crown is
both 'the punk's fee and the punk's disease'
(Hunter).

17 **taffety punk** whore dressed showily in taffeta.

17 **Tib's rush** Country girls (for whom 'Tib' is
generic) made rings of reed for love tokens to be
used in rural mock-weddings. Perhaps here and
subsequently Lavatch is glancing obscenely at the
conventional phallic–vulval similitude.

18 **pancake** Eaten traditionally on Shrove
Tuesday, the feasting day before the beginning of
Lent.

18 **morris** Traditional dance for May festivals.

19, 21 **his** its.

19 **quean** hussy.

20 **nun's...mouth** A bawdy version of the
proverb 'as fit as a pudding for a friar's mouth'
(Tilley P620).

21 **pudding** sausage.

LAVATCH From below your duke to beneath your constable, it will fit any question.

COUNTESS It must be an answer of most monstrous size that must fit all demands. 25

LAVATCH But a trifle neither, in good faith, if the learned should speak truth of it. Here it is, and all that belongs to't. Ask me if I am a courtier: it shall do you no harm to learn.

COUNTESS To be young again, if we could! I will be a fool in question, hoping to be the wiser by your answer. I pray you, sir, are you a courtier? 30

LAVATCH O Lord, sir! – There's a simple putting off. More, more, a hundred of them.

COUNTESS Sir, I am a poor friend of yours that loves you. 35

LAVATCH O Lord, sir! – Thick, thick, spare not me.

COUNTESS I think, sir, you can eat none of this homely meat.

LAVATCH O Lord, sir! – Nay, put me to't, I warrant you.

COUNTESS You were lately whipped, sir, as I think.

LAVATCH O Lord, sir! – Spare not me. 40

COUNTESS Do you cry, 'O Lord, sir!' at your whipping, and 'Spare not me'? Indeed your 'O Lord, sir!' is very sequent to your whipping; you would answer very well to a whipping, if you were but bound to't.

LAVATCH I ne'er had worse luck in my life in my 'O Lord, sir!' I see things may serve long, but not serve ever. 45

COUNTESS I play the noble housewife with the time,
  To entertain it so merrily with a fool.

LAVATCH O Lord, sir! – Why, there't serves well again.

COUNTESS An end, sir; to your business: give Helen this, 50
  And urge her to a present answer back.
  Commend me to my kinsmen and my son.
  This is not much.

31 I pray] F3; *La.* I pray F   47–8] *As verse, Knight; as prose, F*   50 An end, sir; to] *Rowe³;* And end sir to F; And end; sir to F3

23 **below…constable** With a sexual innuendo, as perhaps in the Countess's rejoinder.

27 **neither** on the contrary (intensifying Lavatch's negative answer).

30 **be…question** ask questions like a fool.

33 **O Lord, sir** A fashionable expletive used to evade an awkward question. Compare Parolles at 4.3.259.

33 **putting off** evasion.

36 **Thick** Quickly.

37 **homely meat** plain food.

42 **is very sequent to** follows logically on (because it constitutes a plea for mercy).

43 **answer…to** (1) have a good reply to, (2) be a suitable subject for.

44 **bound to't** (1) compelled by oath to answer, (2) tied to the whipping-post.

51 **present** immediate.

52 **Commend me** My greetings.

LAVATCH Not much commendation to them.
COUNTESS Not much employment for you. You understand me?   55
LAVATCH Most fruitfully. I am there before my legs.
COUNTESS Haste you again.

Exeunt

[2.3] *Enter* COUNT [BERTRAM], LAFEW, *and* PAROLLES

LAFEW They say miracles are past, and we have our philosophical
    persons, to make modern and familiar, things supernatural and
    causeless. Hence is it that we make trifles of terrors, ensconcing
    ourselves into seeming knowledge, when we should submit ourselves
    to an unknown fear.   5
PAROLLES Why, 'tis the rarest argument of wonder that hath shot out
    in our latter times.
BERTRAM And so 'tis.
LAFEW To be relinquished of the artists –
PAROLLES So I say, both of Galen and Paracelsus.   10
LAFEW Of all the learned and authentic fellows –
PAROLLES Right, so I say.
LAFEW That gave him out incurable –
PAROLLES Why, there 'tis, so say I too.
LAFEW Not to be helped –   15

55 me?] *Capell;* me. F   56 legs] F3; legegs F; legges F2   Act 2, Scene 3   2.3] *Capell; not in* F   1 SH LAFEW] *Rowe;*
Ol. Laf. F *(and subst. through scene)*   2 familiar,] *Theobald;* familiar F   8 SH BERTRAM] *Rowe; Ros.* F   10 say,] *Rowe;*
say F

55 **understand** Lavatch in what follows picks
this up in the sense of 'stand' = erect penis, and so
introduces a bawdy quibble on 'fruitfully' meaning
'abundantly' but also 'sexually fruitful'.
    56 **there** i.e. in understanding. Also 'in Paris',
to which he has been commended.
    57 **again** back home again.

Act 2, Scene 3
    2.3 Editors, following Capell, locate the scene in
the King's palace, Paris.
    2 **modern** commonplace.
    3 **causeless** inexplicable.
    3–4 **ensconcing ourselves into** fortifying our-
selves with.
    5 **an unknown fear** fear of the unknown, i.e.
of the inexplicable things and 'terrors' of 2–3.
    6 **rarest argument** most extraordinary subject.
    6 **shot out** i.e. like a nova or blazing star.

7 **latter** recent.
    8 **And so 'tis** Bertram is given enough words to
draw attention to his passivity and silence, distinguishing it from the parasitic volubility of Parolles.
    9 **relinquished...artists** abandoned by the
scholars (i.e. physicians).
    10 **Galen and Paracelsus** The ancient and
modern schools of medicine. Galen, the Greek
physician of the second century A.D., was the
principal medical authority of Shakespeare's time.
Paracelsus (Theophrastus Bombastus von Hohen-
heim), a Swiss alchemist and physician of the early
sixteenth century, propounded new theories of
treating disease.
    11 **authentic fellows** qualified members of the
medical profession. Possibly alluding to 'Fellows'
of the Royal College of Physicians.
    13 **gave him out** proclaimed him.
    15 **helped** cured.

PAROLLES Right, as 'twere a man assured of a –

LAFEW Uncertain life, and sure death.

PAROLLES Just, you say well; so would I have said.

LAFEW I may truly say it is a novelty to the world.

PAROLLES It is indeed; if you will have it in showing, you will read   20
it in what-do-ye-call there.

LAFEW [*Reading*] 'A showing of a heavenly effect in an earthly actor'.

PAROLLES That's it I would have said, the very same.

LAFEW Why, your dolphin is not lustier. 'Fore me, I speak in respect –

PAROLLES Nay, 'tis strange, 'tis very strange, that is the brief and the   25
tedious of it, and he's of a most facinerious spirit that will not
acknowledge it to be the –

LAFEW Very hand of heaven.

PAROLLES Ay, so I say.

LAFEW In a most weak –   30

PAROLLES And debile minister, great power, great transcendence,
which should indeed give us a further use to be made than alone
the recovery of the king, as to be –

LAFEW Generally thankful.

Enter KING, HELENA, *and* ATTENDANTS

PAROLLES I would have said it; you say well. Here comes the king.   35

LAFEW *Lustique*, as the Dutchman says; I'll like a maid the better whilst
I have a tooth in my head. Why, he's able to lead her a coranto.

PAROLLES *Mor du vinager*! is not this Helen?

LAFEW 'Fore God, I think so.

20 indeed;] *Hanmer;* indeede F   21 what-do-ye-call] *Case, conj. Glover;* what do ye call F   22 SD] *Alexander; not in*
F   23 it] *Var. 78;* it, F   24 'Fore] *Capell;* fore F   36 Lustique] Lustique F, Lustick F3   38 *Mor du vinager*] F (vinager,);
*Mort du Vinaigre / Rowe*³

18 **Just** Exactly.

20 **in showing** visible (by being printed).

21 **what…there** Parolles presumably indicates
a ballad Lafew is holding, and the title of which he
proceeds to read.

24 **dolphin** Emblematic of lustiness (and
perhaps punning on the French Dauphin, regularly
anglicised by the Elizabethans as 'Dolphin', the
form in the Folio).

24 **'Fore** Before. A mild oath, like 'Upon my
soul' or ''Fore God' (39).

25–6 **brief…tedious** short and long. (Parolles
lapses, as often, into affected speech.)

26 **facinerious** Form of 'facinorous' ('most
wicked'); the word was commoner then, but still
highfalutin.

31 **debile minister** weak agent.

34 **Generally** Universally.

36 *Lustique* Frolicsome.

37 **tooth** sweet tooth (for girls).

37 **coranto** spirited dance.

38 *Mor du vinager*! Pseudo-French. Editors who
translate this mock oath (e.g. as 'death of the
vinegar') and refer it to the Crucifixion are being
over-literal.

39 **'Fore…so** Lafew ignores Parolles (whose eye
is on the lady) and continues to marvel at the King's
fitness. Some productions have found occasion in
Lafew's 'coranto' (37) to have the King and Helena
enter dancing.

KING Go call before me all the lords in court.   40
    Sit, my preserver, by thy patient's side,
    And with this healthful hand, whose banished sense
    Thou hast repealed, a second time receive
    The confirmation of my promised gift,
    Which but attends thy naming.   45

Enter three or four LORDS

    Fair maid, send forth thine eye. This youthful parcel
    Of noble bachelors stand at my bestowing,
    O'er whom both sovereign power and father's voice
    I have to use. Thy frank election make;
    Thou hast power to choose, and they none to forsake.   50
HELENA To each of you one fair and virtuous mistress
    Fall, when Love please! Marry, to each but one!
LAFEW I'd give bay curtal and his furniture,
    My mouth no more were broken than these boys',
    And writ as little beard.
KING   Peruse them well.   55
    Not one of those but had a noble father.
HELENA (*She addresses her to a Lord*) Gentlemen,
    Heaven hath through me restored the king to health.
ALL We understand it, and thank heaven for you.
HELENA I am a simple maid, and therein wealthiest   60
    That I protest I simply am a maid.

---

51 mistress] *Rowe;* Mistris; F   53 curtal] F; Curtal *Evans*   54 boys'] *Capell;* boyes F   57 SD] *Placed as* F; *following*
stream *(70)* NS   57–8 Gentlemen...health] *As verse, Capell; as prose,* F

42 healthful healthy.

42 banished sense lost power of feeling.

43 repealed called back (from banishment).

45 attends waits on.

45 SD The permissive form of F's SD suggests tentative first thoughts. Productions usually require at least half a dozen lords to form the 'youthful parcel'. The FIRST and SECOND LORD at 71 and 77 may or may not be the Lords Dumaine; they are not marked *G* and *E* in the Folio.

46 parcel small group.

47 stand...bestowing are in my power to give in marriage. The bachelors being wards of the King, he could marry them as he pleased so long as he did not give them to a commoner. Shakespeare deliberately ignores this proviso.

49 frank election free choice.

50 A hexameter line.

50 forsake refuse.

52 to...one (1) only one to each, (2) excepting one of you (whom I choose).

53 Lafew here, and in his speeches down to 93, speaks aside – to himself or to the audience.

53 bay...furniture my bay horse with the docked tail and his trappings.

54 My...than If I were still as sexually vigorous as. Literally, Lafew is saying: 'If I still had all my teeth' (compare 37 above). Residually, he is remembering his bay curtal: a 'broken' horse because its mouth is furnished with a bit.

55 writ (1) proclaimed, (2) showed.

57 SD *She...Lord* 'She squares up to the first candidate while speaking to them all' (Hunter, justifying the singular 'Lord' of the Folio SD).

61 protest avow.

Please it your majesty, I have done already.
The blushes in my cheeks thus whisper me,
'We blush that thou shouldst choose; but be refused,
Let the white death sit on thy cheek for ever,   65
We'll never come there again.'

KING   Make choice and see,
Who shuns thy love shuns all his love in me.

HELENA Now, Dian, from thy altar do I fly,
And to imperial Love, that god most high,
Do my sighs stream. [*To a first Lord*] Sir, will you hear my
suit?   70

FIRST LORD And grant it.

HELENA   Thanks, sir; all the rest is mute.

LAFEW I had rather be in this choice than throw ames-ace for my life.

HELENA [*To a second Lord*] The honour, sir, that flames in your fair
eyes,
Before I speak, too threat'ningly replies.
Love make your fortunes twenty times above   75
Her that so wishes, and her humble love!

SECOND LORD No better, if you please.

HELENA   My wish receive,
Which great love grant, and so I take my leave.

LAFEW Do all they deny her? And they were sons of mine, I'd have
them whipped, or I would send them to th'Turk to make eunuchs   80
of.

HELENA [*To a third Lord*] Be not afraid that I your hand should take,
I'll never do you wrong for your own sake.

---

64 choose; but be refused,] *After Rann;* choose, but be refused; F 69 imperiall Love] *Pope;* imperiall loue F;
imperiall Ioue F2; impartiall Ioue F3   70 SD] *Capel; not in* F   72] *As prose, Pope; as verse,* F   73 SD] *Capell; not in* F
79 And] F; An *Capell*   82 SD] *Capell; not in* F

63 **whisper** whisper to.
64 **be** if you are.
68–96 Stage-productions have often turned the
parade of nobles from which Helena makes choice
into a dance or musical game. For dialogue and
dance compare *Ado* 2.1.85–154.
68 **Dian...fly** I desert the goddess of chastity.
71 **all...mute** I have no more to say.
72 **throw...life** stake my life on throwing two
aces at dice ('ames-ace', or 'ambs-ace', is a term for
a pair of aces). Lafew says ironically that he would
rather take his chance with the bachelors than play
at Russian roulette.

73 **honour** (1) high station, (2) willingness to do
me the honour of marrying me. If the first reading
is right, 'threat'ningly' (74) signifies disdain on the
part of the second Lord, and this is Lafew's
understanding (79 ff.). But 'threat'ningly' can also
mean that Helena feels herself in danger of being
accepted by the wrong suitor, as in fact she is (77).
76 **so** thus.
77 **No better** i.e. than you.
77 **receive** accept.
78 **great love** As distinct from Helena's 'humble
love' (76). Some read 'Love', supposing Helena to
refer to the goddess of love.

Blessing upon your vows, and in your bed
Find fairer fortune, if you ever wed!   85
LAFEW These boys are boys of ice, they'll none have her. Sure they are
  bastards to the English, the French ne'er got 'em.
HELENA [*To a fourth Lord*] You are too young, too happy, and too good,
  To make yourself a son out of my blood.
FOURTH LORD Fair one, I think not so.   90
LAFEW There's one grape yet; I am sure thy father drunk wine – but
  if thou be'st not an ass, I am a youth of fourteen. I have known
  thee already.
HELENA [*To Bertram*] I dare not say I take you, but I give
  Me and my service, ever whilst I live,   95
  Into your guiding power. – This is the man.
KING Why then, young Bertram, take her, she's thy wife.
BERTRAM My wife, my liege? I shall beseech your highness,
  In such a business, give me leave to use
  The help of mine own eyes.
KING   Know'st thou not, Bertram,   100
  What she has done for me?
BERTRAM   Yes, my good lord,
  But never hope to know why I should marry her.
KING Thou know'st she has raised me from my sickly bed.
BERTRAM But follows it, my lord, to bring me down
  Must answer for your raising? I know her well;   105
  She had her breeding at my father's charge –
  A poor physician's daughter my wife? Disdain
  Rather corrupt me ever!
KING 'Tis only title thou disdain'st in her, the which
  I can build up. Strange is it that our bloods,   110
  Of colour, weight, and heat, poured all together,

---

86 her] F2; heere F   88 SH HELENA] F3; *La.* F   88 SD] *Capell; not in* F   94 SD] *Rowe; not in* F
100–2 Know'st...her] *As verse, Pope; as prose,* F

87 **got** begot.
91 **grape** scion of a good stock.
91 **wine** Which, proverbially, makes good blood. Compare Falstaff on the virtues of sherris sack, *2H4* 4.3.89–125.
92 **known** seen through. Lafew may be covertly addressing Bertram.
98 **liege** Sovereign lord to whom allegiance is due.

104–5 **to...raising** With a sexual quibble, which justifies the eccentric-seeming association, at 2.1.93, of Lafew with Pandarus.
106 **charge** expense.
107–8 **Disdain...ever** Instead let my disdain of her ruin my fortunes forever.
109 **title** lack of title (as with 'name' at 116).

Would quite confound distinction, yet stands off
In differences so mighty. If she be
All that is virtuous – save what thou dislik'st,
A poor physician's daughter – thou dislik'st   115
Of virtue for the name. But do not so.
From lowest place, whence virtuous things proceed,
The place is dignified by th'doer's deed.
Where great additions swell's, and virtue none,
It is a dropsied honour. Good alone   120
Is good, without a name; vileness is so:
The property by what it is should go,
Not by the title. She is young, wise, fair,
In these to nature she's immediate heir;
And these breed honour. That is honour's scorn   125
Which challenges itself as honour's born
And is not like the sire. Honours thrive,
When rather from our acts we them derive
Than our foregoers. The mere word's a slave
Debauched on every tomb, on every grave   130
A lying trophy, and as oft is dumb
Where dust and damned oblivion is the tomb
Of honoured bones indeed. What should be said?
If thou canst like this creature as a maid,
I can create the rest. Virtue and she   135
Is her own dower; honour and wealth from me.
BERTRAM I cannot love her, nor will strive to do't.

---

117 place, whence] F; place when *Theobald, conj. Thirlby*   120–1 alone Is good, without a name; vileness] *Capell;* a lone, Is good without a name? Vilenesse F   122 it is] F2; is is F   125 honour's] *Rowe³;* honours F   129 word's a] F2; words, a F   130 Debauched] Deboshed F   130 grave] *Knight;* graue: F   132–3 tomb Of...indeed. What] *Theobald;* Tombe. Of...indeed, what F

---

112 **confound distinction** i.e. could not be distinguished in colour, weight and heat.

112–13 **stands...mighty** they stand separated (in your judgement) by such great differences in pedigree. The singular form 'stands' is influenced by 'distinction'.

117 **whence** The Folio reading, generally emended to 'when'.

117 **proceed** come forth.

119 **additions** titles.

119 **swell's** swell us up.

120 **dropsied** swollen unhealthily (by excess fluid).

120 **alone** (1) lacking a title or 'name', (2) in itself, (3) only (as opposed to all other things, except 'vileness').

121 **vileness is so** i.e. vileness is vile in itself.

122 **property** intrinsic nature.

122 **by** for (as at 123).

122 **go** be accepted.

124 She inherits these qualities directly from nature.

125–7 **That...sire** That which proclaims itself honourable by virtue of ancestry and does not justify its claim by honourable behaviour is scorned by true honour.

129 **foregoers** ancestors.

132–3 **Where...indeed** i.e. where truly honourable persons lie in (unremembered) death.

135 **she** i.e. her intrinsic qualities.

137 **strive** attempt.

KING Thou wrong'st thyself, if thou shouldst strive to choose.
HELENA That you are well restored, my lord, I'm glad.
　　　　Let the rest go.   140
KING My honour's at the stake, which to defeat,
　　　　I must produce my power. Here, take her hand,
　　　　Proud scornful boy, unworthy this good gift,
　　　　That dost in vile misprision shackle up
　　　　My love and her desert; that canst not dream,   145
　　　　We poising us in her defective scale,
　　　　Shall weigh thee to the beam; that wilt not know
　　　　It is in us to plant thine honour where
　　　　We please to have it grow. Check thy contempt;
　　　　Obey our will, which travails in thy good;   150
　　　　Believe not thy disdain, but presently
　　　　Do thine own fortunes that obedient right
　　　　Which both thy duty owes and our power claims;
　　　　Or I will throw thee from my care for ever
　　　　Into the staggers and the careless lapse   155
　　　　Of youth and ignorance, both my revenge and hate
　　　　Loosing upon thee, in the name of justice,
　　　　Without all terms of pity. Speak, thine answer.
BERTRAM Pardon, my gracious lord; for I submit
　　　　My fancy to your eyes. When I consider   160
　　　　What great creation and what dole of honour
　　　　Flies where you bid it, I find that she, which late
　　　　Was in my nobler thoughts most base, is now
　　　　The praisèd of the king, who so ennobled,
　　　　Is as 'twere born so.

155 careless] F; cureless *Dyce²*, *conj. W. S. Walker*   158 Speak, thine] F; Speak thine F3   160 eyes. When] *Rowe*; eies, when F

138 **choose** i.e. for yourself.
139 **restored** cured.
141 **at the stake** tied to the post (i.e. like a bear baited by dogs).
141 **which** i.e. which menace.
143 **boy** A term of contempt.
144 **misprision** (1) mistaking, (2) scorn (and with a quibble on 'false imprisonment', hence introducing 'shackle up').
146 **We** The royal pronoun, as the King puts on his power. So again at 148–9.
146 **poising...scale** adding in the balance our weight to her lightness (she having no title).
147 **weight...beam** outweigh you and tip your scale up to the cross-beam.

147 **that thou** that.
149 **Check** Restrain.
150 **travails in** works for.
151 **Believe not** Deny.
151 **presently** immediately (as again at 2.4.43).
152 Do right by your fortunes by being obedient.
155 **staggers** giddiness.
155 **careless lapse** fall into recklessness.
158 **all terms of pity** pity in any form.
160 **fancy** love.
161 **great creation** creation of greatness.
161 **dole** dealing out.
162 **which late** who recently.
164 **who** i.e. Helena.
164 **so** being so.

KING   Take her by the hand,   165
       And tell her she is thine; to whom I promise
       A counterpoise – if not to thy estate,
       A balance more replete.
BERTRAM   I take her hand.
KING   Good fortune and the favour of the king
       Smile upon this contràct, whose ceremony   170
       Shall seem expedient on the now-born brief,
       And be performed tonight. The solemn feast
       Shall more attend upon the coming space,
       Expecting absent friends. As thou lov'st her,
       Thy love's to me religious; else, does err.   175

                                                    Exeunt

       Lafew and Parolles stay behind, commenting of this wedding

LAFEW   Do you hear, monsieur? A word with you.
PAROLLES   Your pleasure, sir?
LAFEW   Your lord and master did well to make his recantation.
PAROLLES   Recantation? My lord? My master?
LAFEW   Ay; is it not a language I speak?   180
PAROLLES   A most harsh one, and not to be understood without bloody
       succeeding. My master?
LAFEW   Are you companion to the Count Rossillion?
PAROLLES   To any count, to all counts: to what is man.
LAFEW   To what is count's man. Count's master is of another style.   185
PAROLLES   You are too old, sir; let it satisfy you, you are too old.
LAFEW   I must tell thee, sirrah, I write man; to which title age cannot
       bring thee.

167–8 estate, A] F; estate A *Evans*   171 now-born] *Rowe*; now borne F

---

166 whom Presumably Helena, conceivably
Bertram.
  167 A counterpoise An equal weight (recurring
to the image of balance, 146–7).
  167–8 if...replete (1) which, if not greater than
your possessions, will be more fully matched; (2)
which will be, not equal to your possessions, but
more abundant. (*OED* supports both readings of
'replete'.)
  170 ceremony marriage ceremony (which enacts
'this contract').
  171 seem...brief This difficult passage may
mean: 'follow expeditiously on my royal command,
now uttered'. (*OED* sb 1.1 glosses 'brief' as 'royal
mandate'.)
  172 solemn solemnising.
  173–4 more...friends wait through a longer

interval for the arrival of expected friends now
absent.
  175 to me as far as I'm concerned.
  175 religious i.e. holy and true.
  175 does err i.e. is errant and treacherous.
  175 SD.2 of on.
  179 Parolles is taken aback by Lafew's treatment
of Bertram both as a repentant heretic and as
Parolles's master.
  182 succeeding consequences.
  183 companion Lafew intends the old sense
'rascal' as well as the current one 'associate'.
  185 man servant. Lafew sets aside Parolles's
claim to be on equal terms with all men.
  187 sirrah Used to an inferior (as again at 222).
  187 write call myself a.

PAROLLES What I dare too well do, I dare not do.

LAFEW I did think thee, for two ordinaries, to be a pretty wise fellow. 190
Thou didst make tolerable vent of thy travel; it might pass: yet the
scarfs and the bannerets about thee did manifoldly dissuade me
from believing thee a vessel of too great a burden. I have now found
thee. When I lose thee again, I care not; yet art thou good for
nothing but taking up, and that thou'rt scarce worth. 195

PAROLLES Hadst thou not the privilege of antiquity upon thee –

LAFEW Do not plunge thyself too far in anger, lest thou hasten thy trial;
which if – Lord have mercy on thee for a hen! So, my good window
of lattice, fare thee well. Thy casement I need not open, for I look
through thee. Give me thy hand. 200

PAROLLES My lord, you give me most egregious indignity.

LAFEW Ay, with all my heart, and thou art worthy of it.

PAROLLES I have not, my lord, deserved it.

LAFEW Yes, good faith, every dram of it, and I will not bate thee a
scruple. 205

PAROLLES Well, I shall be wiser.

LAFEW Even as soon as thou canst, for thou hast to pull at a smack
a'th'contrary. If ever thou be'st bound in thy scarf and beaten, thou
shalt find what it is to be proud of thy bondage. I have a desire
to hold my acquaintance with thee, or rather my knowledge, that 210

---

190 ordinaries,] *Theobald;* ordinaries: F; ordinaries F2   195 thou'rt] F3, th'ourt F   198 hen!] *Theobald;* hen, F;
hen; F3

189 i.e. I have courage enough to beat you only
too well, but dare not because of your age.

190 **for two ordinaries** i.e. for two mealtimes
spent in Parolles's company. An ordinary was a
tavern.

191 **make**...of talk passably about.

192 **scarfs**...**bannerets** Denoting the military man and worn to excess by Parolles, so
suggesting to Lafew an inconsiderable ship
bedecked with pennants – like the 'scarfed bark' of
MV 2.6.14–15.

193 **of too**...**burden** i.e. carrying a valuable
cargo. Lafew means that Parolles would not
advertise himself or show off if he had something
precious to hide.

193 **found** found out. Introduces a quibble on
'lose' = 'get rid of'. Compare 2.4.25.

195 **taking up** picking up (in contrast to 'lose');
also 'calling to account'.

196 **privilege of antiquity** licence of age.

198 **which if** i.e. you are put to your trial or
testing.

198 **hen** Perhaps alluding to Parolles's 'plumage'
as well as to his fussiness and his timidity.

199 **lattice** With a possible suggestion of the
red-lattice windows which denoted a common
alehouse.

199 **casement** window.

201 **egregious** flagrant (but used here to
exemplify Parolles's highfalutin diction).

204 **bate** abate.

205 **scruple** tiniest part (literally, one-third of a
dram).

206 **wiser** i.e. by avoiding in future creatures like
you. Lafew in his reply picks up the conventional
sense.

207–8 **pull**...**contrary** swallow a large dose of
your foolishness (before you grow wise).

209 **bondage** i.e. the scarves which he has bound
about him.

210 **hold** continue.

I may say in the default, 'He is a man I know.'

PAROLLES My lord, you do me most insupportable vexation.

LAFEW I would it were hell-pains for thy sake, and my poor doing
eternal; for doing I am past, as I will by thee, in what motion age
will give me leave.   *Exit*   215

PAROLLES Well, thou hast a son shall take this disgrace off me, scurvy,
old, filthy, scurvy lord! Well, I must be patient, there is no fettering
of authority. I'll beat him, by my life, if I can meet him with any
convenience, and he were double and double a lord. I'll have no
more pity of his age than I would have of – I'll beat him, and if   220
I could but meet him again.

Enter LAFEW

LAFEW Sirrah, your lord and master's married, there's news for you.
You have a new mistress.

PAROLLES I most unfeignedly beseech your lordship to make some
reservation of your wrongs. He is my good lord; whom I serve above   225
is my master.

LAFEW Who? God?

PAROLLES Ay, sir.

LAFEW The devil it is that's thy master. Why dost thou garter up thy
arms a'this fashion? Dost make hose of thy sleeves? Do other   230
servants so? Thou wert best set thy lower part where thy nose
stands. By mine honour, if I were but two hours younger, I'd beat
thee. Methink'st thou art a general offence, and every man should
beat thee. I think thou wast created for men to breathe themselves
upon thee.   235

PAROLLES This is hard and undeserved measure, my lord.

LAFEW Go to, sir, you were beaten in Italy for picking a kernel out of

---

211 **in the default** when you default (i.e. show
yourself empty when you are brought to trial, 197).
The Clarkes (cited Hunter) suggest a legal allusion:
'when you fail to appear in court'. Compare *MM*
5.1.126, 144.

211 **I know** i.e. know for what he is (compare
MM 5.1.126).

213 **my...doing** i.e. my inadequate power to
inflict vexation. Lafew would like to impose eternal
damnation (with a quibble on 'do' = 'copulate').

214 **will by** will pass by (picking up 'past' in the
preceding clause).

214–15 **motion...leave** movement my
'antiquity' permits.

216 **a son** Whom Parolles will beat in retaliation.

218–19 **with any convenience** on a suitable
occasion.

219 **and** though.

220 **and if** if.

224–5 **make...wrongs** qualify your insults.

225 **good lord** patron (merely).

229–30 **garter...sleeves** i.e. Parolles wears
scarves around his sleeves as others wear garters on
their stockings.

233 **Methink'st** It seems to me that.

234 **breathe** exercise (by beating him).

236 **measure** treatment (meted out).

237–8 **picking...pomegranate** i.e. nothing at
all; the most trivial kind of offence.

a pomegranate. You are a vagabond and no true traveller. You are
more saucy with lords and honourable personages than the
commission of your birth and virtue gives you heraldry. You are   240
not worth another word, else I'd call you knave. I leave you. *Exit*

Enter [BERTRAM] *Count Rossillion*

PAROLLES Good, very good, it is so then. Good, very good, let it be
    concealed awhile.
BERTRAM Undone, and forfeited to cares for ever!
PAROLLES What's the matter, sweet heart?   245
BERTRAM Although before the solemn priest I have sworn,
    I will not bed her.
PAROLLES What, what, sweet heart?
BERTRAM O my Parolles, they have married me!
    I'll to the Tuscan wars, and never bed her.   250
PAROLLES France is a dog-hole, and it no more merits
    The tread of a man's foot. To th'wars!
BERTRAM There's letters from my mother; what th'import is,
    I know not yet.
PAROLLES Ay, that would be known. To th'wars, my boy, to
    th'wars!   255
    He wears his honour in a box unseen,
    That hugs his kicky-wicky here at home,
    Spending his manly marrow in her arms,
    Which should sustain the bound and high curvet
    Of Mars's fiery steed. To other regions!   260
    France is a stable, we that dwell in't jades,
    Therefore to th'war!
BERTRAM It shall be so. I'll send her to my house,
    Acquaint my mother with my hate to her,
    And wherefore I am fled; write to the king   265

---

244 SH BERTRAM] *Rowe; Ros.* F *(and subst. through scene)*   246–7 Although…her] *As verse, Rowe³; as prose,* F

238 **vagabond** mere tramp, vagrant (as opposed
to a 'true traveller' who required a licence to travel).
240 **commission** warrant.
240 **heraldry** entitlement.
249 **Parolles** Trisyllabic.
253 **letters** a letter (Latin *litterae*).
256 **box unseen** With an allusion to the female
genital organs.
257 **kicky-wicky** Otherwise unknown but
meaning generically and jocosely 'mistress'.

258 **Spending** Expending, wasting.
258 **manly marrow** i.e. semen, but with a
general reference to the virile energies that 'sustain'
the soldier and his steed.
259 **curvet** A leap of a horse when all four legs
are off the ground at once.
261 **jades** inferior horses (as opposed to the 'fiery
steed' of 260).

That which I durst not speak. His present gift
Shall furnish me to those Italian fields
Where noble fellows strike. Wars is no strife
To the dark house and the detested wife.

PAROLLES Will this caprichio hold in thee, art sure?   270

BERTRAM Go with me to my chamber, and advise me.
I'll send her straight away. Tomorrow,
I'll to the wars, she to her single sorrow.

PAROLLES Why, these balls bound, there's noise in it. 'Tis hard!
A young man married is a man that's marred;   275
Therefore away, and leave her bravely; go.
The king has done you wrong; but hush, 'tis so.

Exeunt

[2.4] *Enter* HELENA *and* [LAVATCH, *the*] *Clown*

HELENA My mother greets me kindly. Is she well?

LAVATCH She is not well, but yet she has her health. She's very merry,
but yet she is not well; but thanks be given, she's very well, and
wants nothing i'th'world; but yet she is not well.

HELENA If she be very well, what does she ail that she's not very well?   5

LAVATCH Truly, she's very well indeed, but for two things.

HELENA What two things?

LAVATCH One, that she's not in heaven, whither God send her quickly!
the other, that she's in earth, from whence God send her quickly!

Enter PAROLLES

PAROLLES Bless you, my fortunate lady!   10

---

269 detested] *Rowe;* detected F   271 advise] F3; aduice F   277 SD *Exeunt*] *Rowe; Exit* F   Act 2, Scene 4   2.4] *Capell;*
not in F

266 **present gift** The 'counterpoise' of 167.
267 **furnish me** to equip me for.
269 **To** Compared to.
269 **dark house** (1) gloomy house, (2) lunatic asylum (like the 'hideous darkness' where Malvolio is laid: *TN* 4.2.30).
270 **caprichio** whim. Parolles again uses affected diction.
270 **hold** be maintained.
272 **straight** immediately.
274 **balls** tennis balls (stuffed with hair and covered with leather).
274 **bound...hard** Bertram is spirited, and

now playing the game properly, with bounding returns.
275 After the proverb 'Marrying is marring' (Tilley M701).
276 **bravely** with spirit.

Act 2, Scene 4
2.4 Editors, following Capell, locate the scene in the King's palace, Paris.
1 **kindly** affectionately.
2 **not well** i.e. 'not in heaven' (8).
4 **wants** lacks.
5 **what** in what.

HELENA I hope, sir, I have your good will to have mine own good
　　fortune.
PAROLLES You had my prayers to lead them on, and to keep them on,
　　have them still. O, my knave, how does my old lady?
LAVATCH So that you had her wrinkles and I her money, I would she　　15
　　did as you say.
PAROLLES Why, I say nothing.
LAVATCH Marry, you are the wiser man; for many a man's tongue
　　shakes out his master's undoing. To say nothing, to do nothing, to
　　know nothing, and to have nothing, is to be a great part of your　　20
　　title, which is within a very little of nothing.
PAROLLES Away, th'art a knave.
LAVATCH You should have said, sir, 'Before a knave th'art a knave',
　　that's 'Before me th'art a knave.' This had been truth, sir.
PAROLLES Go to, thou art a witty fool, I have found thee.　　25
LAVATCH Did you find me in yourself, sir, or were you taught to find
　　me? The search, sir, was profitable, and much fool may you find
　　in you, even to the world's pleasure and the increase of laughter.
PAROLLES A good knave, i'faith, and well fed.
　　　　Madam, my lord will go away tonight,　　30
　　　　A very serious business calls on him.
　　　　The great prerogative and rite of love,
　　　　Which, as your due time claims, he does acknowledge,
　　　　But puts it off to a compelled restraint;
　　　　Whose want, and whose delay, is strewed with sweets,　　35
　　　　Which they distill now in the curbèd time,
　　　　To make the coming hour o'erflow with joy,

---

12 fortune] F; fortunes *Evans, conj. Heath*　27 The search] *Rowe;* Clo. The search F

13 them i.e. her good fortune. Perhaps Heath's
conjecture 'fortunes' should be preferred.
18 man (1) human being, (2) servant.
19 shakes out causes.
21 title status; and perhaps with a glance at the
name Parolles: (mere) words.
23 Before In the presence of.
24 Before me A mild oath: 'Upon my soul' (and
punning on 'Before', 23). Lavatch is saying that
Parolles is a knave.
25 found thee i.e. seen you for what you are.
This is a significant expression in the play (see
3.6.73, 5.2.35).
26 in yourself by your own efforts (but also with
the sense, which Parolles misses, 'by looking at
yourself').

27 The search The Folio introduces this line
with the speech heading *Clo.[wn]*, which may mean
that a reply by Parolles has dropped out.
28 pleasure entertainment.
29 well fed Resuming the proverb (2.2.3)
'Better fed than taught'.
34 puts...to postpones it because of.
35–8 Whose want...brim i.e. love's rite when
it comes will be sweeter and fuller for the delay, as
perfume is refined from flowers by distillation.
35 sweets flowers.
36 curbèd time time of restraint. The still
holding the distillate was sometimes called a
'cucurbit' (see *OED*).

And pleasure drown the brim.

HELENA   What's his will else?

PAROLLES That you will take your instant leave a'th'king,
    And make this haste as your own good proceeding,   40
    Strengthened with what apology you think
    May make it probable need.

HELENA   What more commands he?

PAROLLES That having this obtained, you presently
    Attend his further pleasure.

HELENA In every thing I wait upon his will.   45

PAROLLES I shall report it so.   *Exit Parolles*

HELENA   I pray you. Come, sirrah.

                                      Exeunt

[2.5] *Enter* LAFEW *and* BERTRAM

LAFEW But I hope your lordship thinks not him a soldier.

BERTRAM Yes, my lord, and of very valiant approof.

LAFEW You have it from his own deliverance.

BERTRAM And by other warranted testimony.

LAFEW Then my dial goes not true. I took this lark for a bunting.   5

BERTRAM I do assure you, my lord, he is very great in knowledge, and
    accordingly valiant.

LAFEW I have then sinned against his experience, and transgressed
    against his valour, and my state that way is dangerous, since I cannot
    yet find in my heart to repent. Here he comes. I pray you make   10
    us friends, I will pursue the amity.

Enter PAROLLES

PAROLLES [*To Bertram*] These things shall be done, sir.

46 you. Come] *Theobald;* you come F   46 *Exeunt*] *Pope; Exit* F   Act 2, Scene 5   2.5] *Capell; not in* F   12 SD] *Capell; not in* F

38 **else** besides.

40 **make...proceeding** represent your hasty departure as your own idea.

42 **it probable need** your hasty departure necessible and plausible.

44 **Attend** Await.

44 **pleasure** command.

Act 2, Scene 5
2.5 Editors, following Capell, locate the scene in the King's palace, Paris.

2 **valiant approof** demonstrated valour.

3 **deliverance** testimony.

5 **dial** pocket watch; as in *AYLI* 2.7.20.

5 **bunting** Which resembles the lark except in its singing. Lafew ironically reverses the proverb 'To take a bunting for a lark' (Tilley B722).

7 **accordingly** correspondingly.

8–10 **sinned...repent** Lafew again gives a religious account of his relationship with Parolles.

10 **find in** find it in.

LAFEW Pray you, sir, who's his tailor?

PAROLLES Sir!

LAFEW O, I know him well, I, sir, he, sir, 's a good workman, a very   15
    good tailor.

BERTRAM [*Aside to Parolles*] Is she gone to the king?

PAROLLES She is.

BERTRAM Will she away tonight?

PAROLLES As you'll have her.   20

BERTRAM I have writ my letters, casketed my treasure,
      Given order for our horses, and tonight,
      When I should take possession of the bride,
      End ere I do begin.

LAFEW A good traveller is something at the latter end of a dinner, but   25
    one that lies three thirds, and uses a known truth to pass a thousand
    nothings with, should be once heard and thrice beaten. God save
    you, captain.

BERTRAM Is there any unkindness between my lord and you, monsieur?

PAROLLES I know not how I have deserved to run into my lord's   30
    displeasure.

LAFEW You have made shift to run into't, boots and spurs and all, like
    him that leapt into the custard; and out of it you'll run again, rather
    than suffer question for your residence.

BERTRAM It may be you have mistaken him, my lord.   35

LAFEW And shall do so ever, though I took him at's prayers. Fare you
    well, my lord, and believe this of me: there can be no kernel in this
    light nut; the soul of this man is his clothes. Trust him not in matter
    of heavy consequence; I have kept of them tame, and know their
    natures. Farewell, monsieur, I have spoken better of you than you   40

---

15 I, sir] I sir F; Ay, 'sir' *Hunter*   15 he, sir, 's] *Capell;* hee sirs F   17 SD] *Rowe; not in* F   24 End] *Collier;* And F
25 traveller] F3, Trauailer F   26 one] *Rowe³;* on F   27 heard] F2; hard F

13 **who's his tailor** Another reference to
Parolles's plumage (as in 2.3.192 and below,
38). Compare *Lear* 2.2.54–5: 'a tailor made
thee'.

15–16 Lafew pretends to take 'Sir' as the
tailor's name.

24 *End Collier's emendation of the Folio 'And'
is generally accepted. It is possible, however, that
the conjunction completes the thought of a line that
has dropped out.

25 **something** i.e. to amuse the table with tall
stories.

32 **made shift** contrived.

33 **him...custard** Referring to the jester who
leaped into an enormous custard pie at the annual
feast of the Lord Mayor of London.

34 **suffer...residence** tolerate enquiry as to
why you are there.

36 **took** Playing on 'mistaken' (35).

39 **heavy** important.

39 **of them tame** some of these creatures as
household pets.

have or will to deserve at my hand, but we must do good against
      evil.   *[Exit]*

PAROLLES An idle lord, I swear.

BERTRAM I think so.

PAROLLES Why, do you not know him?   45

BERTRAM Yes, I do know him well, and common speech
      Gives him a worthy pass. Here comes my clog.

Enter HELENA

HELENA I have, sir, as I was commanded from you,
      Spoke with the king, and have procured his leave
      For present parting; only he desires   50
      Some private speech with you.

BERTRAM   I shall obey his will.
      You must not marvel, Helen, at my course,
      Which holds not colour with the time, nor does
      The ministration and requirèd office
      On my particular. Prepared I was not   55
      For such a business; therefore am I found
      So much unsettled. This drives me to entreat you,
      That presently you take your way for home,
      And rather muse than ask why I entreat you,
      For my respects are better than they seem,   60
      And my appointments have in them a need
      Greater than shows itself at the first view
      To you that know them not. This to my mother.
            [Giving a letter]
      'Twill be two days ere I shall see you, so
      I leave you to your wisdom.

---

41 or will] F; *or wit or will conj. Singer*   42 SD] *Rowe; not in* F   44 I think so] F; *I think not so Singer²*   63 SD]
Rowe; not in F

41 **have...deserve** have deserved or will
deserve.

41 **do good against** return good for. See
1 Thess. 5.15.

43 **idle** foolish.

45 If Bertram's 'I think so' (44) is correct,
Parolles's rejoinder is to be taken, not as a question,
but as an intensifier: 'Come, we know what he is.'

47 **worthy pass** good reputation.

47 **clog** Wooden block tied to an animal to
restrict its movement.

48 **from** by.

50 **present parting** immediate departure.

53 **holds...time** is not in keeping with a
wedding-day.

53–5 **nor...particular** i.e. and does not fulfil
my obligation as a husband.

59 **muse** wonder.

60 **respects** reasons.

61 **appointments** affairs.

HELENA   Sir, I can nothing say,   65
    But that I am your most obedient servant.

BERTRAM Come, come, no more of that.

HELENA   And ever shall
    With true observance seek to eke out that
    Wherein toward me my homely stars have failed
    To equal my great fortune.

BERTRAM   Let that go.   70
    My haste is very great. Farewell; hie home.

HELENA Pray, sir, your pardon.

BERTRAM   Well, what would you say?

HELENA I am not worthy of the wealth I owe,
    Nor dare I say 'tis mine; and yet it is;
    But like a timorous thief, most fain would steal   75
    What law does vouch mine own.

BERTRAM   What would you have?

HELENA Something, and scarce so much; nothing indeed.
    I would not tell you what I would, my lord.
    Faith, yes:
    Strangers and foes do sunder, and not kiss.   80

BERTRAM I pray you stay not, but in haste to horse.

HELENA I shall not break your bidding, good my lord.
    Where are my other men? Monsieur, farewell.   *Exit*

BERTRAM Go thou toward home, where I will never come
    Whilst I can shake my sword or hear the drum.   85
    Away, and for our flight.

PAROLLES   Bravely, *corragio*!

                                 Exeunt

70–1] *As verse, Pope; as prose,* F   78–9] *As Dyce²; as one line,* F   83 Where...men? Monsieur, farewell. *Exit*] F;
BERTRAM Where...Monsieur? – farewell. *Exit Helena* / *conj. Theobald*   86 SD] *Rowe; not in* F

68 observance dutiful service.
68 eke out supplement.
69 my homely stars i.e. my fate which denied
me noble parents.
71 hie hasten.
73 owe own, possess.
75 fain willingly.
76 vouch affirm to be.

80 sunder separate from one another.
81 stay delay.
83 Theobald assigns this line to Bertram. But
though Helena's stars are 'homely' she has status
enough to be attended by a retinue (her 'other
men').
86 Bravely, *corragio*! Bravo, courage (Italian).

3.[1] *Flourish. Enter the* DUKE OF FLORENCE, *the two Frenchmen* [*the*
FIRST *and* SECOND LORDS DUMAINE], *with a troop of soldiers*

DUKE So that from point to point now have you heard
       The fundamental reasons of this war,
       Whose great decision hath much blood let forth
       And more thirsts after.
FIRST LORD   Holy seems the quarrel
       Upon your grace's part; black and fearful   5
       On the opposer.
DUKE Therefore we marvel much our cousin France
       Would in so just a business shut his bosom
       Against our borrowing prayers.
SECOND LORD   Good my lord,
       The reasons of our state I cannot yield   10
       But like a common and an outward man
       That the great figure of a council frames
       By self-unable motion, therefore dare not
       Say what I think of it, since I have found
       Myself in my incertain grounds to fail   15
       As often as I guessed.
DUKE   Be it his pleasure.
FIRST LORD But I am sure the younger of our nature,
       That surfeit on their ease, will day by day
       Come here for physic.
DUKE   Welcome shall they be;

Act 3, Scene 1   3.1] *Rowe; Actus Tertius.* F   0 SD *Frenchmen*] F; *French Lords / Rowe*   9 SH SECOND LORD] *Rowe;*
French E. F   13 self-unable] F4; selfe vnable F   17 SH FIRST LORD] *Cam.; Fren. G.* F   17 nature] F; *Nation Rowe*

Act 3, Scene 1
   3.1 Editors, following Capell, locate the scene in
Florence, the Duke's palace.
   3 **Whose great decision** The violent deciding
of which.
   4 **more thirsts after** is still thirsty for more
(blood).
   4–9 **Holy...prayers** Shakespeare draws attention to the contrast between the aloof attitude of the
King of France to the Italian wars and that of his
committed nobles. Compare 1.2.1–17 and 2.1.1–5.
   6 **the opposer** the enemy's part.
   7 **cousin** fellow ruler.
   8 **bosom** heart.
   9 **borrowing prayers** entreaties for assistance.

   10 **yield** produce.
   11 **Except** as a commoner who stands outside
(state councils).
   12 **figure** scheme.
   12 **frames** constructs.
   13 **self-unable motion** (his own) inadequate
thought. 'Motion' = 'agitation of the mind' (*OED*
Motion *sb* 4).
   16 **guessed** conjectured.
   16 **Be...pleasure** Let it be as he will.
   17 **nature** temperament.
   18 **surfeit on** grow sick with. Compare *MM*
1.2.126.
   19 **for physic** to be cured by bloodletting.

And all the honours that can fly from us   20
Shall on them settle. – You know your places well;
When better fall, for your avails they fell.
Tomorrow to th'field.

Flourish. [Exeunt]

[3.2] *Enter* COUNTESS *and [*LAVATCH, *the*] *Clown*

COUNTESS It hath happened all as I would have had it, save that he
  comes not along with her.
LAVATCH By my troth, I take my young lord to be a very melancholy
  man.
COUNTESS By what observance, I pray you?   5
LAVATCH Why, he will look upon his boot and sing, mend the ruff and
  sing, ask questions and sing, pick his teeth and sing. I know a man
  that had this trick of melancholy sold a goodly manor for a song.
COUNTESS Let me see what he writes, and when he means to come.
  [Opening the letter]
LAVATCH I have no mind to Isbel since I was at court. Our old lings 10
  and our Isbels a'th'country are nothing like your old ling and your
  Isbels a'th'court. The brains of my Cupid's knocked out, and I
  begin to love, as an old man loves money, with no stomach.
COUNTESS What have we here?
LAVATCH E'en that you have there.   *Exit* 15

23 to th'] *After* F2 *(to the)*; to'th the F   **Act 3, Scene 2**   3.2] *Pope; not in* F   8 sold] F3; hold F   9 SH COUNTESS]
Rowe; Lad. F *(and subst. through scene, with / Old La. / at 57)*   9 SD] *Capell; not in* F   10 lings] F; Ling F2
15 E'en] *Theobald; In* F

20 can...us i.e. we can bestow.
22 better fall better places fall vacant.
22 for...fell i.e. they will have become vacant
for you to fill. The Duke's words link this scene with
the opening of 3.3 on the battlefield, where the
'general of our horse' leaves a vacancy for Bertram.

Act 3, Scene 2
3.2 Editors, following Capell, locate the scene in
Rossillion, the Count's palace.
1 all altogether.
3 troth faith.
5 observance observation (of him).
6 mend adjust.
6 ruff Either the frilled collar worn by men and
women in Shakespeare's time, or the ruffle or
turned-over flap at the top of a boot.

7 pick his teeth Like the affected traveller with
his toothpick, 1.1.134.
8 trick quirk.
8 *sold The reading of F3 is supported by the
proverb, current in Shakespeare's time, 'sold for a
song' (Tilley s636).
10 old lings salt cod. 'Salt' can mean lecherous
and 'cod' (as in cod-piece) can mean scrotum; the
Clown's joke remains obscure, but it appears to
suggest that his own appetites have become more
sophisticated since he was at court.
11 country Perhaps continuing the obscene
quibble. Compare *Ham.* 3.2.116.
12 brains...out i.e. my old love is finished.
13 stomach appetite.
15 E'en As Hunter remarks, F's 'In' appears to be
a variant spelling of 'E'en' (= even).

[COUNTESS] [*Reads*] *a letter* 'I have sent you a daughter-in-law; she
   hath recovered the king, and undone me. I have wedded her, not
   bedded her, and sworn to make the "not" eternal. You shall hear
   I am run away; know it before the report come. If there be breadth
   enough in the world, I will hold a long distance. My duty to you.   20
                                        Your unfortunate son,
                                                   Bertram.'
         This is not well, rash and unbridled boy,
         To fly the favours of so good a king,
         To pluck his indignation on thy head   25
         By the misprising of a maid too virtuous
         For the contempt of empire.

                  Enter [LAVATCH, *the*] *Clown*

LAVATCH O madam, yonder is heavy news within between two soldiers
   and my young lady!
COUNTESS What is the matter?   30
LAVATCH Nay, there is some comfort in the news, some comfort. Your
   son will not be killed so soon as I thought he would.
COUNTESS Why should he be killed?
LAVATCH So say I, madam, if he run away, as I hear he does. The
   danger is in standing to't; that's the loss of men, though it be the   35
   getting of children. Here they come will tell you more. For my part,
   I only hear your son was run away.

   Enter HELENA *and two Gentlemen* [*the* FIRST *and* SECOND LORDS
                           DUMAINE]

SECOND LORD 'Save you, good madam.
HELENA Madam, my lord is gone, for ever gone.
FIRST LORD Do not say so.   40
COUNTESS Think upon patience. Pray you, gentlemen,
         I have felt so many quirks of joy and grief

---

16 SD COUNTESS *Reads*] *Rowe³; not in* F   37 SD *the French* LORDS] *Neilson; not in* F   38 SH SECOND LORD] *Kittredge;*
French E. F *(and subst. through scene)*   40 SH FIRST LORD] *Kittredge; French G.* F *(and subst. through scene, with* / I.G. /
at 55)   41 patience.] *Capell;* patience, F; patience; F3

17 **recovered** cured.   35 **standing to't** staying put (with a quibble on
18 **'not'** With a pun on the hymeneal knot.   tumescence, as in *TGV* 2.5.22–3).
25 **pluck** draw down.   36 **getting** begetting.
26 **misprising** scorning (as at 2.3.144).   37 **run away** Most editors, beginning with
27 **the...empire** even an emperor to disdain   Capell, make the Clown leave at this point, though
her.   there is no direction in the Folio.
28 **heavy** sad.   42 **quirks** sudden strokes.

That the first face of neither on the start
Can woman me unto't. Where is my son, I pray you?
FIRST LORD Madam, he's gone to serve the Duke of Florence.   45
We met him thitherward, for thence we came;
And after some dispatch in hand at court,
Thither we bend again.
HELENA Look on his letter, madam, here's my passport.
[*Reads*] 'When thou canst get the ring upon my finger, which never   50
shall come off, and show me a child begotten of thy body that I
am father to, then call me husband; but in such a "then" I write
a "never".' This is a dreadful sentence.
COUNTESS Brought you this letter, gentlemen?
FIRST LORD Ay, madam, and for the contents' sake are sorry for our   55
pains.
COUNTESS I prithee, lady, have a better cheer;
If thou engrossest all the griefs are thine,
Thou robb'st me of a moiety. He was my son,
But I do wash his name out of my blood,   60
And thou art all my child. Towards Florence is he?
FIRST LORD Ay, madam.
COUNTESS   And to be a soldier?
FIRST LORD Such is his noble purpose, and believe't,
The duke will lay upon him all the honour
That good convenience claims.
COUNTESS   Return you thither?   65
SECOND LORD Ay, madam, with the swiftest wing of speed.
HELENA [*Reads*] 'Till I have no wife, I have nothing in France.'
'Tis bitter.
COUNTESS   Find you that there?
HELENA   Ay, madam.
SECOND LORD 'Tis but the boldness of his hand haply, which his heart
was not consenting to.   70

---

50 SD] *Capell; not in* F   58 engrossest all] F4; *engrossest, all* F   67 SD] *After Rowe; not in* F   68 'Tis...madam] *As
verse, Var. 93; as prose,* F

43 **face** appearance.
43–4 **first...unto't** i.e. the startling first
appearance of neither joy nor grief can surprise me
into womanish weeping.
44 **woman me unto't** make me behave like a
weeping woman.
46 **thitherward** on his way thither.
47 **dispatch in hand** urgent business.
49 **passport** licence to wander from home.

58 **thou engrossest** you monopolise.
58 **are** that are.
59 **a moiety** half. More generally, a part.
61 **art** all only are.
65 **good convenience claims** he can in
propriety claim.
67 '**Till...France**' i.e. while Bertram has a wife
living in France he will not return there.
69 **haply** perhaps.

COUNTESS Nothing in France, until he have no wife!
    There's nothing here that is too good for him
    But only she, and she deserves a lord
    That twenty such rude boys might tend upon,
    And call her hourly mistress. Who was with him?   75
SECOND LORD A servant only, and a gentleman
    Which I have sometime known.
COUNTESS   Parolles, was it not?
SECOND LORD Ay, my good lady, he.
COUNTESS A very tainted fellow, and full of wickedness.
    My son corrupts a well-derivèd nature   80
    With his inducement.
SECOND LORD   Indeed, good lady,
    The fellow has a deal of that too much,
    Which holds him much to have.
COUNTESS   Y'are welcome, gentlemen.
    I will entreat you, when you see my son,
    To tell him that his sword can never win   85
    The honour that he loses. More I'll entreat you
    Written to bear along.
FIRST LORD   We serve you, madam,
    In that and all your worthiest affairs.
COUNTESS Not so, but as we change our courtesies.
    Will you draw near?   90
                    Exit [with the Lords Dumaine]
HELENA 'Till I have no wife, I have nothing in France.'
    Nothing in France, until he has no wife!
    Thou shalt have none, Rossillion, none in France;
    Then hast thou all again. Poor lord, is't I
    That chase thee from thy country, and expose   95
    Those tender limbs of thine to the event
    Of the none-sparing war? And is it I
    That drive thee from the sportive court, where thou

81–8] *As verse, Capell; as prose,* F   82 that] *Rowe³; that,* F   90 SD *with Lords] Neilson, after Rowe; not in* F

79 **tainted** corrupt.
80 **a well-derivèd nature** i.e. the good nature which he has inherited.
82 **that** power of inducement, persuasiveness.
83 **holds...have** i.e. stands him in good stead. 'Holds' = 'supports', 'maintains' (*OED v* 3d).
87 **Written** In writing.

89 i.e. you serve me only to the extent that we exchange civilities.
90 **draw near** come along (with me).
93–4 **none in...again** Helena will not live in France and Bertram will be free to come home (112).
96 **event** hazard.

Wast shot at with fair eyes, to be the mark
Of smoky muskets? O you leaden messengers,   100
That ride upon the violent speed of fire,
Fly with false aim, move the still-piercing air
That sings with piercing, do not touch my lord.
Whoever shoots at him, I set him there;
Whoever charges on his forward breast,   105
I am the caitiff that do hold him to't;
And though I kill him not, I am the cause
His death was so effected. Better 'twere
I met the ravin lion when he roared
With sharp constraint of hunger; better 'twere   110
That all the miseries which nature owes
Were mine at once. No, come thou home, Rossillion,
Whence honour but of danger wins a scar,
As oft it loses all. I will be gone.
My being here it is that holds thee hence.   115
Shall I stay here to do't? No, no, although
The air of paradise did fan the house,
And angels officed all. I will be gone,
That pitiful rumour may report my flight
To consolate thine ear. Come night, end day!   120
For with the dark, poor thief, I'll steal away.   *Exit*

---

102 still-piercing] F2; still-peering F; still-piecing *Var. 78*; still-'pearing *Delius*   118 angels] F2; Angles F

99 mark target.
100 leaden messengers i.e. bullets.
102 move (1) stir (to pity), (2) displace.
102 *still-piercing. The Folio text reads 'still-peering'. Among many emendations, the most popular is Steevens's 'still-piecing', i.e. always closing up again. Alternatively, the compound can mean 'always looking on' or 'still appearing'. But 'piercing' in the line that follows suggests a deliberate repetition of the gerund, with the emphatic word being 'sings'. It seems tenable, therefore, to read 'still-piercing', i.e. always invading to the quick, and this reading is supported by F2.
103 sings with piercing i.e. in token of its indifference or malignity; alternatively, as the bullets pierce it, or as it derides their piercing. Compare *Rom.* 1.1.111–12.

105 forward (1) facing the enemy, (2) pressing forward.
106 caitiff wretch.
106 hold compel.
109 ravin ravening.
111 owes owns, possesses.
113 Whence From the war (where).
113 but...scar (1) only from danger wins a scar, (2) wins from danger only a scar.
114 As...all And often loses life itself.
115 holds keeps.
116 do't i.e. keep thee hence.
118 officed all had the office of all the household duties.
119 pitiful full of pity (for Bertram).
121 thief Helena, who has 'stolen' the title of wife, and whose resolution recapitulates Bertram's at 2.1.33.

[3.3] *Flourish. Enter the* DUKE OF FLORENCE, [BERTRAM, *Count of*]
Rossillion, Drum and Trumpets, Soldiers, PAROLLES

DUKE The general of our horse thou art, and we,
      Great in our hope, lay our best love and credence
      Upon thy promising fortune.
BERTRAM   Sir, it is
      A charge too heavy for my strength, but yet
      We'll strive to bear it for your worthy sake   5
      To th'extreme edge of hazard.
DUKE   Then go thou forth,
      And Fortune play upon thy prosperous helm
      As thy auspicious mistress!
BERTRAM   This very day,
      Great Mars, I put myself into thy file;
      Make me but like my thoughts, and I shall prove   10
      A lover of thy drum, hater of love.

                                  Exeunt

[3.4] *Enter* COUNTESS *and* [RINALDO, *the*] *Steward*

COUNTESS Alas! and would you take the letter of her?
      Might you not know she would do as she has done
      By sending me a letter? Read it again.
[RINALDO] [*Reads*] *letter*
      'I am Saint Jaques' pilgrim, thither gone.

Act 3, Scene 3 3.3] *Capell; not in* F   0 SD BERTRAM, *Count of*] *After Rowe; not in* F   Act 3, Scene 4 3.4] *Capell;
not in* F   1 SH COUNTESS] *Rowe; La.* F *(through scene)*   4 SD STEWARD *Reads*] *Collier; not in* F

Act 3, Scene 3
  3.3 Evidently located on a Florentine battlefield
(see 3.1.23).
  0 SD The appearance of Parolles at the end of the
parade is probably calculated.
  0 SD *Drum and Trumpets* Drummers and
trumpeters.
  2 **Great in** Swelling with (like a pregnant
woman).
  2 **lay** wager.
  2 **credence** trust.
  3 **promising fortune** promise of good fortune
to come.
  6 **extreme...hazard** utmost limit of danger.
'Hazard', signifying a game of chance, also picks up
the Duke's 'lay' at 2. See 2.1.49 n.

7 **helm** helmet.
9 **file** ranks.

Act 3, Scene 4
  3.4 Editors, following Capell, locate the scene in
Rossillion, the Count's palace.
  4–17 **I...free** These fourteen lines make a
Shakespearean sonnet.
  4 **Saint Jaques' pilgrim** A pilgrim to the shrine
of Santiago de Compostella, a famous place of
pilgrimage in north-western Spain where St James
the Greater is buried. 'Jaques' is pronounced as a
disyllable. For the sense of 'pilgrim', see Dante,
Vita Nuova, XL: 'in a specific sense "pilgrim"
means only one who travels to or returns from the
house of St James'.

  Ambitious love hath so in me offended   5
  That barefoot plod I the cold ground upon
  With sainted vow my faults to have amended.
  Write, write, that from the bloody course of war
  My dearest master, your dear son, may hie.
  Bless him at home in peace, whilst I from far   10
  His name with zealous fervour sanctify.
  His taken labours bid him me forgive;
  I, his despiteful Juno, sent him forth
  From courtly friends, with camping foes to live,
  Where death and danger dogs the heels of worth.   15
  He is too good and fair for death and me,
  Whom I myself embrace to set him free.'
COUNTESS Ah, what sharp stings are in her mildest words!
  Rinaldo, you did never lack advice so much
  As letting her pass so. Had I spoke with her,   20
  I could have well diverted her intents,
  Which thus she hath prevented.
RINALDO   Pardon me, madam,
  If I had given you this at overnight,
  She might have been o'erta'en; and yet she writes,
  Pursuit would be but vain.
COUNTESS   What angel shall   25
  Bless this unworthy husband? He cannot thrive,
  Unless her prayers, whom heaven delights to hear
  And loves to grant, reprieve him from the wrath
  Of greatest justice. Write, write, Rinaldo,
  To this unworthy husband of his wife.   30
  Let every word weigh heavy of her worth,
  That he does weigh too light. My greatest grief,

---

7 have] F2; *hane* F 10 peace, whilst] F3; peace. Whilst F 18 SH COUNTESS] *Capell; not in* F

---

 7 sainted (1) holy, (2) made to a saint.
 7 to have amended to cause to be amended (see Abbott 360).
 8 course Possibly punning on 'curse'.
 9 hie hasten.
 10 Bless him Let him be blessed.
 10 in peace i.e. both safe from the war and his unwanted wife.
 11 sanctify invoke blessings on.
 12 His taken labours As for the labours he has undertaken.
 13 despiteful spiteful.

 13 Juno Whose enmity imposed on Hercules his celebrated labours.
 17 Whom i.e. death.
 19 advice considered judgement.
 22 prevented forestalled.
 23 at overnight last evening.
 27 whom i.e. both Helena and her prayers.
 30 unworthy...wife husband unworthy of his wife.
 31 weigh heavy of emphasise.
 32 greatest very great.

Though little he do feel it, set down sharply.
Dispatch the most convenient messenger.
When haply he shall hear that she is gone, 35
He will return, and hope I may that she,
Hearing so much, will speed her foot again,
Led hither by pure love. Which of them both
Is dearest to me, I have no skill in sense
To make distinction. Provide this messenger. 40
My heart is heavy, and mine age is weak;
Grief would have tears, and sorrow bids me speak.

Exeunt

[3.5] *A tucket afar off. Enter old* WIDOW *of Florence, her daughter*
[DIANA], VIOLENTA, *and* MARIANA, *with other* CITIZENS

WIDOW Nay, come, for if they do approach the city, we shall lose all
the sight.
DIANA They say the French count has done most honourable service.
WIDOW It is reported that he has taken their great'st commander, and
that with his own hand he slew the duke's brother. 5
[*Tucket*]
We have lost our labour, they are gone a contrary way. Hark! you
may know by their trumpets.
MARIANA Come, let's return again and suffice ourselves with the report
of it. Well, Diana, take heed of this French earl. The honour of
a maid is her name, and no legacy is so rich as honesty. 10
WIDOW I have told my neighbour how you have been solicited by a
gentleman his companion.

Act 3, Scene 5 3.5] *Capell; not in* F o SD DIANA] *Rowe; not in* F 1–12] *As prose, Pope;* Nay...come, / ...Citty,
/ ...sight. / ...done / ...service. / ...reported, / ...Commander, / ...slew / ...labour, / ...harke, / ...Trumpets.
/ ...againe, / ...it. / ...Earle, / ...name, / ...rich / ...honestie. / ...neighbour / ...Gentleman /...Companion. F
5 SD] *Capell; not in* F

33 **sharply** emphatically, so that he will feel it.
35 **When haply** Perhaps when.
39 **skill in sense** ability in terms of what I feel.
40 **Provide** Equip.

Act 3, Scene 5
3.5 Editors, following Capell, locate the scene
outside Florence.
o SD *tucket* A series of notes on the trumpet.
o SD VIOLENTA This character does not speak.

Violenta appears in William Painter's *Palace of
Pleasure* (1566, 1569, 1575), in the 37th and 42nd
novelle, and may represent the name Shakespeare
originally intended for the Widow's daughter, or an
abandoned intention to create another character
here.
4 **their** i.e. the Senoys'.
8 **suffice** content.
10 **name** reputation (as maiden or virgin).
10 **honesty** chastity (as again at 55).

MARIANA I know that knave, hang him! one Parolles, a filthy officer
he is in those suggestions for the young earl. Beware of them, Diana;
their promises, enticements, oaths, tokens, and all these engines of   15
lust, are not the things they go under. Many a maid hath been
seduced by them, and the misery is, example, that so terrible shows
in the wrack of maidenhood, cannot for all that dissuade succession,
but that they are limed with the twigs that threatens them. I hope
I need not to advise you further, but I hope your own grace will   20
keep you where you are, though there were no further danger known
but the modesty which is so lost.
DIANA You shall not need to fear me.

Enter HELENA

WIDOW I hope so. Look, here comes a pilgrim. I know she will lie at
my house; thither they send one another. I'll question her. God   25
save you, pilgrim, whither are bound?
HELENA To Saint Jaques le Grand.
    Where do the palmers lodge, I do beseech you?
WIDOW At the Saint Francis here beside the port.
HELENA Is this the way?   30
A march afar
WIDOW Ay, marry, is't. Hark you, they come this way.
    If you will tarry, holy pilgrim,
    But till the troops come by,
    I will conduct you where you shall be lodged,
    The rather for I think I know your hostess   35
    As ample as myself.

17 is,] *Rowe*³; is F   23 SD *Enter* HELENA] F; *Enter* HELENA *disguised like a Pilgrim.* / *Rowe*   26 whither] F2; whether
F   26 are] F; are you F2   27 le] F3; la F

13 **officer** agent.
14 **suggestions for** solicitings on behalf of.
15 **engines** schemes.
16 **go under** pretend to be.
17–18 **example…maidenhood** that previous
examples will illustrate so terribly the ruin of
virginity.
18 **dissuade succession** prevent other maids
from taking the same course.
19 **but that** but for all that (wealth of example).
See Abbott 122 on 'but' as signifying prevention.
19 **limed…twigs** caught in the trap (as birds are
snared by birdlime smeared on twigs).
19 **threatens** Elizabethan usage sanctions a
singular verb with a plural subject.
23 **fear** fear for, worry about.

24 **lie** lodge.
26 **are** are you.
28 **palmers** Pilgrims who carried a palm leaf in
token of having visited the Holy Sepulchre in
Jerusalem.
29 **Saint Francis** An inn with the sign of St
Francis.
29 **port** city gate. It is likely that the main doors
of the façade of the tiring-house served to represent
it.
30–3 Hunter suggests that the short lines may
represent a compositor's attempt to regularise
confused copy. In any case, the dialogue is
punctuated by the sound of the approaching band.
36 **ample** amply.

HELENA   Is it yourself?

WIDOW If you shall please so, pilgrim.

HELENA I thank you, and will stay upon your leisure.

WIDOW You came, I think, from France?

HELENA   I did so.

WIDOW Here you shall see a countryman of yours   40
    That has done worthy service.

HELENA   His name, I pray you?

DIANA The Count Rossillion. Know you such a one?

HELENA But by the ear, that hears most nobly of him.
    His face I know not.

DIANA   Whatsome'er he is,
    He's bravely taken here. He stole from France,   45
    As 'tis reported, for the king had married him
    Against his liking. Think you it is so?

HELENA Ay, surely, mere the truth, I know his lady.

DIANA There is a gentleman that serves the count
    Reports but coarsely of her.

HELENA   What's his name?   50

DIANA Monsieur Parolles.

HELENA   O, I believe with him.
    In argument of praise, or to the worth
    Of the great count himself, she is too mean
    To have her name repeated. All her deserving
    Is a reservèd honesty, and that   55
    I have not heard examined.

DIANA   Alas, poor lady,
    'Tis a hard bondage to become the wife
    Of a detesting lord.

WIDOW I write 'good creature', wheresoe'er she is,
    Her heart weighs sadly. This young maid might do her   60
    A shrewd turn, if she pleased.

HELENA   How do you mean?

---

59 I write] F; I right F2; Ah! right *Rowe*; A right *Var. 78*; I warrant, *Globe*   59 'good creature',] *This edn*; good creature, F

---

38 **stay upon** await.
44 **Whatsome'er** Whatever.
45 **bravely taken** highly regarded.
46 **for** because.
48 **mere** absolutely.
52 **In…or** With respect to her merit, or in comparison.
53 **mean** low born.

54 **All her deserving** Her only merit.
55 **reservèd** strictly preserved.
56 **examined** called in question.
59 **write** style her. The Globe emendation 'warrant' is generally preferred to the Folio reading. But compare *MM* 2.4.16 and *Ado* 4.3.86–7.
60 **weighs sadly** is heavy.
61 **shrewd** (1) curst, (2) hurtful.

May be the amorous count solicits her
In the unlawful purpose?

WIDOW   He does indeed,
And brokes with all that can in such a suit
Corrupt the tender honour of a maid.   65
But she is armed for him, and keeps her guard
In honestest defence.

Drum and Colours. Enter [BERTRAM] *Count Rossillion,* PAROLLES,
and the whole army

MARIANA   The gods forbid else!
WIDOW So, now they come.
That is Antonio, the duke's eldest son,
That, Escalus.

HELENA   Which is the Frenchman?
DIANA   He,   70
That with the plume; 'tis a most gallant fellow.
I would he loved his wife. If he were honester
He were much goodlier. Is't not a handsome gentleman?
HELENA I like him well.
DIANA 'Tis pity he is not honest. Yond's that same knave   75
That leads him to these places. Were I his lady,
I would poison that vile rascal.
HELENA   Which is he?
DIANA That jack-an-apes with scarfs. Why is he melancholy?
HELENA Perchance he's hurt i'th'battle.
PAROLLES Lose our drum! Well.   80
MARIANA He's shrewdly vexed at something. Look, he has spied us.
WIDOW Marry, hang you!
MARIANA And your courtesy, for a ring-carrier!
                        Exeunt [*Bertram, Parolles, and army*]

67 SD BERTRAM] *Rowe; not in* F   69 Antonio] F2; *Anthonio* F   75 Yond's] *Rowe;* yonds F   83 SD *Exeunt...army*]
After Rowe; Exit F

64 **brokes** bargains, like a go-between or bawd.
Compare *Tro.* 5.10.33.
66 **guard** ward. A term from weaponry
signifying defence. Compare *Tro.* 1.2.263.
67 **honestest** most chaste.
67 SD.1 *Colours* Colour-bearer (i.e.
standard-bearer).
67 **else** that it should be otherwise.
72 **honester** more honourable.
73 **were** would be.
75 **Yond's** Not an adverb but a demonstrative
pronoun: 'That one there is'.

78 **jack-an-apes** monkey.
80 **drum** As much a symbol of regimental honour
as the regiment's colours.
81 **shrewdly** keenly.
83 **courtesy** Alluding to the bow or curtsy
Parolles makes to the ladies.
83 **ring-carrier** Go-between who carries presents
or tenders of marriage between his master and the
woman marked down for prey.

WIDOW The troop is past. Come, pilgrim, I will bring you
  Where you shall host. Of enjoined penitents   85
  There's four or five, to great Saint Jaques bound,
  Already at my house.
HELENA   I humbly thank you.
  Please it this matron and this gentle maid
  To eat with us tonight, the charge and thanking
  Shall be for me, and to requite you further,   90
  I will bestow some precepts of this virgin
  Worthy the note.
BOTH   We'll take your offer kindly.

Exeunt

[3.6] *Enter* [BERTRAM] *Count Rossillion and the Frenchmen* [*the* FIRST
and SECOND LORDS DUMAINE], *as at first*

SECOND LORD Nay, good my lord, put him to't; let him have his way.
FIRST LORD If your lordship find him not a hilding, hold me no more
  in your respect.
SECOND LORD On my life, my lord, a bubble.
BERTRAM Do you think I am so far deceived in him?   5
SECOND LORD Believe it, my lord, in mine own direct knowledge,
  without any malice, but to speak of him as my kinsman, he's a most

Act 3, Scene 6   3.6] *Capell; not in* F   0 SD BERTRAM] *Rowe; not in* F   1 SH SECOND LORD] *Capell; Cap.E.* F *(and
subst. through scene)*   2 SH FIRST LORD] *Capell; Cap.G.* F *(through scene)*   5] *As prose, Pope;* Do...farre /
Deceiued...him. F

85 **host** lodge.
85 **enjoined penitents** Persons vowed to
undertake a pilgrimage in penance for their sins.
88 **Please it** If it please.
89–90 **charge...me** i.e. I shall pay the bill and
be grateful too.
91 **precepts** advice.
91 **of** on.
92 **Worthy the note** (1) 'worth listening to'
(modifying 'precepts'), (2) 'worth looking at'
(modifying 'virgin').
92 **kindly** gratefully.

Act 3, Scene 6
3.6 Editors, following Capell, locate the scene in
the Florentine camp.
0 SD *as at first* Recalls their previous appearance
at 3.2.37.
1 **to't** to the test.

2 *For SECOND LORD in the first speech heading
and FIRST LORD in the second, F reads,
respectively, '*Cap.E.*' and '*Cap.G.*' These F
designations continue for SECOND LORD at 1, 4, 6,
31, 67, 77 and 85. At 17 he is simply '*C.E.*' At 87
however, he becomes '*Cap.G.*' FIRST LORD is
designated '*Cap.G.*' by F at 2, 11, 15, 26, 35, 39, 71
and 81, but becomes '*Cap.E.*' at 89 and 95. In
the text of the present scene all Es have, with three
exceptions, been interpreted as SECOND LORD and
all Gs as FIRST LORD. For the exceptions see notes
on SHS 87, 89 and 95. For an account of the
confusion between the two lords and their relation
to the letters that designate them in F, see Textual
Analysis, pp. 156–7 below.
2 **hilding** coward.
4 **bubble** glittering and empty cheat.
7 **as** as if he were.

notable coward, an infinite and endless liar, an hourly promise-
breaker, the owner of no one good quality worthy your lordship's
entertainment.   10

FIRST LORD It were fit you knew him, lest reposing too far in his virtue,
     which he hath not, he might at some great and trusty business in
     a main danger fail you.

BERTRAM I would I knew in what particular action to try him.

FIRST LORD None better than to let him fetch off his drum, which you   15
     hear him so confidently undertake to do.

SECOND LORD I, with a troop of Florentines, will suddenly surprise him;
     such I will have, whom I am sure he knows not from the enemy.
     We will bind and hoodwink him so, that he shall suppose no other
     but that he is carried into the leaguer of the adversaries, when we   20
     bring him to our own tents. Be but your lordship present at his
     examination, if he do not, for the promise of his life, and in the
     highest compulsion of base fear, offer to betray you, and deliver all
     the intelligence in his power against you, and that with the divine
     forfeit of his soul upon oath, never trust my judgement in anything.   25

FIRST LORD O, for the love of laughter, let him fetch his drum; he says
     he has a stratagem for't. When your lordship sees the bottom of
     his success in't, and to what metal this counterfeit lump of ore will
     be melted, if you give him not John Drum's entertainment, your
     inclining cannot be removed. Here he comes.   30

Enter PAROLLES

SECOND LORD O, for the love of laughter, hinder not the honour of his
     design. Let him fetch off his drum in any hand.

BERTRAM How now, monsieur? This drum sticks sorely in your
     disposition.

FIRST LORD A pox on't, let it go, 'tis but a drum.   35

9 quality worthy] *Rowe*; qualitie, worthy F   28 his] *Rowe*; this F   28 ore] *Theobald*; ours F

10 **entertainment** patronage.
11 **reposing...in** depending too much on.
12 **trusty** needing trustworthiness.
14 **try** test.
15 **fetch off** retrieve.
17 **surprise** capture.
19 **hoodwink** blindfold.
20 **leaguer** camp.
24 **intelligence...power** information he possesses.
27 **bottom** extent.
28 *his F's 'this' looks like a misreading.

28 **counterfeit ... ore** lump of counterfeit ore.
28 *ore F's 'ours' makes limp sense, and 'ours'
may be a misreading of 'oure', a variant spelling of
'ore'; here, as in *Ham.* 4.1.25, it means 'gold' (by
confusion with 'or' in heraldry).
29 **John Drum's entertainment** Proverbial for
being turned out of doors (Tilley J12).
30 **inclining** partiality (to Parolles).
32 **in any hand** in any case.
33–4 **sticks...disposition** annoys you sorely.
35 **pox on't** plague take it.

PAROLLES But a drum! Is't but a drum? A drum so lost! There was excellent command, to charge in with our horse upon our own wings, and to rend our own soldiers!

FIRST LORD That was not to be blamed in the command of the service; it was a disaster of war that Caesar himself could not have 40 prevented, if he had been there to command.

BERTRAM Well, we cannot greatly condemn our success. Some dishonour we had in the loss of that drum, but it is not to be recovered.

PAROLLES It might have been recovered.

BERTRAM It might, but it is not now. 45

PAROLLES It is to be recovered. But that the merit of service is seldom attributed to the true and exact performer, I would have that drum or another, or *hic jacet*.

BERTRAM Why, if you have a stomach, to't, monsieur: if you think your mystery in stratagem can bring this instrument of honour again 50 into his native quarter, be magnanimous in the enterprise and go on; I will grace the attempt for a worthy exploit. If you speed well in it, the duke shall both speak of it, and extend to you what further becomes his greatness, even to the utmost syllable of your worthiness. 55

PAROLLES By the hand of a soldier, I will undertake it.

BERTRAM But you must not now slumber in it.

PAROLLES I'll about it this evening, and I will presently pen down my dilemmas, encourage myself in my certainty, put myself into my mortal preparation; and by midnight look to hear further from me. 60

BERTRAM May I be bold to acquaint his grace you are gone about it?

PAROLLES I know not what the success will be, my lord, but the attempt I vow.

---

49 stomach, to't] F; stomack to't *Capell*   51 magnanimous] magnanimious F

38 **wings** flanks.
39 **command...service** military orders.
42 **greatly...success** feel too bad about the outcome (as at 62).
46 **But** Were it not.
48 *hic jacet* here lies (the inscription on a tombstone).
49 **a stomach** the courage.
50 **mystery** technical knowledge, as of a craft.
52 **grace** support.
52 **speed** succeed.
54 **becomes** does credit to.

54 **syllable** Perhaps Bertram is glancing satirically at the name 'Parolles'.
58 **presently** immediately.
58 **pen down** (1) write out, (2) confine, as in a pen.
59 **dilemmas** (1) alternative and equally unfavourable arguments (whence the 'horns' of a dilemma), (2) perplexities.
59 **certainty** i.e. of success (and opposing the 'dilemmas' of 59).
60 **mortal preparation** (1) preparation for my death, (2) preparation for the deaths of others (whom Parolles is about to slay).

BERTRAM I know th'art valiant, and to the possibility of thy soldiership
    will subscribe for thee. Farewell.   65
PAROLLES I love not many words.   *Exit*
SECOND LORD No more than a fish loves water. Is not this a strange
    fellow, my lord, that so confidently seems to undertake this
    business, which he knows is not to be done, damns himself to do,
    and dares better be damned than to do't?   70
FIRST LORD You do not know him, my lord, as we do. Certain it is that
    he will steal himself into a man's favour, and for a week escape a
    great deal of discoveries, but when you find him out, you have him
    ever after.
BERTRAM Why, do you think he will make no deed at all of this that   75
    so seriously he does address himself unto?
SECOND LORD None in the world, but return with an invention, and
    clap upon you two or three probable lies. But we have almost
    embossed him, you shall see his fall tonight; for indeed he is not
    for your lordship's respect.   80
FIRST LORD We'll make you some sport with the fox ere we case him.
    He was first smoked by the old Lord Lafew. When his disguise and
    he is parted, tell me what a sprat you shall find him, which you
    shall see this very night.
SECOND LORD I must go look my twigs. He shall be caught.   85
BERTRAM Your brother, he shall go along with me.
SECOND LORD As't please your lordship. I'll leave you.   [*Exit*]
BERTRAM Now will I lead you to the house, and show you
        The lass I spoke of.
FIRST LORD   But you say she's honest.

64–5] *As prose, Pope;* I...valiant, / And...souldiership, / Will...Farewell. F   87 SH SECOND LORD] *Rowe; Cap.G.*
F; FIRST LORD *Malone*   87 SD] *Theobald; not in* F   89, 95 SH FIRST LORD] *Rowe³; Cap.E.* F; SECOND LORD *Malone*

64 **possibility** utmost capacity.
65 **subscribe** vouch.
69 **damns** swears (perjured) oaths.
73 **have him** perceive his true character.
75 **make no deed** perform no part.
77 **an invention** a fabricated tale.
78 **probable** plausible.
79 **embossed him** (1) driven him into a corner,
(2) made him foam at the mouth like an exhausted
animal. (It seems likely that the verb conflates both
meanings.)
  80 **respect** regard.
  81 **case** skin (hence 'unmask').
  82 **smoked** (1) smelled out, (2) driven out of his
hole by smoke (as again at 4.1.21).

83 **sprat** small fry, contemptible creature.
85 **look** overlook.
85 **twigs** i.e. trap (the twigs being smeared
with birdlime as a snare).
87 SH *SECOND LORD F's assignment of this line
to *Cap.G.* (usually signifying the FIRST LORD) is
inconsistent with 17 SH and 85 SH, which require
the initiative in the plot against Parolles to be taken
by *Cap.E.* (the SECOND LORD).
  89 SH, 95 SH *FIRST LORD F's assignment of
these lines to the SECOND LORD (*Cap.E.*) is
inconsistent with 17, 85 and 86.
  89 **honest** chaste.

BERTRAM That's all the fault. I spoke with her but once,   90
    And found her wondrous cold, but I sent to her,
    By this same coxcomb that we have i'th'wind,
    Tokens and letters which she did re-send,
    And this is all I have done. She's a fair creature;
    Will you go see her?
FIRST LORD   With all my heart, my lord.   95

                            Exeunt

[3.7] *Enter* HELENA *and* WIDOW

HELENA If you misdoubt me that I am not she,
    I know not how I shall assure you further
    But I shall lose the grounds I work upon.
WIDOW Though my estate be fall'n, I was well born,
    Nothing acquainted with these businesses,   5
    And would not put my reputation now
    In any staining act.
HELENA   Nor would I wish you.
    First give me trust, the count he is my husband,
    And what to your sworn counsel I have spoken
    Is so from word to word; and then you cannot,   10
    By the good aid that I of you shall borrow,
    Err in bestowing it.
WIDOW   I should believe you,
    For you have showed me that which well approves
    Y'are great in fortune.
HELENA   Take this purse of gold,
    And let me buy your friendly help thus far,   15
    Which I will over-pay and pay again

Act 3, Scene 7   3.7] *Capell; not in* F

92 **coxcomb** fool.
92 **have…wind** are to the windward of (i.e. we can track him without being scented by him).

Act 3, Scene 7
3.7 Editors, following Capell, locate the scene in Florence, the Widow's house.
1 **misdoubt** doubt.
3 **But…lose** Without losing. Helena fears she might give away her position ('grounds').

4 **estate be fall'n** worldly fortune has declined.
8 **trust** belief.
9 **sworn counsel** private hearing, backed by a vow to be secret.
10 **from…word** word by word.
11 **By** With regard to.
13 **approves** proves.
16 **over-pay…again** doubly recompense.

When I have found it. The count he woos your daughter,
Lays down his wanton siege before her beauty,
Resolved to carry her. Let her in fine consent,
As we'll direct her how 'tis best to bear it.   20
Now his important blood will naught deny
That she'll demand. A ring the county wears,
That downward hath succeeded in his house
From son to son, some four or five descents,
Since the first father wore it. This ring he holds   25
In most rich choice; yet in his idle fire,
To buy his will, it would not seem too dear,
Howe'er repented after.

WIDOW   Now I see
The bottom of your purpose.

HELENA You see it lawful then. It is no more   30
But that your daughter, ere she seems as won,
Desires this ring; appoints him an encounter;
In fine, delivers me to fill the time,
Herself most chastely absent. After,
To marry her, I'll add three thousand crowns   35
To what is passed already.

WIDOW   I have yielded.
Instruct my daughter how she shall persever,
That time and place with this deceit so lawful
May prove coherent. Every night he comes
With musics of all sorts, and songs composed   40
To her unworthiness. It nothing steads us
To chide him from our eaves, for he persists
As if his life lay on't.

---

19 Resolved] *Collier;* Resolue F; Resolves F2   28–9 Now...purpose] *As Capell; as one line,* F   34 After,] *Hunter;* after
F; after this F2   41 steads] F4; steeds F

17 **found** received.
18 **wanton** lecherous.
19 **carry** conquer (the looked-for result of the
siege).
19 **fine** so many words (as again at 33).
20 **bear it** conduct the business.
21 **important** importunate.
21 **blood** passion.
26 **rich choice** high regard.
26 **idle fire** worthless passion.
27 **buy his will** achieve the object of his lust.
29 **bottom** extent.

30 **lawful** i.e. to be lawful.
32 **encounter** assignation.
35 **marry her** enable her to get married (by
furnishing her with a dowry).
36 **is passed** has been given.
37 **persèver** carry herself.
39 **coherent** in accord.
40 **musics** musicians.
40–1 **composed...unworthiness** (1) leading to
her disrepute, (2) addressed to her (socially) inferior
person.
41 **nothing steads us** does us no good.
43 **lay** depended.

HELENA   Why then tonight
    Let us assay our plot, which if it speed,
    Is wicked meaning in a lawful deed,   45
    And lawful meaning in a lawful act,
    Where both not sin, and yet a sinful fact.
    But let's about it.

                                [Exeunt]

4.[1] *Enter one of the Frenchmen [the* SECOND LORD DUMAINE], *with
five or six other* SOLDIERS *in ambush*

SECOND LORD He can come no other way but by this hedge corner.
    When you sally upon him, speak what terrible language you will.
    Though you understand it not yourselves, no matter; for we must
    not seem to understand him, unless some one among us, whom we
    must produce for an interpreter.   5
FIRST SOLDIER Good captain, let me be th'interpreter.
SECOND LORD Art not acquainted with him? Knows he not thy voice?
FIRST SOLDIER No, sir, I warrant you.
SECOND LORD But what linsey-woolsey hast thou to speak to us again?
FIRST SOLDIER E'en such as you speak to me.   10
SECOND LORD He must think us some band of strangers i'th'adversary's
    entertainment. Now he hath a smack of all neighbouring languages;
    therefore we must every one be a man of his own fancy, not to know
    what we speak to one another; so we seem to know, is to know

48 SD] *Rowe; not in* F   Act 4, Scene 1 4.1] *Rowe; Actus Quartus.* F 0 SD *the* SECOND LORD] *After Cam; not in* F
1 SH SECOND LORD] *Cam.; 1.Lord E.* F *(and subst. through scene)* 6 captain] F3; Captaiue F

44 **assay** try.
44 **speed** succeed.
45 **meaning** intention (on Bertram's part).
45 **a lawful deed** i.e. Helena cohabiting with her husband.
46 **meaning** intention (on Helena's part).
47 **In which**, notwithstanding Bertram's conviction that he is committing adultery, neither party is guilty of adulterous behaviour.
47 **fact** act, deed.

Act 4, Scene 1
4.1. Editors, following Capell, locate the scene outside the Florentine camp. In 1 'this hedge corner' reminds us that the stage was provided with hiding-places for the soldiers who enter 'in ambush'.

1 SH SECOND LORD F in this scene uses the anomalous SH *1.Lord E* at 1, 7, 9, 11, and *Lor.E, Lo.E.* or *L.E.* to the end of the scene. For consistency with 3.6, all Es in the present scene have been interpreted as SECOND LORD.
2 **terrible** ferocious.
4 **unless** except for.
9 **linsey-woolsey** hodgepodge (of words). Literally, cloth made of a mixture of linen and wool.
11–12 **some...entertainment** foreign troops in the service of the enemy.
12 **smack** smattering.
13 **to know** knowing.
14–15 **know...purpose** see our intention effected at once.

straight our purpose: choughs' language, gabble enough, and good   15
enough. As for you, interpreter, you must seem very politic. But
couch ho, here he comes, to beguile two hours in a sleep, and then
to return and swear the lies he forges.

Enter PAROLLES

PAROLLES Ten a'clock: within these three hours 'twill be time enough
to go home. What shall I say I have done? It must be a very plausive   20
invention that carries it. They begin to smoke me, and disgraces
have of late knocked too often at my door. I find my tongue is too
foolhardy, but my heart hath the fear of Mars before it, and of his
creatures, not daring the reports of my tongue.

SECOND LORD This is the first truth that e'er thine own tongue was   25
guilty of.

PAROLLES What the devil should move me to undertake the recovery
of this drum, being not ignorant of the impossibility, and knowing
I had no such purpose? I must give myself some hurts, and say
I got them in exploit. Yet slight ones will not carry it. They will   30
say, 'Came you off with so little?' And great ones I dare not give;
wherefore what's the instance? Tongue, I must put you into a
butter-woman's mouth, and buy myself another of Bajazeth's mule,

15 choughs'] *Dyce,* Choughs F   33 Bajazeth's] *Baiazeths* F; Bajazet's *Rowe;* Balaam's *Lowes, conj. Addis*   33 mule]
F; mute *Hanmer, conj. Warburton*

15 **choughs'** jackdaws'.
17 **couch** lie down. (Presumably the soldiers conceal themselves about the stage.)
17 **beguile** idle away.
20 **plausive** plausible.
21 **carries it** i.e. makes my lies believable (as again at 30).
23–4 **his creatures** i.e. soldiers (Mars being the god of war).
24 **not...tongue** being afraid to bear out my bragging.
32 **instance** (1) motive (i.e. 'What the devil should move me...?'), (2) proof (of my sufficient 'hurts...in exploit').
33 **butter-woman's** dairy-woman's. Some editors (e.g. Evans, Kittredge) associate this with garrulity. A 'butter-whore' is a scolding butter-woman (*OED* Butter *sb*¹ 5). Parolles, wanting to get rid of his prattling tongue, will give it to a loquacious butter-woman who can make better use of it.
33 **Bajazeth's mule** Bajazeth defies Tamburlaine when he is taken prisoner (in Marlowe's *Tamburlaine*), and perhaps Parolles is thinking of the mule's

defiance of any master, and associates Bajazeth and the mule. Inconsequently, he himself is found out to be an ass at 4.3.282–3. Steevens notes (Var. 73): 'In one of our old Turkish histories, there is a pompous description of Bajazet riding on a mule to Divan.' None of these associations is inevitable or fully clarifies an allusion to Bajazeth's mule. It is possible, however, that Shakespeare is remembering, not Marlowe's Bajazeth, but Bajazeth the son of Suleyman the Magnificent, who was strangled by the royal mutes with their bowstrings at the order of his father, 25 September 1561. If it is this event that Shakespeare is remembering, Hanmer's emendation of F 'mule' to 'mute' will be the preferred reading. Painter, in the penultimate tale (34) in Volume II of his *Palace of Pleasure,* tells how Suleyman had the mutes strangle his eldest son Mustapha, and Painter recalls in passing the murder of Sultan Bajazeth by his son Selim the Grim, the father of Suleyman. These atrocities, perhaps conflated or confused and engendering the image of the 'malignant and turbaned Turk', were notorious in sixteenth-century England, and their currency in the literature of the period has been documented by if you prattle me into these perils.

SECOND LORD Is it possible he should know what he is, and be that 35
he is?

PAROLLES I would the cutting of my garments would serve the turn,
or the breaking of my Spanish sword.

SECOND LORD We cannot afford you so.

PAROLLES Or the baring of my beard, and to say it was in stratagem. 40

SECOND LORD 'Twould not do.

PAROLLES Or to drown my clothes, and say I was stripped.

SECOND LORD Hardly serve.

PAROLLES Though I swore I leapt from the window of the citadel –

SECOND LORD How deep? 45

PAROLLES Thirty fathom.

SECOND LORD Three great oaths would scarce make that be believed.

PAROLLES I would I had any drum of the enemy's. I would swear I
recovered it.

SECOND LORD You shall hear one anon. 50

PAROLLES A drum now of the enemy's –

Alarum within

SECOND LORD *Throca movousus, cargo, cargo, cargo.*

ALL *Cargo, cargo, cargo, villianda par corbo, cargo.*

PAROLLES O ransom, ransom! Do not hide mine eyes.

[They blindfold him]

INTERPRETER *Boskos thromuldo boskos.* 55

PAROLLES I know you are the Muskos' regiment,
    And I shall lose my life for want of language.
    If there be here German, or Dane, Low Dutch,
    Italian, or French, let him speak to me,
    I'll discover that which shall undo the Florentine. 60

INTERPRETER *Boskos vauvado.* I understand thee, and can speak thy
tongue. *Kerelybonto*, sir, betake thee to thy faith, for seventeen
poniards are at thy bosom.

PAROLLES O!

46 fathom] fadom F   48, 51 enemy's] *Malone*; enemies F   54] *As one line, Pope*; O…ransome, / Do…eyes. F
54 SD] *After Rowe; not in* F   55 SH INTERPRETER] F; *First Soldier* / *Capell*   56 Muskos'] *Capell*; Muskos F

Samuel C. Chew, *The Crescent and the Rose*, 1937.
The Turk was evidently in Shakespeare's mind
when he wrote this play. See e.g. 2.3.80 and
4.4.7. For the conjunction of mutes and Turks, see
TN 1.2.62: 'Be you his eunuch, and your mute I'll
be.'

35 **that** what.

37 **serve the turn** suffice.

39 **afford you so** let you off like that.

40 **baring** shaving.

40 **in stratagem** an act of cunning.

46 **fathom** A measure of six feet.

52 'Choughs' language'.

56 **Muskos'** Muscovites'.

60 **discover** reveal.

62 **betake…faith** fall to your prayers.

63 **poniards** daggers.

INTERPRETER O, pray, pray, pray! *Manka revania dulche.*   65
SECOND LORD *Oscorbidulchos volivorco.*
INTERPRETER The general is content to spare thee yet,
    And hoodwinked as thou art, will lead thee on
    To gather from thee. Haply thou mayst inform
    Something to save thy life.
PAROLLES   O, let me live,   70
    And all the secrets of our camp I'll show,
    Their force, their purposes; nay, I'll speak that
    Which you will wonder at.
INTERPRETER   But wilt thou faithfully?
PAROLLES If I do not, damn me.
INTERPRETER   *Acordo linta.*
    Come on, thou art granted space.   75

                   Exit [with Parolles]
       A short alarum within
SECOND LORD Go tell the Count Rossillion, and my brother,
    We have caught the woodcock, and will keep him muffled
    Till we do hear from them.
SOLDIER   Captain, I will.
SECOND LORD 'A will betray us all unto ourselves:
    Inform on that.
SOLDIER   So I will, sir.   80
SECOND LORD Till then I'll keep him dark and safely locked.

                       Exeunt

[4.2] *Enter* BERTRAM *and the maid called* DIANA

BERTRAM They told me that your name was Fontybell.
DIANA No, my good lord, Diana.
BERTRAM   Titled goddess,

65] *As Staunton;* Oh...pray, / *Manka reuania dulche.* F   75 art] F3; *are* F   75 SD *with Parolles*] *After Capell; not in* F
78, 80 SH SOLDIER] *Sol.* F; *Second Soldier / Capell*   81 SD] *Rowe; not in* F   Act 4, Scene 2   4.2] *Pope; not in* F

    68 hoodwinked blindfolded; with residual sense
of 'deceived', as in *Mac.* 4.3.72.
    69 gather get information.
    69 Haply Perhaps.
    73 faithfully truthfully; with the ironic sense of
'loyally'.
    75 space a reprieve.
    77 woodcock A proverbially foolish bird.
Compare *Ham.* 5.2.306.

    77 muffled blindfolded.
    80 Inform on Report.

Act 4, Scene 2
    1 They...Fontybell A haunting line. The name
Fontybell means 'beautiful fountain'.
    2–3 Titled...addition! You bear the name of
the goddess (of chastity), and deserve the name,
with additional marks of distinction.

And worth it, with addition! But, fair soul,
In your fine frame hath love no quality?
If the quick fire of youth light not your mind,   5
You are no maiden, but a monument.
When you are dead, you should be such a one
As you are now; for you are cold and stern,
And now you should be as your mother was
When your sweet self was got.   10

DIANA She then was honest.

BERTRAM   So should you be.

DIANA   No;
My mother did but duty, such, my lord,
As you owe to your wife.

BERTRAM   No more a' that.
I prithee do not strive against my vows.
I was compelled to her, but I love thee   15
By love's own sweet constraint, and will for ever
Do thee all rights of service.

DIANA   Ay, so you serve us
Till we serve you; but when you have our roses,
You barely leave our thorns to prick ourselves,
And mock us with our bareness.

BERTRAM   How have I sworn!   20

DIANA 'Tis not the many oaths that makes the truth,
But the plain single vow that is vowed true.
What is not holy, that we swear not by,
But take the High'st to witness. Then pray you tell me,
If I should swear by Jove's great attributes   25
I loved you dearly, would you believe my oaths
When I did love you ill? This has no holding,

---

6 monument.] F2 *(subst.)*; monument F

4 **quality** part.
5 **quick** lively.
6 **monument** lifeless effigy.
10 **got** begotten.
14 **vows** i.e. resolution to live apart from Helena.
16 **constraint** compulsion which wedded him to Helena.
18 **serve** gratify (sexually).
19 i.e. once you have denuded us of roses you leave our thorns exposed to prick us.
22 **single** As opposed to 'double' = 'equivocal'.
23–4 **What...witness** A self-evident observation, perhaps meant in ironic response to Bertram's 'How have I sworn!' (20): 'We do not swear (whatever our vicious purpose) by the devil but by God' – with the implication: 'So much for your pious asseverations!'
24 **High'st** F does not capitalise the name of God here, or the pronoun 'Him' at 28 and 29.
25 **Jove's** Perhaps replacing 'God's' to accord with the statute of 1606 which forbade the profane use of the Lord's name in plays. However, Shakespeare and his contemporaries routinely allow Christian attributes to pagan deities.
27 **ill** (1) indifferently (as opposed to 'dearly', 26), (2) wickedly.
27 **has no holding** is not tenable.

To swear by Him whom I protest to love
That I will work against Him. Therefore your oaths
Are words and poor conditions, but unsealed –   30
At least in my opinion.

BERTRAM   Change it, change it!
Be not so holy-cruel. Love is holy,
And my integrity ne'er knew the crafts
That you do charge men with. Stand no more off,
But give thyself unto my sick desires,   35
Who then recovers. Say thou art mine, and ever
My love, as it begins, shall so persèver.

DIANA I see that men make rope's in such a scarre,
That we'll forsake ourselves. Give me that ring.

BERTRAM I'll lend it thee, my dear; but have no power   40
To give it from me.

DIANA   Will you not, my lord?

BERTRAM It is an honour 'longing to our house,
Bequeathèd down from many ancestors,
Which were the greatest obloquy i'th'world
In me to lose.

DIANA   Mine honour's such a ring,   45
My chastity's the jewel of our house,
Bequeathèd down from many ancestors,
Which were the greatest obloquy i'th'world
In me to lose. Thus your own proper wisdom
Brings in the champion Honour on my part,   50
Against your vain assault.

BERTRAM   Here, take my ring!
My house, mine honour, yea, my life, be thine,
And I'll be bid by thee.

28, 29 Him...Him] *Neilson;* him...him F   42 'longing] *Rowe;* longing F

28 protest profess.
30 words mere words.
30 poor...unsealed (1) a worthless contract, simply unsealed (i.e. without the seal that would make it valid), (2) but (i.e. only) a worthless unsealed contract.
32 holy-cruel cruel in your holiness.
33 crafts craftiness.
36 Who then recovers Which then recover.
38 make...scarre This, perhaps the most notorious crux in the Folio, has been frequently emended, e.g. 'make Hopes in such Affairs' (Rowe); 'make hopes in such a scene' (Malone);

'may cope's in such a stir' (Tannenbaum). The best emendation seems that proposed by P. A. Daniel in 1870 and followed by Sisson in his edition, 'may rope's in such a snare' (i.e. may rope us in such a snare). The text, however, is probably irrecoverably corrupt.
41 from away from.
42 honour 'longing source or token of honour belonging.
45 honour's chastity's.
49 proper personal (peculiar to you).
50 part side.
53 bid commanded.

DIANA When midnight comes, knock at my chamber window;
       I'll order take my mother shall not hear.   55
       Now will I charge you in the band of truth,
       When you have conquered my yet maiden bed,
       Remain there but an hour, nor speak to me.
       My reasons are most strong, and you shall know them
       When back again this ring shall be delivered;   60
       And on your finger in the night I'll put
       Another ring, that what in time proceeds
       May token to the future our past deeds.
       Adieu till then, then fail not. You have won
       A wife of me, though there my hope be done.   65
BERTRAM A heaven on earth I have won by wooing thee.   *Exit*
DIANA For which live long to thank both heaven and me!
       You may so in the end.
       My mother told me just how he would woo,
       As if she sat in's heart. She says all men   70
       Have the like oaths. He had sworn to marry me
       When his wife's dead; therefore I'll lie with him
       When I am buried. Since Frenchmen are so braid,
       Marry that will, I live and die a maid.
       Only in this disguise I think't no sin   75
       To cozen him that would unjustly win.   *Exit*

---

57 maiden bed] *Theobald;* maiden-bed F   66 SD] F2; *not in* F   70 sat] *Warburton;* sate F

55 **order take** insure that.
56 **band** bond.
57 **yet** still.
62 **Another ring** By exchanging rings, Diana means to signify their betrothal.
62 **what...proceeds** whatever may fall out in future.
63 **token** betoken.
64–5 **You...done** Diana is deliberately cryptic. She may mean 'You have made me yield to you as a wife when I cannot hope to marry you'; but her first words could mean 'You have won a wife through my agency' and her last could allude to the

forfeiture of her chastity, spoiling her hope of wedlock.
71–2 **had...dead** We do not hear him so swear, but it appears at 5.3.139–40 and 166–73 that he does so when they exchange rings; 'had' could mean 'would have', but some have emended to 'has'.
73 **braid** twisted, like plaited braid.
74 **that** who.
75 **disguise** assumed role. Compare *MM* 3.2.262–3.
76 **cozen** deceive.

[4.3] *Enter the two French Captains [the* FIRST *and* SECOND LORDS DUMAINE] *and some two or three* SOLDIERS

FIRST LORD You have not given him his mother's letter?

SECOND LORD I have delivered it an hour since. There is something in't that stings his nature; for on the reading it he changed almost into another man.

FIRST LORD He has much worthy blame laid upon him for shaking off   5
so good a wife and so sweet a lady.

SECOND LORD Especially he hath incurred the everlasting displeasure of the king, who had even tuned his bounty to sing happiness to him. I will tell you a thing, but you shall let it dwell darkly with you.   10

FIRST LORD When you have spoken it, 'tis dead, and I am the grave of it.

SECOND LORD He hath perverted a young gentlewoman here in Florence, of a most chaste renown, and this night he fleshes his will in the spoil of her honour. He hath given her his monumental ring,   15
and thinks himself made in the unchaste composition.

FIRST LORD Now God delay our rebellion! As we are ourselves, what things are we!

SECOND LORD Merely our own traitors. And as in the common course of all treasons, we still see them reveal themselves, till they attain   20
to their abhorred ends, so he that in this action contrives against his own nobility in his proper stream o'erflows himself.

Act 4, Scene 3   4.3] *Pope; not in* F   0 SD *Captains]* F; Lords *Rowe*   1 SH FIRST LORD] *Rowe; Cap.G* F *(through scene, except 70, 104)*   1 letter?] *Rowe;* letter. F   2 SH SECOND LORD] *Rowe; Cap.E.* F *(through scene, except 263, 265)*
22 stream o'erflows] *Theobald;* streame, ore-flowes F

Act 4, Scene 3

4.3 Apparently a street scene, as suggested by another encounter reported in 65, but editors, following Capell, locate it in the Florentine camp.

2 since ago.

4 another man i.e. his mood completely changed.

5 worthy deserved.

9 darkly secretly.

13 perverted corrupted (i.e. seduced).

14 renown reputation.

14 fleshes his will rewards and so stimulates his lust (as hounds or hawks are fleshed or fed with a piece of meat from the animal they have hunted down).

15 spoil Concretely, 'the dead prey'; by analogy, 'the entity (honour) that has been destroyed'.

15 monumental i.e. which serves as a token of his identity (see *OED adj* 2b).

16 made a made man.

16 composition bargain (with a play on 'composition' as something made).

17 delay our rebellion quench our rebellious appetites. See *OED* Delay v². The modern sense of 'delay' as 'postpone' is also quite possible, a mere postponing being the best human nature can look for.

17 ourselves i.e. not supported by God's grace.

19 Merely Simply.

20 still always.

21 abhorred ends damnable objectives; i.e. their deaths, which put an end to their revelations.

21–2 contrives...nobility is a traitor to his station.

22 his proper...himself This may mean

FIRST LORD Is it not meant damnable in us, to be trumpeters of our
  unlawful intents? We shall not then have his company tonight?

SECOND LORD Not till after midnight; for he is dieted to his hour.   25

FIRST LORD That approaches apace. I would gladly have him see his
  company anatomised, that he might take a measure of his own
  judgements, wherein so curiously he had set this counterfeit.

SECOND LORD We will not meddle with him till he come; for his
  presence must be the whip of the other.   30

FIRST LORD In the mean time, what hear you of these wars?

SECOND LORD I hear there is an overture of peace.

FIRST LORD Nay, I assure you a peace concluded.

SECOND LORD What will Count Rossillion do then? Will he travel
  higher, or return again into France?   35

FIRST LORD I perceive by this demand, you are not altogether of his
  council.

SECOND LORD Let it be forbid, sir. So should I be a great deal of his
  act.

FIRST LORD Sir, his wife some two months since fled from his house.   40
  Her pretence is a pilgrimage to Saint Jaques le Grand, which holy
  undertaking with most austere sanctimony she accomplished; and
  there residing, the tenderness of her nature became as a prey to her
  grief; in fine, made a groan of her last breath, and now she sings
  in heaven.   45

SECOND LORD How is this justified?

FIRST LORD The stronger part of it by her own letters, which makes
  her story true, even to the point of her death. Her death itself, which

---

27 anatomised] *Rowe;* anathomiz'd F   37 council] *Rowe³;* councell F; counsel *Rowe*

either (1) his self-revealing discourse is like a body
of water which exceeds its appointed limit and so
forfeits its integrity; or (2) he does not confine
himself to the proper course of his own nobility but
allows the treacheries of his nature to overflow. For
(1) compare *Ham.* 4.5.100–1.

23–4 Is it...intents Is it not meant to be
damnable sin in us to proclaim our unlawful
intentions?

25 dieted...hour restricted to his appointed
time; continuing residually the play at 14 on eating
or fleshing.

27 company companion.

27 anatomised dissected, laid open to
inspection.

28 curiously carefully.

28 set this counterfeit i.e. as a fake stone is
placed in an elaborate setting or foil.

29 him...he Parolles...Bertram.

29–30 his...the other Bertram's...Parolles.

33 Nay i.e. more than an overture.

35 higher farther; perhaps into the mountains.
See 2.1.12 n.

36 demand question.

36–7 of his council in his confidence. The
spelling of Rowe³, followed here, conveys either
'council' (a deliberative body) or 'counsel'
(confidence).

38–9 a great...act deeply involved as an
accessory in his affairs (with a play on 'act' and
'council' as in 'acts of the Council').

41 pretence intention.

41 is i.e. was.

42 sanctimony sanctity.

44 fine sum.

46 justified proved.

could not be her office to say is come, was faithfully confirmed by
the rector of the place.   50

SECOND LORD Hath the count all this intelligence?

FIRST LORD Ay, and the particular confirmations, point from point, to
the full arming of the verity.

SECOND LORD I am heartily sorry that he'll be glad of this.

FIRST LORD How mightily sometimes we make us comforts of our   55
losses!

SECOND LORD And how mightily some other times we drown our gain
in tears! The great dignity that his valour hath here acquired for
him shall at home be encountered with a shame as ample.

FIRST LORD The web of our life is of a mingled yarn, good and ill   60
together: our virtues would be proud, if our faults whipped them
not, and our crimes would despair, if they were not cherished by
our virtues.

Enter a [SERVANT as] Messenger

How now? where's your master?

SERVANT He met the duke in the street, sir, of whom he hath taken   65
a solemn leave. His lordship will next morning for France. The duke
hath offered him letters of commendations to the king.

SECOND LORD They shall be no more than needful there, if they were
more than they can commend.

Enter [BERTRAM] Count Rossillion

FIRST LORD They cannot be too sweet for the king's tartness. Here's   70
his lordship now. How now, my lord, is't not after midnight?

BERTRAM I have tonight dispatched sixteen businesses, a month's
length apiece, by an abstract of success: I have congied with the

---

63 SD SERVANT *as*] *Kittredge; not in* F   65 SH SERVANT] F; *Messenger / Neilson*   69 SD BERTRAM] *Rowe; not in* F
70 SH FIRST LORD] *Rowe; Ber.* F; *Cap.G.* F3

49 **office** function (she being dead).
50 **rector** priest (recalling 'office' in the
preceding line).
51 **intelligence** information.
53 **arming...verity** strengthening of the truth
against attack.
58 **dignity** honour.
59 **encountered** met.
62 **crimes** sins.
62 **cherished** entertained kindly (i.e. palliated).
But carries also the sense of 'accommodation', or
happy mingling.

66 **solemn** formal.
66 **will** i.e. will depart.
67 **offered** given.
68–9 **if...commend** even if they commended
Bertram more strongly than he deserves.
70 **for** i.e. to balance.
73 **by...success** Meaning either (1) summarily
and successfully, or (2) to give a brief account of my
success – or a brief account of the successive items.
(The account then follows.)
73 **congied with** taken leave of.

duke, done my adieu with his nearest; buried a wife, mourned for
her, writ to my lady mother I am returning, entertained my convoy, 75
and between these main parcels of dispatch effected many nicer
needs. The last was the greatest, but that I have not ended yet.

SECOND LORD If the business be of any difficulty, and this morning
your departure hence, it requires haste of your lordship.

BERTRAM I mean the business is not ended, as fearing to hear of it 80
hereafter. But shall we have this dialogue between the fool and the
soldier? Come, bring forth this counterfeit module, h'as deceived
me like a double-meaning prophesier.

SECOND LORD Bring him forth.

[Exeunt Soldiers]

H'as sat in th'stocks all night, poor gallant knave. 85

BERTRAM No matter, his heels have deserved it, in usurping his spurs
so long. How does he carry himself?

SECOND LORD I have told your lordship already: the stocks carry him.
But to answer you as you would be understood, he weeps like a
wench that had shed her milk. He hath confessed himself to 90
Morgan, whom he supposes to be a friar, from the time of his
remembrance to this very instant disaster of his setting i'th'stocks;
and what think you he hath confessed?

BERTRAM Nothing of me, has'a?

SECOND LORD His confession is taken, and it shall be read to his face. 95
If your lordship be in't, as I believe you are, you must have the
patience to hear it.

Enter PAROLLES *with his* INTERPRETER

BERTRAM A plague upon him! Muffled! He can say nothing of me.

FIRST LORD Hush, hush! Hoodman comes! *Portotartarossa.*

---

76 effected] F3; affected F   82 h'as] *Rowe*³, ha s F   84 SD] *Capell; not in* F   85 H'as] *Rowe*, Ha's F   99 SH FIRST LORD] *Rann; not in* F

---

75 **entertained my convoy** seen to my escort.
Compare 4.4.10.

76 **between...dispatch** in between these major
items of business.

76 **nicer** more delicate.

77 **The last** i.e. his supposed conquest of Diana.

80–1 **as...hereafter** Bertram fears that Diana
may in future claim him for a husband.

82 **module** model (of a soldier).

83 **double meaning prophesier** equivocal
oracle. see *Mac.* 5.8.19–22.

85 **gallant** showy in appearance.

86 **usurping his spurs** wrongly laying claim
to the trappings of knightly valour.

87 **carry** comport (with a play on 'carry', 88)

90 **shed** spilled.

91–2 **from...remembrance** as far back as he can
remember.

92 **very instant disaster** misfortune in the
immediate present.

98 **Muffled** Blindfolded.

99 *Hush, hush Assigned to Bertram in F, but
an interruption is more probable.

99 **Hoodman** The blindfolded player in the
game of hoodman blind (blind man's buff).

INTERPRETER He calls for the tortures. What will you say without 'em? 100
PAROLLES I will confess what I know without constraint. If ye pinch
    me like a pasty, I can say no more.
INTERPRETER *Bosko chimurcho.*
FIRST LORD *Boblibindo chicurmurco.*
INTERPRETER You are a merciful general. Our general bids you answer 105
    to what I shall ask you out of a note.
PAROLLES And truly, as I hope to live.
INTERPRETER [*Reads*] 'First demand of him, how many horse the duke
    is strong.' What say you to that?
PAROLLES Five or six thousand, but very weak and unserviceable. The 110
    troops are all scattered, and the commanders very poor rogues, upon
    my reputation and credit, and as I hope to live.
INTERPRETER Shall I set down your answer so?
PAROLLES Do, I'll take the sacrament on't, how and which way you
    will. 115
BERTRAM All's one to him. What a past-saving slave is this!
FIRST LORD Y'are deceived, my lord, this is Monsieur Parolles, the
    gallant militarist – that was his own phrase – that had the whole
    theoric of war in the knot of his scarf, and the practice in the chape
    of his dagger. 120
SECOND LORD I will never trust a man again for keeping his sword
    clean, nor believe he can have everything in him by wearing his
    apparel neatly.
INTERPRETER Well, that's set down.
PAROLLES 'Five or six thousand horse', I said – I will say true – 'or 125
    thereabouts', set down, for I'll speak truth.
FIRST LORD He's very near the truth in this.
BERTRAM But I con him no thanks for't, in the nature he delivers it.
PAROLLES 'Poor rogues', I pray you say.

---

104 SH FIRST LORD] *Rowe; Cap.* F   108, 133, 146, 175 SD *Reads*] *Cam.; not in* F   116 SD BERTRAM] *Capell; not in* F

102 **pasty** A kind of pie which has the crusts
pinched together.
  106 **note** list (of questions).
  108 **horse** horsemen.
114–15 **how...will** according to whatever rite
you choose.
116 ***All's...him** It's all the same to him. These
words are assigned to Parolles in F.
118 **militarist** expert in military affairs.
  119 **theoric...practice** Hunter, citing
Hoby's *Theorique and Practice of Warre* (1597) and
Barret's *The Theorike and Practice of Modern*

Warres (1598), sees these words as technical terms
for the division of military (and other) science.
  119 **chape** The metal plate covering the point of
a scabbard.
121–3 W. S. Walker suggests that these lines
should be assigned to Bertram.
  121 **for keeping** because he keeps.
  122 **clean** polished.
  123 **neatly** elegantly.
  128 **I con...it** I know no reason to thank him
for speaking that manner of truth.

INTERPRETER Well, that's set down.   130

PAROLLES I humbly thank you, sir. A truth's a truth, the rogues are
marvellous poor.

INTERPRETER [*Reads*] 'Demand of him, of what strength they are
afoot.' What say you to that?

PAROLLES By my troth, sir, if I were to live this present hour, I will   135
tell true. Let me see: Spurio, a hundred and fifty; Sebastian, so
many; Corambus, so many; Jaques, so many; Guiltian, Cosmo,
Lodowick, and Gratii, two hundred fifty each; mine own company,
Chitopher, Vaumond, Bentii, two hundred fifty each; so that the
muster-file, rotten and sound, upon my life, amounts not to fifteen   140
thousand pole, half of the which dare not shake the snow from off
their cassocks, lest they shake themselves to pieces.

BERTRAM What shall be done to him?

FIRST LORD Nothing, but let him have thanks. Demand of him my
condition, and what credit I have with the duke.   145

INTERPRETER Well, that's set down. [*Reads*] 'You shall demand of
him, whether one Captain Dumaine be i'th'camp, a Frenchman;
what his reputation is with the duke; what his valour, honesty, and
expertness in wars; or whether he thinks it were not possible with
well-weighing sums of gold to corrupt him to a revolt.' What say   150
you to this? What do you know of it?

PAROLLES I beseech you let me answer to the particular of the
inter'gatories. Demand them singly.

INTERPRETER Do you know this Captain Dumaine?

PAROLLES I know him. 'A was a botcher's prentice in Paris, from   155
whence he was whipped for getting the shrieve's fool with child,
a dumb innocent that could not say him nay.

BERTRAM Nay, by your leave, hold your hands – though I know his
brains are forfeit to the next tile that falls.

INTERPRETER Well, is this captain in the Duke of Florence's camp?   160

PAROLLES Upon my knowledge, he is, and lousy.

---

135 live i.e. live only until.
136–7 so many as many.
140 muster-file total roll.
140 rotten and sound sick (with disease) and well.
141 pole poll (i.e. heads).
142 cassocks military cloaks.
145 condition military character.
150 well-weighing (1) heavy, (2) influential.
152 particular particular items.

153 inter'gatories interrogatories. A syncopated form, now obsolete.
155 botcher's patcher's. Referring to a tailor or cobbler who does rough repair work.
156 shrieve's fool idiot girl ('innocent') in the care of the sheriff.
158 Bertram addresses the First Lord ('Captain Dumaine').
158–9 his...falls i.e. he is in danger of death from the next accident.

FIRST LORD Nay, look not so upon me; we shall hear of your lordship
    anon.
INTERPRETER What is his reputation with the duke?
PAROLLES The duke knows him for no other but a poor officer of mine,   165
    and writ to me this other day to turn him out a'th'band. I think
    I have his letter in my pocket.
INTERPRETER Marry, we'll search.
PAROLLES In good sadness, I do not know. Either it is there, or it is
    upon a file with the duke's other letters in my tent.   170
INTERPRETER Here 'tis, here's a paper. Shall I read it to you?
PAROLLES I do not know if it be it or no.
BERTRAM Our interpreter does it well.
FIRST LORD Excellently.
INTERPRETER [*Reads*] 'Dian, the count's a fool, and full of gold' –   175
PAROLLES That is not the duke's letter, sir; that is an advertisement
    to a proper maid in Florence, one Diana, to take heed of the
    allurement of one Count Rossillion, a foolish idle boy, but for all
    that very ruttish. I pray you, sir, put it up again.
INTERPRETER Nay, I'll read it first, by your favour.   180
PAROLLES My meaning in't, I protest, was very honest in the behalf
    of the maid; for I knew the young count to be a dangerous and
    lascivious boy, who is a whale to virginity, and devours up all the
    fry it finds.
BERTRAM Damnable both-sides rogue!   185
INTERPRETER [*Reads the*] letter
    'When he swears oaths, bid him drop gold, and take it;
    After he scores, he never pays the score.
    Half won is match well made; match, and well make it;
    He ne'er pays after-debts, take it before,
    And say a soldier, Dian, told thee this: 190
    Men are to mell with, boys are not to kiss;

---

162 lordship] *Pope*; Lord F   186 SD *Reads the*] *Rowe*; not in F

169 **good sadness** all seriousness.
176 **advertisement** advice, warning.
177 **proper** respectable.
179 **ruttish** lustful.
179 **up again** back.
180 **favour** leave.
184 **fry** small fish.
187 **scores** (1) hits the mark, (2) incurs (scores
up) a debt.
187 **score** bill.

188 **Half...made** i.e. a bargain will turn out
successfully in so far as the conditions are agreed
in advance. The 'match' is the prospective union
of Diana and Bertram.
189 **after-debts** obligations still outstanding
(after the goods have been delivered).
191 **mell** meddle (in the sense of sexual
intercourse).
191 **boys** i.e. like Bertram as opposed to Parolles.

For count of this, the count's a fool, I know it,
Who pays before, but not when he does owe it.
　　　　　　　Thine, as he vowed to thee in thine ear,
　　　　　　　　　　　　Parolles.' 195

BERTRAM He shall be whipped through the army with this rhyme in's
forehead.

SECOND LORD This is your devoted friend, sir, the manifold linguist
and the armipotent soldier.

BERTRAM I could endure anything before but a cat, and now he's a cat 200
to me.

INTERPRETER I perceive, sir, by the general's looks, we shall be fain
to hang you.

PAROLLES My life, sir, in any case! Not that I am afraid to die, but
that my offences being many, I would repent out the remainder of 205
my nature. Let me live, sir, in a dungeon, i'th'stocks, or anywhere,
so I may live.

INTERPRETER We'll see what may be done, so you confess freely;
therefore once more to this Captain Dumaine. You have answered
to his reputation with the duke, and to his valour. What is his 210
honesty?

PAROLLES He will steal, sir, an egg out of a cloister. For rapes and
ravishments he parallels Nessus. He professes not keeping of oaths;
in breaking 'em he is stronger than Hercules. He will lie, sir, with
such volubility, that you would think truth were a fool. Drunkenness 215
is his best virtue, for he will be swine-drunk, and in his sleep he
does little harm, save to his bed-clothes about him; but they know
his conditions, and lay him in straw. I have but little more to say,

---

199 armipotent] *Capell,* army-potent F　202 the] F3; your F

<table>
<tr><td>

192 **For count** Therefore take note.

193 **pays before** i.e. if you can compel him to make prior payment.

193 **when...it** (1) after he owes payment for his debt, (2) after he has possessed the desired thing (Diana's virginity).

196 **in** on.

198 **manifold linguist** speaker of many languages.

199 **armipotent** powerful in action.

202 *the F reads 'your', which could mean 'the general concerned' (*OED* Your 5). Compare 1.1.135–6 n.

202 **fain** obliged.

205–6 **would...nature** want to devote the rest of my life to repenting.

</td><td>

207 **so** provided that.

212 **an...cloister** 'He will steal anything, however trifling, from any place, however holy' (Johnson).

213 **Nessus** The Centaur, half-man, half-horse, who tried to rape Hercules' wife Dejanira. The Centaurs, ravishers of the women at the Feast of the Lapithae, figure as an emblem of lust.

213 **professes not** makes no practice of.

214 **stronger** i.e. however strong the oaths.

215 **volubility** facility in expression.

215 **a fool** i.e. because so easily put down or discredited.

217 **they** i.e. the attendants who put him to bed.

218 **conditions** habits.

</td></tr>
</table>

sir, of his honesty. He has everything that an honest man should
not have; what an honest man should have, he has nothing.   220

FIRST LORD I begin to love him for this.

BERTRAM For this description of thine honesty? A pox upon him for
me, he's more and more a cat.

INTERPRETER What say you to his expertness in war?

PAROLLES Faith, sir, h'as led the drum before the English tragedians.   225
To belie him I will not, and more of his soldiership I know not,
except in that country he had the honour to be the officer at a place
there called Mile-end, to instruct for the doubling of files. I would
do the man what honour I can, but of this I am not certain.

FIRST LORD He hath out-villained villainy so far, that the rarity   230
redeems him.

BERTRAM A pox on him, he's a cat still.

INTERPRETER His qualities being at this poor price, I need not to ask
you if gold will corrupt him to revolt.

PAROLLES Sir, for a cardecue he will sell the fee-simple of his   235
salvation, the inheritance of it, and cut th'entail from all remainders,
and a perpetual succession for it perpetually.

INTERPRETER What's his brother, the other Captain Dumaine?

SECOND LORD Why does he ask him of me?

INTERPRETER What's he?   240

PAROLLES E'en a crow a'th'same nest; not altogether so great as the
first in goodness, but greater a great deal in evil. He excels his
brother for a coward, yet his brother is reputed one of the best that
is. In a retreat he outruns any lackey; marry, in coming on he has
the cramp.   245

INTERPRETER If your life be saved, will you undertake to betray the
Florentine?

PAROLLES Ay, and the captain of his horse, Count Rossillion.

INTERPRETER I'll whisper with the general, and know his pleasure.

---

225 h'as] *Rowe;* ha's F   235 cardecue] F2; Cardceue F

225 **drum** Which went before troops of actors
advertising their performances; i.e. so much for his
'expertness in war'.

226 **To...not** I will not belie him. An old use
of 'to'; see Abbott 357.

228 **Mile-end** An open field east of the City of
London where the citizen-militia, an inconsiderable
force, received its training.

228 **doubling of files** A simple kind of military
marching drill.

235 **cardecue** *quart d'écu.* A French coin of slight
value.

235 **fee-simple** absolute possession (of land).

236–7 **cut...perpetually** break the reversion
of property rights ('remainders') not only to his
immediate heir but to all heirs to the end of time.

244 **lackey** servant who ran errands.

244 **coming on** advancing.

246 **undertake** commit yourself.

PAROLLES I'll no more drumming, a plague of all drums! Only to seem   250
    to deserve well, and to beguile the supposition of that lascivious
    young boy the count, have I run into this danger. Yet who would
    have suspected an ambush where I was taken?
INTERPRETER There is no remedy, sir, but you must die. The general
    says, you that have so traitorously discovered the secrets of your   255
    army, and made such pestiferous reports of men very nobly held,
    can serve the world for no honest use; therefore you must die.
    Come, headsman, off with his head.
PAROLLES O Lord, sir, let me live, or let me see my death!
INTERPRETER That shall you, and take your leave of all your friends.   260
                        [Unmuffling him]
    So, look about you. Know you any here?
BERTRAM Good morrow, noble captain.
SECOND LORD God bless you, Captain Parolles.
FIRST LORD God save you, noble captain.
SECOND LORD Captain, what greeting will you to my Lord Lafew? I   265
    am for France.
FIRST LORD Good captain, will you give me a copy of the sonnet you
    writ to Diana in behalf of the Count Rossillion? And I were not
    a very coward, I'd compel it of you, but fare you well.
                        Exeunt [Bertram and Lords]
INTERPRETER You are undone, captain, all but your scarf; that has a   270
    knot on't yet.
PAROLLES Who cannot be crushed with a plot?
INTERPRETER If you could find out a country where but women were
    that had received so much shame, you might begin an impudent
    nation. Fare ye well, sir, I am for France too. We shall speak of   275
    you there.
                        Exit [with Soldiers]
PAROLLES Yet am I thankful. If my heart were great,
    'Twould burst at this. Captain I'll be no more,
    But I will eat, and drink, and sleep as soft

---

260 SD] *Var. 93; not in* F   263, 265 SH SECOND LORD] *Rowe; Lo.E.* F   269 SD *Bertram and Lords] After Capell; not in* F
276 SD *with Soldiers] Cam.; not in* F

251 **beguile the supposition** deceive the
opinion.
  255 **discovered** revealed.
  256 **pestiferous** pernicious.
  256 **held** esteemed.
  265 **will you** do you wish to send.

266 **for off** to.
269 **very** absolute.
270 **undone** (1) ruined, (2) undressed.
273 **but** only.
274 **impudent** shameless.

As captain shall. Simply the thing I am   280
Shall make me live. Who knows himself a braggart,
Let him fear this; for it will come to pass
That every braggart shall be found an ass.
Rust sword, cool blushes, and, Parolles, live
Safest in shame! Being fooled, by fool'ry thrive!   285
There's place and means for every man alive.
I'll after them.   *Exit*

[4.4] *Enter* HELENA, WIDOW, *and* DIANA

HELENA That you may well perceive I have not wronged you,
One of the greatest in the Christian world
Shall be my surety; 'fore whose throne 'tis needful,
Ere I can pèrfect mine intents, to kneel.
Time was, I did him a desirèd office,   5
Dear almost as his life, which gratitude
Through flinty Tartar's bosom would peep forth,
And answer thanks. I duly am informed
His grace is at Marseilles, to which place
We have convenient convoy. You must know   10
I am supposèd dead. The army breaking,
My husband hies him home, where heaven aiding,
And by the leave of my good lord the king,
We'll be before our welcome.
WIDOW   Gentle madam,
You never had a servant to whose trust   15
Your business was more welcome,
HELENA   Nor you, mistress,
Ever a friend whose thoughts more truly labour
To recompense your love. Doubt not but heaven

Act 4, Scene 4   4.4] *Capell; not in* F   3 'fore] F3; for F; fore F2   9 Marseilles] *Pope; Marcellæ* F   16 you] F4; your F

284 Parolles Trisyllabic.
285 fooled gulled.

Act 4, Scene 4
4.4 Editors, following Capell, locate the scene in
Florence, the Widow's house.
3 surety guarantee.
6 which gratitude gratitude for which.
7 Tartar's Whose heart ('bosom') was prover-

bially hard. This reference to the Tartars is
perhaps evoked unconsciously by association with
Bajazeth (4.1.33), and hence with Tamburlaine,
countryman of Genghis Khan.
  9 Marseilles Pronounced as three syllables, and
spelt 'Marcellus' in F at 4.5.64.
10 convenient convoy suitable transport.
11 breaking disbanding.
14 our welcome i.e. we are expected.

Hath brought me up to be your daughter's dower,
As it hath fated her to be my motive   20
And helper to a husband. But O, strange men,
That can such sweet use make of what they hate,
When saucy trusting of the cozened thoughts
Defiles the pitchy night; so lust doth play
With what it loathes for that which is away –   25
But more of this hereafter. You, Diana,
Under my poor instructions yet must suffer
Something in my behalf.

DIANA   Let death and honesty
Go with your impositions, I am yours
Upon your will to suffer.

HELENA   Yet, I pray you: 30
But with the word the time will bring on summer,
When briers shall have leaves as well as thorns,
And be as sweet as sharp. We must away:
Our wagon is prepared, and time revives us.
All's well that ends well; still the fine's the crown.   35
Whate'er the course, the end is the renown.

                                                  Exeunt

35 fine's] *Theobald;* fines F

20 **motive** Probably 'means', though this sense
is not recorded elsewhere.
23 **saucy...thoughts** wanton abandonment to
deluded appetites.
24 **Defiles...night** Blackens even pitch-black
night, being blacker than it. See *1H4* 2.4.410–13,
where Falstaff quotes the proverb 'Pitch doth
defile' (from Ecclus. 13.1).
25 **for** in place of.
27 **yet** still for a while (as again at 30).
28 **death and honesty** an honest death; i.e. I
am willing to die for you provided I remain chaste.
29 **impositions** The 'instructions' of 27.
30 **Upon your will** At your pleasure.

31 **the word** Variously glossed: 'in a word'; 'as
the proverb has it'; 'as I have promised'. It is hard
not to feel that there are deeper intimations here,
and that 'the word' is analogous in power to Holy
Writ.
32 **leaves** petals.
33 **sweet** sweet-smelling.
34 **revives** i.e. will revive.
35 **All's...well** Proverbial from at least the
beginning of the fourteenth century.
35 **the...crown** Also proverbial and a familiar
commonplace to Shakespeare, e.g. in *Tro.* 4.5.224.
35 **fine's** end's.
36 **is the renown** determines the praise.

[4.5] *Enter* [LAVATCH, *the*] *Clown, old Lady* [COUNTESS], *and* LAFEW

LAFEW No, no, no, your son was misled with a snipped-taffeta fellow
there, whose villainous saffron would have made all the unbaked
and doughy youth of a nation in his colour. Your daughter-in-law
had been alive at this hour, and your son here at home, more
advanced by the king than by that red-tailed humble-bee I speak   5
of.

COUNTESS I would I had not known him; it was the death of the most
virtuous gentlewoman that ever nature had praise for creating. If
she had partaken of my flesh, and cost me the dearest groans of a
mother, I could not have owed her a more rooted love.   10

LAFEW 'Twas a good lady, 'twas a good lady. We may pick a thousand
sallets ere we light on such another herb.

LAVATCH Indeed, sir, she was the sweet marjoram of the sallet, or rather
the herb of grace.

LAFEW They are not herbs, you knave, they are nose-herbs.   15

LAVATCH I am no great Nebuchadnezzar, sir, I have not much skill in
grace.

LAFEW Whether dost thou profess thyself – a knave or a fool?

LAVATCH A fool, sir, at a woman's service, and a knave at a man's.

LAFEW Your distinction?   20

LAVATCH I would cozen the man of his wife and do his service.

Act 4, Scene 5   o SD COUNTESS] *Rowe; not in* F   7 SH COUNTESS] *Rowe; La.* F *(and subst. through scene)*   17 grace]
F; grass *Rowe*

Act 4, Scene 5

4.5 Editors, following Capell, locate the scene in
Rossillion, the Count's palace.

1 with by.

1 snipped-taffeta flashy. Literally, silk slashed
to allow the rich underlining to show through.

2 saffron A yellow dye (yellow denoting
cowards) used to colour the starch of ruffs and
collars, also to colour pastries.

2–3 unbaked and doughy immature and
unformed. Continuing the culinary figure suggested
by 'saffron'.

5 red-tailed humble-bee brightly coloured
insect, showy fellow of no consequence (with an
allusion to Parolles's gaudy apparel). Elsewhere
Shakespeare calls the humble-bee 'red-hipped'
(*MND* 4.1.11).

9 dearest direst, but with suggestion of 'most
precious'.

12 sallets salads.

14 herb of grace rue (not marjoram), signifying
repentance.

15 herbs salad herbs.

15 nose-herbs Cultivated for their fragrance
rather than for eating.

16 Nebuchadnezzar The Babylonian king who
ate grass like the oxen. See Dan. 4.

17 grace Picking up 14, also punning on 'grass'
(the pronunciation being presumably the same), and
introducing the graceless cozenage Lavatch
imputes to himself in the lines that follow.

18 Whether Which.

19 service With the sense of sexual intercourse.

21 cozen cheat.

LAFEW So you were a knave at his service indeed.

LAVATCH And I would give his wife my bauble, sir, to do her service.

LAFEW I will subscribe for thee, thou art both knave and fool.

LAVATCH At your service.   25

LAFEW No, no, no.

LAVATCH Why, sir, if I cannot serve you, I can serve as great a prince
as you are.

LAFEW Who's that? A Frenchman?

LAVATCH Faith, sir, 'a has an English maine, but his fisnomy is more   30
hotter in France than there.

LAFEW What prince is that?

LAVATCH The black prince, sir, alias the prince of darkness, alias the
devil.

LAFEW Hold thee, there's my purse. I give thee not this to suggest thee   35
from thy master thou talk'st of; serve him still.

LAVATCH I am a woodland fellow, sir, that always loved a great fire,
and the master I speak of ever keeps a good fire. But sure he is the
prince of the world; let his nobility remain in's court. I am for the
house with the narrow gate, which I take to be too little for pomp   40
to enter. Some that humble themselves may, but the many will be
too chill and tender, and they'll be for the flowery way that leads
to the broad gate and the great fire.

LAFEW Go thy ways, I begin to be aweary of thee, and I tell thee so
before, because I would not fall out with thee. Go thy ways, let my   45
horses be well looked to, without any tricks.

---

30 maine] F; name *Rowe*   36 of] F3; off F

23 **bauble** The Fool's staff, topped with a knob, and suggesting an obscene quibble on 'penis'. See *Rom.* 2.3.91–3.

24 **subscribe** vouch.

30 **maine** Of doubtful meaning. Variously glossed as: (1) retinue, (2) domicile, (3) quality. Most editors, following Rowe, emend to 'name'. *OED* allows the first two readings, however, under 'meinie', and the third under 'maine', as in the collocation 'main bread' or 'pain-demaine'. See 41 n.

30 **fisnomy** In Shakespeare's time an acceptable (not illiterate) form of 'physiognomy', here meaning the characteristic expression of the face.

30–1 **more hotter** (1) because inflamed by the 'French disease', (2) because Edward, the Black Prince (33) of England, was such a scourge to the French.

35 **suggest** tempt.

39 **prince...world** A familiar appellation for the devil. See John 12.31, 14.30.

40 **narrow gate** A reminiscence of Matt. 7.13.

41 **many** multitude. 'Many' and 'meiny' are interchangeable in this sense.

42 **chill and tender** sensitive to cold (so preferring the 'good fire' of hell) and loving their comfort.

42 **flow'ry way** As in *Mac* 2.3.19: 'the primrose way to th'everlasting bonfire'.

44 **Go thy ways** Go along.

45 **before** i.e. before quarrelling.

46 **tricks** Like buttering hay to save on supplies. (Horses will not eat buttered hay.) Compare *Lear* 2.4.125–6. [L]

LAVATCH If I put any tricks upon 'em, sir, they shall be jades' tricks,
   which are their own right by the law of nature.   *Exit*
LAFEW A shrewd knave and an unhappy.
COUNTESS So 'a is. My lord that's gone made himself much sport out   50
   of him. By his authority he remains here, which he thinks is a patent
   for his sauciness, and indeed he has no pace, but runs where he
   will.
LAFEW I like him well, 'tis not amiss. And I was about to tell you, since
   I heard of the good lady's death, and that my lord your son was   55
   upon his return home, I moved the king my master to speak in the
   behalf of my daughter, which in the minority of them both, his
   majesty, out of a self-gracious remembrance, did first propose. His
   highness hath promised me to do it, and to stop up the displeasure
   he hath conceived against your son, there is no fitter matter. How   60
   does your ladyship like it?
COUNTESS With very much content, my lord, and I wish it happily
   effected.
LAFEW His highness comes post from Marseilles, of as able body as
   when he numbered thirty. 'A will be here tomorrow, or I am   65
   deceived by him that in such intelligence hath seldom failed.
COUNTESS It rejoices me, that I hope I shall see him ere I die. I have
   letters that my son will be here tonight. I shall beseech your
   lordship to remain with me till they meet together.
LAFEW Madam, I was thinking with what manners I might safely be   70
   admitted.
COUNTESS You need but plead your honourable privilege.
LAFEW Lady, of that I have made a bold charter, but I thank my God
   it holds yet.

64 Marseilles] *Pope; Marcellus* F *; Marsellis* F2   67 It] F3 *; Ir* F

47 **jades' tricks** i.e. the tricks played by ill-bred
or exhausted horses. Lavatch sees himself as
'jaded' like his charges.
   49 **shrewd** curst, biting.
   49 **unhappy** sharp, mischievous (inflicting
unhappiness with his keen wit).
   51 **patent** warrant.
   52 **has no pace** will not move as the reins direct
him. The Countess reverts to the horse-talk of
45–8. See 2.1.49 n.
   54 **'tis not amiss** there's no harm done.
   56 **upon his return** returning.
   57 **in…both** when they were children.

58 **self-gracious remembrance** a kindness
which needed no prompting.
   64 **post** speedily.
   65 **numbered thirty** was thirty years old.
   66 **him** i.e. an unnamed intelligencer or supplier
of information.
   67 **I hope** I can hope.
   70 **with…safely** how I might properly.
   71 **admitted** i.e. to the meeting of Bertram and
the King.
   72 **your honourable privilege** the privilege
done to your honoured self.
   73 **made … charter** too boldly put forward my
claim.

Enter [LAVATCH, *the*] *Clown*

LAVATCH O madam, yonder's my lord your son with a patch of velvet   75
on's face. Whether there be a scar under't or no, the velvet knows,
but 'tis a goodly patch of velvet. His left cheek is a cheek of two
pile and a half, but his right cheek is worn bare.

LAFEW A scar nobly got, or a noble scar, is a good livery of honour;
so belike is that.   80

LAVATCH But it is your carbonadoed face.

LAFEW Let us go see your son, I pray you. I long to talk with the young
noble soldier.

LAVATCH Faith, there's a dozen of 'em, with delicate fine hats, and most
courteous feathers, which bow the head, and nod at every man.   85

Exeunt

5.[1] *Enter* HELENA, WIDOW, *and* DIANA, *with two* ATTENDANTS

HELENA But this exceeding posting day and night
Must wear your spirits low; we cannot help it.
But since you have made the days and nights as one,
To wear your gentle limbs in my affairs,
Be bold you do so grow in my requital   5
As nothing can unroot you.

Enter [GENTLEMAN,] *a* GENTLE ASTRINGER

In happy time!
This man may help me to his majesty's ear,

79–80] *As prose, Pope;* A...got, / Or...honor, / So...that. F   79 livery] liv'ry F   82–3] *As prose, Pope;* Let...see
/ your...talke / With...souldier. F   Act 5, Scene 1   5.1] *Rowe; Actus Quintus.* F   6 SD] *Placed as Kittredge; follows*
6 *in* F   6 SD *a* GENTLE ASTRINGER] F; *a gentle Astranger* F2; *a Gentleman a stranger* F3; *a Gentleman* / *Rowe*

75 **patch of velvet** Used impartially to cover
honourable wounds and the carbonadoes or
incisions which were supposed to relieve syphilis.
Hence the joke at 81.

76 **scar** wound.

77–8 **two...half** i.e. thickly bandaged (the
thickest velvet being three-piled).

78 **is worn bare** has no patch.

79 **livery** Distinctive costume or insignia.

80 **belike** probably.

Act 5, Scene 1

5.1 Editors, following Capell, locate the scene in
Marseilles.

1 **posting** speedy travelling.

4 **wear** weary.

5 **bold** assured.

5 **requital** obligation to requite you.

6 SD *a* GENTLE ASTRINGER a gentleman
falconer (literally, a keeper of goshawks). See
illustration 2, p. 9 above. Why this character's
occupation is stipulated has never been obvious to
editors, who frequently emend to 'a Gentleman, a
stranger'. The only warrant for this, however, is F2's
corrupt reading 'Astranger'. It seems best, then, to
stay with the Folio text – not least because the noun,
being so eccentric a word, probably reflects
deliberate intention.

6 **In happy time!** Most opportunely!

If he would spend his power. God save you, sir.

GENTLEMAN And you.

HELENA Sir, I have seen you in the court of France.   10

GENTLEMAN I have been sometimes there.

HELENA I do presume, sir, that you are not fall'n
From the report that goes upon your goodness,
And therefore goaded with most sharp occasions,
Which lay nice manners by, I put you to   15
The use of your own virtues, for the which
I shall continue thankful.

GENTLEMAN   What's your will?

HELENA That it will please you
To give this poor petition to the king,
And aid me with that store of power you have   20
To come into his presence.

GENTLEMAN The king's not here.

HELENA   Not here, sir?

GENTLEMAN   Not indeed.
He hence removed last night, and with more haste
Than is his use.

WIDOW   Lord, how we lose our pains!

HELENA All's well that ends well yet,   25
Though time seem so adverse and means unfit.
I do beseech you, whither is he gone?

GENTLEMAN Marry, as I take it, to Rossillion,
Whither I am going.

HELENA   I do beseech you, sir,
Since you are like to see the king before me,   30
Commend the paper to his gracious hand,
Which I presume shall render you no blame,
But rather make you thank your pains for it.
I will come after you with what good speed
Our means will make us means.

GENTLEMAN   This I'll do for you.   35

HELENA And you shall find yourself to be well thanked,

---

8 **spend** expend.

12–13 **are…goodness** have not changed in your behaviour from your reputation for goodness.

14 **sharp occasions** urgent necessities. See illustration 1, p. 6 above.

15 **lay . . . by** put aside finicking politeness.

15 **put** press.

16 **virtues** powers.

23 **removed** departed.

24 **use** custom.

35 **Our means…means** Our resources will facilitate.

Whate'er falls more. We must to horse again.
Go, go, provide.

[*Exeunt*]

[5.2] *Enter* [LAVATCH, *the*] *Clown and* PAROLLES

PAROLLES Good Master Lavatch, give my Lord Lafew this letter. I
have ere now, sir, been better known to you, when I have held
familiarity with fresher clothes; but I am now, sir, muddied in
Fortune's mood, and smell somewhat strong of her strong
displeasure.   5
LAVATCH Truly, Fortune's displeasure is but sluttish if it smell so
strongly as thou speak'st of. I will henceforth eat no fish of
Fortune's buttering. Prithee allow the wind.
PAROLLES Nay, you need not to stop your nose, sir; I spake but by
a metaphor.   10
LAVATCH Indeed, sir, if your metaphor stink, I will stop my nose, or
against any man's metaphor. Prithee get thee further.
PAROLLES Pray you, sir, deliver me this paper.
LAVATCH Foh, prithee stand away. A paper from Fortune's close-stool
to give to a nobleman! Look here he comes himself.   15

Enter LAFEW

Here is a purr of Fortune's, sir, or of Fortune's cat – but not a
musk-cat – that has fall'n into the unclean fishpond of her
displeasure, and as he says, is muddied withal. Pray you, sir, use
the carp as you may, for he looks like a poor, decayed, ingenious,

---

38 SD] F2; *not in* F   Act 5, Scene 2   5.2] *Pope; not in* F   1 Master] *Neilson;* Mr F; M. F2   8 buttering] butt'ring F
16 Here] *Theobald;* Clo. Heere F   17 musk-cat] *Theobald;* Muscat F   19 ingenious] F; ingenerous NS. *conj.*
Brigstocke

37 **falls more** else should happen.

Act 5, Scene 2
5.2 Editors, following Capell, locate the scene in
Rossillion, the Count's palace.
1 Lavatch No one has explained why the Clown
should be named here for the first and only time in
the play. His name suggests French *la vache* =
'cow', or Italian *lavaccio* = 'lavage' or 'slop'.
4 mood displeasure (perhaps with a play on
'muddied', 'mood' being pronounced 'mud').
7–8 of Fortune's buttering prepared by
Fortune (see Tilley F305).
8 allow the wind stand to the windward of me
(so I don't smell you).
14 close-stool privy.

16 purr (1) the knave or jack in the card-game
of post and pair (see *OED* Pur), (2) piece of animal
excrement, (3) the sound made by a cat.
17 musk-cat Perfume was made from secretions
of the civet cat and musk deer. Lavatch,
conflating them, says that Parolles is not
sweet-smelling.
18 withal with it.
19 carp (1) a fish raised in manured ponds, (2)
a person who carps or chatters.
19 ingenious An unexpectedly generous word in
the context and Hunter may be right to interpret
as 'un-genious', i.e. without intellectual capacity.
But Parolles, like Helena, is in many things
contradictory, and Lafew may be commending
Parolles as a resourceful rascal.

foolish, rascally knave. I do pity his distress in my similes of comfort,   20
and leave him to your lordship.   [*Exit*]

PAROLLES My lord, I am a man whom Fortune hath cruelly scratched.

LAFEW And what would you have me to do? 'Tis too late to pare her
nails now. Wherein have you played the knave with Fortune that
she should scratch you, who of herself is a good lady, and would   25
not have knaves thrive long under her? There's a cardecue for you.
Let the justices make you and Fortune friends; I am for other
business.

PAROLLES I beseech your honour to hear me one single word.

LAFEW You beg a single penny more. Come, you shall ha't; save your   30
word.

PAROLLES My name, my good lord, is Parolles.

LAFEW You beg more than 'word' then. Cox my passion! give me your
hand. How does your drum?

PAROLLES O my good lord, you were the first that found me!   35

LAFEW Was I, in sooth? And I was the first that lost thee.

PAROLLES It lies in you, my lord, to bring me in some grace, for you
did bring me out.

LAFEW Out upon thee, knave! Dost thou put upon me at once both the
office of God and the devil? One brings thee in grace, and the other   40
brings thee out.

                    [*Trumpets sound*]

The king's coming, I know by his trumpets. Sirrah, enquire further
after me. I had talk of you last night; though you are a fool and
a knave, you shall eat. Go to, follow.

PAROLLES I praise God for you.   45

                                    [*Exeunt*]

---

20 similes] *Theobald, conj. Warburton;* smiles F   21 SD] *Capell; not in* F   26 her] F2; *not in* F   33 than] F4; then F
33 'word'] *Cam.;* word F; one word F3   39 Dost] *Rowe,* doest F   41 SD] *After Theobald; not in* F   42 coming,] F3,
comming F   45 SD] *Rowe; not in* F

20 *similes Because Parolles is said to be 'like'
a knave rather than the thing itself. F's reading is
indefensible and looks like a minim error.

22 scratched Fortune has become the cat.

26 cardecue The small coin of 4.3.235.

27 justices i.e. justices of the peace, who were
responsible for beggars under the Elizabethan poor
law.

33 more than 'word' more than one word (since
your name signifies 'words').

33 Cox Cock's (God's). A casual oath.

35 found me found me out.

36 lost See 2.3.193–4.

37 in some grace into some favour. Lafew in
rejoining plays on 'grace' as the grace of God.

42–3 enquire further after come later to see.

[5.3] *Flourish. Enter* KING, *old Lady* [COUNTESS], LAFEW, *the two French Lords* [*the* FIRST *and* SECOND LORDS DUMAINE], *with* ATTENDANTS

KING We lost a jewel of her, and our esteem
    Was made much poorer by it; but your son,
    As mad in folly, lacked the sense to know
    Her estimation home.
COUNTESS   'Tis past, my liege,
    And I beseech your majesty to make it   5
    Natural rebellion, done i'th'blade of youth,
    When oil and fire, too strong for reason's force,
    O'erbears it, and burns on.
KING   My honoured lady,
    I have forgiven and forgotten all,
    Though my revenges were high bent upon him,   10
    And watched the time to shoot.
LAFEW   This I must say –
    But first I beg my pardon – the young lord
    Did to his majesty, his mother, and his lady
    Offence of mighty note; but to himself
    The greatest wrong of all. He lost a wife   15
    Whose beauty did astonish the survey
    Of richest eyes, whose words all ears took captive,
    Whose dear perfection hearts that scorned to serve
    Humbly called mistress.
KING   Praising what is lost
    Makes the remembrance dear. Well, call him hither,   20
    We are reconciled, and the first view shall kill
    All repetition. Let him not ask our pardon,

Act 5, Scene 3   5.3] *Pope; not in* F   0 SD COUNTESS] *Rowe; not in* F   4 SH COUNTESS] *Rowe; Old La.* F *(through scene except 193)*   6 blade] F; *blaze Capell, conj. Theobald*

Act 5, Scene 3
5.3 Editors locate the scene as 5.2.
1 of in.
1 our esteem my value.
3 As Being.
4 estimation home worth to the full.
6 Natural rebellion i.e. of the natural passions against 'reason's force' (7).
6 blade green shoot (i.e. immaturity).
10 high bent i.e. like a tautened bow.

11 watched waited for.
12 But...pardon Perhaps recurring to the excessive boldness Lafew acknowledges in himself at 4.5.73
16–17 astonish...eyes dumbfound the gazing of even those most experienced in beholding beautiful women.
21–2 kill...repetition cancel any reviewing of past wrongs.

The nature of his great offence is dead,
And deeper than oblivion we do bury
Th'incensing relics of it. Let him approach   25
A stranger, no offender; and inform him
So 'tis our will he should.

GENTLEMAN   I shall, my liege.   [*Exit*]

KING What says he to your daughter? Have you spoke?

LAFEW All that he is hath reference to your highness.

KING Then shall we have a match. I have letters sent me   30
    That sets him high in fame.

Enter COUNT BERTRAM

LAFEW   He looks well on't.

KING I am not a day of season,
    For thou mayst see a sunshine and a hail
    In me at once. But to the brightest beams
    Distracted clouds give way, so stand thou forth,   35
    The time is fair again.

BERTRAM   My high-repented blames,
    Dear sovereign, pardon to me.

KING   All is whole,
    Not one word more of the consumèd time.
    Let's take the instant by the forward top;
    For we are old, and on our quick'st decrees   40
    Th'inaudible and noiseless foot of time
    Steals ere we can effect them. You remember
    The daughter of this lord?

BERTRAM Admiringly, my liege. At first

---

27 SD] *Capell; not in* F   28] *As Theobald;* What…daughter. / Haue…spoke? F   30–1] *As verse, Pope; as prose,* F
44 Admiringly, my liege.] *Rowe;* Admiringly my Liege, F

---

23 **nature…dead** i.e. just what it was the king
has already forgotten.

25 **incensing relics** reminders that would
rekindle anger. With an unexpected quibble on
perfuming or censing, the offence being understood
as somehow palliating itself.

26 **stranger** i.e. one newly arrived, his past
unknown.

29 **hath reference to** is at the disposal of.

30 **letters** a letter (as at 2.3.253).

31 **on't** i.e. after his recent experience.

32 **of season** of one season (i.e. I am not
altogether a summer's or a winter's day).

34 **at once** simultaneously.

35 **Distracted** Broken (i.e. the clouds will break
when the sun shines).

36 **high-repented blames** deeply repented sins.

37 **to** in.

39 **forward top** forelock. The only way to
grasp Opportunity or Occasion, who is generally
figured as being bald behind. See illustration 1, p. 6
above.

40 **quick'st** (1) most urgent, (2) most quick with
life.

44 **Admiringly** With wonder.

I stuck my choice upon her, ere my heart   45
Durst make too bold a herald of my tongue;
Where the impression of mine eye infixing,
Contempt his scornful pèrspective did lend me,
Which warped the line of every other favour,
Scorned a fair colour, or expressed it stol'n,   50
Extended or contracted all proportions
To a most hideous object. Thence it came
That she whom all men praised, and whom myself,
Since I have lost, have loved, was in mine eye
The dust that did offend it.

KING   Well excused.   55
That thou didst love her, strikes some scores away
From the great compt; but love that comes too late,
Like a remorseful pardon slowly carried,
To the great sender turns a sour offence,
Crying, 'That's good that's gone.' Our rash faults   60
Make trivial price of serious things we have,
Not knowing them until we know their grave.
Oft our displeasures, to ourselves unjust,
Destroy our friends, and after weep their dust;
Our own love waking cries to see what's done,   65
While shameful hate sleeps out the afternoon.
Be this sweet Helen's knell, and now forget her.
Send forth your amorous token for fair Maudlin.

58 carried,] *Rowe;* carried F   59 sender turns] *Theobald;* sender, turnes F   65 done] F2; don,e F

45 **stuck** fixed.

45–6 ere...tongue (1) before I dared say what
I feel in my heart (for Lafew's daughter), (2) before
I, in my rashness, allowed my tongue to say what
I felt (about Helena).

47 **Where** i.e. in the heart.

47 **impression...infixing** image beheld by my
eye impressing itself.

48 **pèrspective** The ordinary perspective glass
was a convex mirror bringing a whole scene into
view and helping the artist to compose it. But this
is 'Contempt's perspective'. See M. M. Martinet,
Le Miroir de l'esprit dans le théâtre Elisabéthain,
1981, p. 317 n. 29 (discussion of 'le prisme de
Dédain').

49 **favour** face.

50 **fair colour** beautiful complexion.

50 **expressed it stol'n** said that it was painted
on.

51–2 Extended...object Distorted all shapes,

as by elongating or shortening them, so that they
became an ugly sight.

53 **she** i.e. Helena.

56 **scores** debts. In alehouses they were scored
up on a slate.

57 **compt** account (with a residual suggestion of
the Day of Judgement).

59 **turns...offence** becomes offensive to, goes
sour on – the pardon arriving too late to save the
victim whom 'the great sender' wished to save.

61 **Make...of** Put a trifling value on.

62 **know their grave** have lost them forever.

64 **weep their dust** mourn over their remains.

65 **cries to see** i.e. is saddened by seeing.

66 **sleeps...afternoon** enjoys an untroubled
repose.

68 **Maudlin** So pronounced but signifying
'Magdalen'. Perhaps an unconscious reminiscence
of Mary Magdalene. See p. 3 above.

The main consents are had, and here we'll stay
To see our widower's second marriage day.   70
COUNTESS Which better than the first, O dear heaven, bless!
Or, ere they meet, in me, O nature, cesse!
LAFEW Come on, my son, in whom my house's name
Must be digested; give a favour from you
To sparkle in the spirits of my daughter,   75
That she may quickly come.
                    [*Bertram gives a ring*]
                                        By my old beard,
And every hair that's on't, Helen, that's dead,
Was a sweet creature; such a ring as this,
The last that e'er I took her leave at court,
I saw upon her finger.
BERTRAM   Hers it was not.   80
KING Now pray you let me see it; for mine eye,
While I was speaking, oft was fastened to't.
This ring was mine, and when I gave it Helen,
I bade her, if her fortunes ever stood
Necessitied to help, that by this token   85
I would relieve her. Had you that craft to reave her
Of what should stead her most?
BERTRAM   My gracious sovereign,
Howe'er it pleases you to take it so,
The ring was never hers.
COUNTESS   Son, on my life,
I have seen her wear it, and she reckoned it   90
At her life's rate.
LAFEW   I am sure I saw her wear it.
BERTRAM You are deceived, my lord, she never saw it.
In Florence was it from a casement thrown me,
Wrapped in a paper, which contained the name

---

71 SH COUNTESS] *Theobald; not in* F   72 meet,…nature,] *Rowe;* meete…Nature F   76 SD] *Hanmer; not in* F
91 life's] liues F

69 The…had i.e. all the interested parties have   74 favour love-token.
agreed to the marriage.   79 last last time.
71–2 *Given by F to the King, but most follow   79 took her leave took leave of her.
Theobald and reassign to the Countess. The King   85 Necessitied to In need of.
has already spoken the couplet that signals the   86 reave deprive.
conclusion of his speech (69–70).   87 stead benefit.
   72 cesse cease.   90 reckoned esteemed.
   74 digested absorbed (since his daughter's name   91 At As highly as.
will be lost in marriage).

Of her that threw it. Noble she was, and thought   95
I stood ingaged; but when I had subscribed
To mine own fortune, and informed her fully
I could not answer in that course of honour
As she had made the overture, she ceased
In heavy satisfaction, and would never   100
Receive the ring again.

KING   Plutus himself,
That knows the tinct and multiplying med'cine,
Hath not in nature's mystery more science
Than I have in this ring. 'Twas mine, 'twas Helen's,
Whoever gave it you. Then if you know   105
That you are well acquainted with yourself,
Confess 'twas hers, and by what rough enforcement
You got it from her. She called the saints to surety
That she would never put it from her finger,
Unless she gave it to yourself in bed,   110
Where you have never come, or sent it us
Upon her great disaster.

BERTRAM   She never saw it.

KING Thou speak'st it falsely, as I love mine honour,
And mak'st conjectural fears to come into me,
Which I would fain shut out. If it should prove   115
That thou art so inhuman – 'twill not prove so;
And yet I know not: thou didst hate her deadly,
And she is dead, which nothing but to close
Her eyes myself could win me to believe,
More than to see this ring. Take him away.   120
My fore-past proofs, howe'er the matter fall,

---

101 Plutus] *Rowe³, Platus* F   113 falsely,] *Rowe;* falsely: F   114 conjectural] F2 *(subst.);* connecturall F
115 out.] *Singer²;* out, F; out; F4   116–17 inhuman–...not:] *After Rowe;* inhumane,...not, F

96 **ingaged** pledged (to her), as by giving his gage. The figure, continued with 'subscribed' and 'course of honour', is from duelling.

96–7 **subscribed To** given her an account of.

98–9 **in...As** with the like honour with which.

100 **heavy satisfaction** sad conviction.

101 **Plutus** The god of riches and skilled in alchemical lore (102).

102 **tinct...med'cine** tincture and elixir which (as the alchemists supposed) converted base metals to gold, thus multiplying gold indefinitely.

103 **science** knowledge.

105–6 **if...yourself** This contingent phrase is ironic, for Bertram does not know himself.

108 **surety** bear witness.

112 **Upon...disaster** In the event of some great misfortune overtaking her.

114 **conjectural fears** surmises full of foreboding.

121 **My fore-past proofs** The evidence I have had already.

121 **fall** turn out.

Shall tax my fears of little vanity,
Having vainly feared too little. Away with him!
We'll sift this matter further.

BERTRAM   If you shall prove
This ring was ever hers, you shall as easy   125
Prove that I husbanded her bed in Florence,
Where yet she never was.

                                        [*Exit guarded*]

                    Enter GENTLEMAN

KING I am wrapped in dismal thinkings.
GENTLEMAN   Gracious sovereign,
Whether I have been to blame or no, I know not.
Here's a petition from a Florentine,   130
Who hath for four or five removes come short
To tender it herself. I undertook it,
Vanquished thereto by the fair grace and speech
Of the poor suppliant, who by this I know
Is here attending. Her business looks in her   135
With an importing visage, and she told me,
In a sweet verbal brief, it did concern
Your highness with herself.
[KING] [*Reads*] *a letter* 'Upon his many protestations to marry me when
his wife was dead, I blush to say it, he won me. Now is the Count   140
Rossillion a widower, his vows are forfeited to me, and my honour's
paid to him. He stole from Florence, taking no leave, and I follow
him to his country for justice. Grant it me, O king, in you it best
lies; otherwise a seducer flourishes, and a poor maid is undone.
                                        Diana Capilet.'   145

---

122 tax] F3; taze F; taxe F2   127 SD *Exit guarded*] Rowe; *not in* F   139 SD KING *Reads*] Rowe; *not in* F   141 honour's]
Rowe³; honors F

122–3 **Shall...little** Will suffice to show that my
fears were not foolish; my foolishness consists
rather in not having feared enough.
  124 **sift** examine.
  127 SD GENTLEMAN Presumably the astringer
of 5.1.6 SD.
  131 **removes** Stopping-places in a royal progress.
Helena has just missed or come short of the King
at each of these places.
  133 **Vanquished   thereto** Won   to   the
undertaking.

134 **by this** by this time.
135 **looks** shows itself.
136 **importing** (1) importunate, (2) important.
137 **sweet verbal brief** summary recital, sweetly
delivered.
140–1 **Now...Rossillion** Now that the Count
Rossillion is.
141 **vows...me** promises of marriage are debts
which I may legitimately claim.

LAFEW I will buy me a son-in-law in a fair, and toll for this. I'll none
    of him.
KING The heavens have thought well on thee, Lafew,
        To bring forth this discovery. Seek these suitors.
        Go speedily, and bring again the count.   150

                                       [Exeunt Attendants]

        I am afear'd the life of Helen, lady,
        Was foully snatched.
COUNTESS   Now, justice on the doers!

              Enter BERTRAM [*guarded*]

KING I wonder, sir, since wives are monsters to you,
        And that you fly them as you swear them lordship,
        Yet you desire to marry. What woman's that?   155

              Enter WIDOW, DIANA

DIANA I am, my lord, a wretched Florentine,
        Derivèd from the ancient Capilet.
        My suit, as I do understand, you know,
        And therefore know how far I may be pitied.
WIDOW I am her mother, sir, whose age and honour   160
        Both suffer under this complaint we bring,
        And both shall cease, without your remedy.
KING Come hither, count, do you know these women?
BERTRAM My lord, I neither can nor will deny
        But that I know them. Do they charge me further?   165
DIANA Why do you look so strange upon your wife?
BERTRAM She's none of mine, my lord.
DIANA   If you shall marry,

---

146 toll] *Rowe*, toule F   150 SD] *After Capell; not in* F   152 SD *Enter* BERTRAM] *Placed as Capell; after 150* F
152 SD *guarded*] *Capell; not in* F   153 sir, since wives] *Var. 93, conj. Tyrwhitt;* sir, sir, wiues F; sir, wives F2; sir, sith
wives *Dyce*   155 SD DIANA] *Rowe; Diana, and Parrolles.* F

146 **in** at.
146 **a fair** Which offers the chance of buying a
better husband than Bertram, though sleazy or
stolen goods were often sold there.
146 **toll for this** register Bertram for sale in
the toll-book (where merchandise offered at a
market had to be entered for a fee).
149 **suitors** i.e. the wronged women who sue for
justice.
153 **since* F's reading is a compositor's slip,
possibly for MS. form 'sith' = 'since'.
154 **that** since.

154 **as** as soon as.
154 **swear them lordship** promise them
marriage.
155 SD **Enter* WIDOW, DIANA F adds '*and
Parrolles*'. Does Parolles enter here and sneak away?
Presumably not, since he is summoned for the first
time at 202. Perhaps the confusion represents
an original intention of Shakespeare's preserved in
his working copy but not carried through.
157 **Derivèd** Descended.
162 **both** i.e. age and honour.

You give away this hand, and that is mine;
You give away heaven's vows, and those are mine;
You give away myself, which is known mine;   170
For I by vow am so embodied yours,
That she which marries you must marry me,
Either both or none.

LAFEW Your reputation comes too short for my daughter, you are no
 husband for her.   175

BERTRAM My lord, this is a fond and desperate creature,
 Whom sometime I have laughed with. Let your highness
 Lay a more noble thought upon mine honour
 Than for to think that I would sink it here.

KING Sir, for my thoughts, you have them ill to friend   180
 Till your deeds gain them; fairer prove your honour
 Than in my thought it lies.

DIANA   Good my lord,
 Ask him upon his oath, if he does think
 He had not my virginity.

KING What say'st thou to her?

BERTRAM   She's impudent, my lord,   185
 And was a common gamester to the camp.

DIANA He does me wrong, my lord; if I were so,
 He might have bought me at a common price.
 Do not believe him. O, behold this ring,
 Whose high respect and rich validity   190
 Did lack a parallel; yet for all that
 He gave it to a commoner a'th'camp,
 If I be one.

COUNTESS   He blushes, and 'tis hit.
 Of six preceding ancestors, that gem,
 Conferred by testament to th'sequent issue,   195

---

181 them; fairer] *Theobald²*; them fairer: F

168 **this hand** i.e. Bertram's.
171 **embodied yours** made a part of your body.
176 **fond and desperate** foolish and reckless.
177 **sometime** formerly.
179 **sink** degrade.
180 **you...friend** they are not friendly to you.
181 **them; fairer** This emending by Theobald of F's 'them fairer' is generally accepted. Hunter, who accepts it, suggests, however, that F will make sense if we read '...them fairer. Prove your honour; Then' ('then' and 'than' being interchangeable Elizabethan spellings).

181 **gain them** win their friendship.
185 **impudent** shameless.
186 **gamester** whore.
190 **high...validity** great honour in his regard and high value.
191 **Did...parallel** Was without equal.
193 **'tis hit** Diana has hit the mark.
194 **Of** By.
195 **testament...issue** will to the succeeding heir.

Hath it been owed and worn. This is his wife,
That ring's a thousand proofs.

KING   Methought you said
You saw one here in court could witness it.

DIANA I did, my lord, but loath am to produce
So bad an instrument. His name's Parolles.   200

LAFEW I saw the man today, if man he be.

KING Find him, and bring him hither.

                                  [Exit an Attendant]

BERTRAM   What of him?
He's quoted for a most perfidious slave,
With all the spots a'th'world taxed and debauched,
Whose nature sickens but to speak a truth.   205
Am I or that or this for what he'll utter,
That will speak any thing?

KING   She hath that ring of yours.

BERTRAM I think she has. Certain it is I liked her,
And boarded her i'th'wanton way of youth.
She knew her distance, and did angle for me,   210
Madding my eagerness with her restraint,
As all impediments in fancy's course
Are motives of more fancy, and in fine,
Her insuite cunning, with her modern grace,
Subdued me to her rate. She got the ring,   215
And I had that which any inferior might
At market-price have bought.

---

202 SD] *Dyce; not in* F   202 SH BERTRAM] *Rowe; Ros.* F *(through scene)*   205 sickens but...truth.] *Staunton;* sickens: but...truth, F   214 insuite cunning] *This edn;* insuite comming F; insuit comming F2; insuit coming F4; in suit coming *Hanmer;* inf'nite cunning *conj. W. S. Walker*   215 rate.] rate; F3; rate, F

196 **owed** possessed.

197–8 **Methought...it** We do not hear Diana say this.

203 **quoted for** set down as.

204 **With...debauched** Censured for being debauched with every vice.

205 **but** only.

206 **or...this** either that or this (i.e. anything).

206 **for** by virtue of.

207 **That** Who.

209 **boarded** went aboard (i.e. had intercourse with).

210 **knew her distance** (1) understood the difference in our stations (which might properly have kept her aloof), (2) understood how to keep a teasing distance (the better to draw me on).

211 **Madding** Maddening.

211 **eagerness** sharpness (i.e. of his sexual edge).

212 **fancy's** love's.

213 **motives** occasions.

213 **in fine** to sum up.

214 **insuite cunning** If this reading of F is correct, it represents a Shakespearean coinage from Latin *insuetus* (unusual). Compare English 'insuetude' = 'the quality of being unusual', not in use, a rare substantive but not cited by *OED* before 1824. Editors generally emend to read 'inf'nite'.

214 **modern** commonplace, ordinary. This adjective is conventionally pejorative in Shakespeare and supports the antithesis with 'insuite'.

215 **Subdued...rate** Made me submit to her price.

DIANA   I must be patient.
     You that have turned off a first so noble wife,
     May justly diet me. I pray you yet
     (Since you lack virtue, I will lose a husband)   220
     Send for your ring, I will return it home,
     And give me mine again.
BERTRAM   I have it not.
KING What ring was yours, I pray you?
DIANA   Sir, much like
     The same upon your finger.
KING Know you this ring? This ring was his of late.   225
DIANA And this was it I gave him, being abed.
KING The story then goes false, you threw it him
          Out of a casement.
DIANA   I have spoke the truth.

                    Enter PAROLLES

BERTRAM My lord, I do confess the ring was hers.
KING You boggle shrewdly, every feather starts you.   230
          Is this the man you speak of?
DIANA   Ay, my lord.
KING Tell me, sirrah – but tell me true, I charge you,
          Not fearing the displeasure of your master,
          Which on your just proceeding I'll keep off –
          By him and by this woman here what know you?   235
PAROLLES So please your majesty, my master hath been an honourable
     gentleman. Tricks he hath had in him, which gentlemen have.
KING Come, come, to th'purpose. Did he love this woman?
PAROLLES Faith, sir, he did love her, but how?
KING How, I pray you?   240
PAROLLES He did love her, sir, as a gentleman loves a woman.
KING How is that?
PAROLLES He loved her, sir, and loved her not.
KING As thou art a knave, and no knave. What an equivocal companion
     is this!   245

223–4 Sir...finger] *As Capell; as one line,* F   226 abed] a-bed *Rowe;* a bed F   241 gentleman] *Rowe;* Gent. F
244 knave.] *Rowe (*knave;*);* knave, F

218 a...noble so noble a first.
219 diet me confine me to a lean regimen.
230 boggle shrewdly are quick to shy (like a skittish horse).
230 starts agitates.
235 By...by About...about.

236–7 honourable gentleman True when reductively interpreted – honourable because he is touchy about his reputation and status, a gentleman because he behaves like others of his class.
244 companion fellow (pejorative).

PAROLLES I am a poor man, and at your majesty's command.

LAFEW He's a good drum, my lord, but a naughty orator.

DIANA Do you know he promised me marriage?

PAROLLES Faith, I know more than I'll speak.

KING But wilt thou not speak all thou know'st?   250

PAROLLES Yes, so please your majesty. I did go between them as I said, but more than that, he loved her, for indeed he was mad for her, and talked of Satan and of Limbo and of furies, and I know not what. Yet I was in that credit with them at that time that I knew of their going to bed, and of other motions, as promising her   255 marriage, and things which would derive me ill will to speak of; therefore I will not speak what I know.

KING Thou hast spoken all already, unless thou canst say they are married. But thou art too fine in thy evidence, therefore stand aside.
　　　This ring you say was yours?

DIANA 　　　　　　　　　　　Ay, my good lord.   260

KING Where did you buy it? Or who gave it you?

DIANA It was not given me, nor I did not buy it.

KING Who lent it you?

DIANA 　　　　　　　It was not lent me neither.

KING Where did you find it then?

DIANA 　　　　　　　　　　I found it not.

KING If it were yours by none of all these ways,   265
　　　How could you give it him?

DIANA 　　　　　　　　　　I never gave it him.

LAFEW This woman's an easy glove, my lord, she goes off and on at pleasure.

KING This ring was mine, I gave it his first wife.

DIANA It might be yours or hers for aught I know.   270

KING Take her away, I do not like her now,
　　　To prison with her; and away with him.
　　　Unless thou tell'st me where thou hadst this ring,
　　　Thou diest within this hour.

DIANA 　　　　　　　　　　I'll never tell you.

KING Take her away.

DIANA 　　　　　I'll put in bail, my liege.   275

KING I think thee now some common customer.

252 that,] F3; that F

247 **drum** drummer.
247 **naughty** no good.
254 **credit** confidence.

255 **motions** proposals.
259 **fine** subtle.
276 **common customer** prostitute.

DIANA By Jove, if ever I knew man, 'twas you.
KING Wherefore hast thou accused him all this while?
DIANA Because he's guilty, and he is not guilty.
         He knows I am no maid, and he'll swear to't;   280
         I'll swear I am a maid, and he knows not.
         Great king, I am no strumpet, by my life;
         I am either maid, or else this old man's wife.
                    [*Pointing to Lafew*]
KING She does abuse our ears. To prison with her!
DIANA Good mother, fetch my bail.
                                                      [*Exit Widow*]
                          Stay, royal sir.   285
         The jeweller that owes the ring is sent for,
         And he shall surety me. But for this lord,
         Who hath abused me, as he knows himself,
         Though yet he never harmed me, here I quit him.
         He knows himself my bed he hath defiled,   290
         And at that time he got his wife with child.
         Dead though she be, she feels her young one kick.
         So there's my riddle: one that's dead is quick –
         And now behold the meaning.

                    Enter HELENA *and* WIDOW

KING   Is there no exorcist
         Beguiles the truer office of mine eyes?   295
         Is't real that I see?
HELENA   No, my good lord,
         'Tis but the shadow of a wife you see,
         The name and not the thing.
BERTRAM   Both, both. O, pardon!
HELENA O my good lord, when I was like this maid,
         I found you wondrous kind. There is your ring,   300
         And look you, here's your letter. This it says:
         'When from my finger you can get this ring,
         And are by me with child, etc.' This is done.
         Will you be mine now you are doubly won?

283 SD] *Rowe; not in* F   285 SD] *Pope (after 285), placed as Craig; not in* F   303 are] *Rowe; is* F

277 knew knew sexually.   295 Deceives my eyes' true sight?
289 quit (1) acquit, (2) requite.   297 shadow (1) ghost, shade, (2) imitation.
293 quick alive.   299 was like seemed to you to be. [L]
294 exorcist raiser of spirits.

BERTRAM If she, my liege, can make me know this clearly,   305
　　　　　I'll love her dearly, ever, ever dearly.
HELENA If it appear not plain and prove untrue,
　　　　Deadly divorce step between me and you!
　　　　O my dear mother, do I see you living?
LAFEW Mine eyes smell onions, I shall weep anon.   310
　　　[*To Parolles*] Good Tom Drum, lend me a handkercher. So, I thank
　　　thee; wait on me home, I'll make sport with thee. Let thy curtsies
　　　alone, they are scurvy ones.
KING Let us from point to point this story know,
　　　To make the even truth in pleasure flow.   315
　　　[*To Diana*] If thou beest yet a fresh uncroppèd flower,
　　　Choose thou thy husband, and I'll pay thy dower.
　　　For I can guess that by thy honest aid
　　　Thou kept'st a wife herself, thyself a maid.
　　　Of that and all the progress, more and less,   320
　　　Resolvedly more leisure shall express.
　　　All yet seems well, and if it end so meet,
　　　The bitter past, more welcome is the sweet.
　　　　　　　　　　　　Flourish

[EPILOGUE]

　　　The king's a beggar, now the play is done;
　　　All is well ended, if this suit be won,
　　　That you express content; which we will pay,
　　　With strife to please you, day exceeding day.
　　　Ours be your patience then, and yours our parts;   5
　　　Your gentle hands lend us, and take our hearts.
　　　　　　　　　　　　Exeunt

311 SD] *Rowe; not in* F　311 Good...handkercher.] *As prose, Capell; as verse,* F　316 SD] *Rowe; not in* F　321 Resolvedly] F4*; Resolduedly* F*; Resolv'dly* F3　Epilogue　EPILOGUE] *Rowe; not in* F　4 strife] F2*; strift* F　6 SD *Exeunt*] Exeunt omn. FINIS. F

308 **Deadly divorce** Divorcing death.
312 **wait on me** accompany me (as a servant).
312–13 **Let...ones** Parolles is bowing and scraping.
315 **even** plain, exact.
320 **more and less** both greater and lesser details.
321 **Resolvedly** In a manner which will resolve all questions.
322 **meet** fitly.
323 **past** being past.

Epilogue
1 **king's a beggar** 'Perhaps there is some allusion to the old tale of The King and the Beggar, which was the subject of a ballad' (Malone).
3 **express content** show your satisfaction (by applauding).
4 **strife** striving.
5 Reversing roles, we will be the patient spectators and listen to your applause, you applauding will be the actors.
6 **Your...us** i.e. applaud.
6 **hearts** gratitude.

TEXTUAL ANALYSIS

There are no editions in quarto of *All's Well That Ends Well*, and the basis for any edition of the play is that of its first publication in the Folio of 1623. The Folio text is sometimes carelessly printed, and there are stumbling-places or cruces that require an editor's intervention. (This intervention is not invariably successful.) Examples are Helena musing on her virginity (1.1.140), the King referring cryptically to those who 'inherit but the fall of the last monarchy' (2.1.13–14), Helena on the 'still-peering' air (3.2.102), Parolles invoking 'Bajazeth's mule' (4.1.33), Bertram thinking he knows Diana as 'Fontybell' (4.2.1), and Diana fearing that women will forsake themselves, seeing that men 'make rope's in such a scarre' (4.2.38).

The printing of the Folio text has been assigned by modern editors, such as Hunter, to two compositors, designated A and B, with the latter doing the bulk of the work. Hinman, building on spelling preferences (in *The Printing and Proof-Reading of the First Folio of Shakespeare*, 2 vols., 1963), saw three compositors at work, and he divided the assignment of Compositor A between him and a colleague designated C. Failing a correct discrimination of the parts of the text set by each compositor, it is difficult to speak of compositorial influence on textual readings. But if this discrimination depends on spelling, as it does in the work of Hinman and Alice Walker (*Textual Problems of the First Folio*, 1953), it will necessarily be open to query. The point is made emphatically by T. H. Howard-Hill in an article on 'The compositors of Shakespeare's Folio comedies' (*SB* 26 (1973), 61–106): 'without precise knowledge of the spellings of the copy from which the compositors set their Folio pages, it is hard to identify their shares of text printed from manuscript copy of unknown character'.

How many compositors worked on *All's Well* is uncertain, and so is the order in which they set the play. Shakespeare's great Folio is a 'Folio-in-sixes': three folded sheets are placed one within another at the fold and sewn together to make a quire or gathering of six leaves or twelve pages. In such a gathering, leaves 1 and 6, 2 and 5, and 3 and 4 will be conjugate, i.e. part of the same sheet joined at the fold. According to Hinman (in *SQ* 6 (1955), 259–73), the compositor set the text not by pages but by formes (a unit of two type-pages printed on the same sheet and subsequently locked in the metal rectangular frame that enclosed them). Generally the compositor worked from the inside out, first setting pages 6 and 7, then 5 and 8, then 4 and 9, and continuing in this sequence until he had set 11 and 12. This done, he proceeded to pages 6 and 7 of the next quire. If two compositors were involved, A set page 6 while B set 7, and they continued to divide the work between them, following the sequence outlined above.

In the Folio, *All's Well* extends over 25 pages, encompassing three gatherings which bear the signatures V, X and Y. The text begins on the verso of sig. V1 and continues through the verso of YI. In gathering V (according to Hunter), Compositor A set sigs. v3ᵛ, v4, and probably v3 and v4ᵛ. (Hinman gives v4 and v4ᵛ to Compositor C.) Compositor B set sigs. vIᵛ, v2 and v2ᵛ. The composition of gathering x and the two pages of gathering Y devoted to *All's Well* are also assigned to Compositor B.

Compositor A (Hinman's A and C), though generally characterised as more meticulous than his colleague, is not especially meticulous. For example, he drops words (at 1.3.89), or transposes letters (1.3.143, 2.1.151), or garbles the text (reading ''ton tooth' at 1.3.149), and sometimes his punctuation involves us in difficulties (2.1.3). Compositor B also punctuates carelessly, distorting the sense (2.3.64, 121, 133, 160, 5.3.181). He alters words (4.3.202, 5.3.303), or omits or repeats them (2.3.122, 5.2.26), or he repeats speech headings (2.2.31, 2.4.27), or assigns them incorrectly (4.3.99, 116, 5.3.71). He misreads letters in his copy (2.5.24, 3.2.8, 3.6.28, 3.7.19), or adds letters (3.6.28) or omits letters (5.2.20, 5.3.153).

Compositor B has an indifferent eye for calculating the relation of copy to type. Occasionally the foot of the Folio pages is marred by 'space-losing', as if the compositor had not enquired beforehand how much manuscript copy he needed to fill the printed page. Illustrations of this occur at the foot of sig. v2ᵛ (1.3.12), where the Clown's dialogue is widely spaced to no purpose except to eke out the available space, and the foot of the first column on x5ᵛ (4.5.79–83) where the prose is printed in short lines, presumably to fill the column and allow the second column to begin with Act 5. This makes trouble in the second column, where crowding is apparent. There is crowding again on x6ᵛ and YI (5.3.76–296). On XI at the bottom of the second column, four lines of verse assigned to the Countess are contracted to three lines of prose (3.2.83–6), while on xIᵛ towards the end of the second column, the prose is printed in short lines as if it were verse (3.5.1–12), probably because the compositor lacked sufficient copy to finish his stint. These examples of maladroit composition are described by bibliographers as 'bad casting-off'. Not only do they comment on the compositor: perhaps they attest to the provisional state of the copy from which he was working. In the first column of x2, for instance, short lines recur again (3.5.30–3), and scholars, including Hunter, conjecture that the compositor is seeking to regularise confused copy.

The nature of this copy has been variously described. Arthur Quiller-Couch and J. Dover Wilson, in the New Shakespeare edition of the play (1929), emphasised a mingling of consistency with inconsistency, like our mingled yarn, and they supposed that the Folio text depended on a prompt-book prepared by the company's book-keeper. W. W. Greg detected the book-keeper's intervention in the presence of stage directions such as *Flourish cornets* (1.2 and 2.1) and *Alarum within* (4.1), but he thought that a prompt-copy, being valuable, would have stayed in the archives rather than gone to the printer. Conceivably it was the book-keeper who divided the Folio text into acts, not a rarity in Shakespeare but not customary practice either. The act-division carries right through the Comedies section of the Folio, however, and is more likely to be the work of the Folio editors.

Hypothetically, the prompt-book theory takes support from the use of the letters 'E' and 'G' by which Shakespeare's First and Second Lord are designated throughout. E. K. Chambers (in *William Shakespeare*, 1930) attributed these letters to the book-keeper, who is assumed to have made a transcript of Shakespeare's manuscript. The argument here is that the book-keeper is indicating the names of the actors – Ecclestone and Gough, or Gilburne for Gough – who played the parts in question. It is true that Shakespeare designed his parts, or some of them, for specific members of the company, and in *Much Ado* the first speech of the Constable Verges in 4.2 is assigned in the Folio to 'Cowley', the actor who took this part. But nowhere in Shakespeare, unless in *All's Well*, does a single letter denote a particular actor. Also, the letters 'E' and 'G' seem to be used indifferently for First and Second Lord, an intolerable confusion with which editors must cope but with which the book-keeper, whose intervention used to be hypothesised, evidently declined to cope.

Spelling in the Folio text is not notably peculiar, and this might support the hypothesising of a scribe (whether the book-keeper or somebody else), intervening between the manuscript and printed text. Shakespeare's spelling, as represented in the autograph customarily attributed to him (Hand D of the play of *Sir Thomas More*), is certainly peculiar. Final consonants are often doubled, final 'e' is omitted after 'c' ('obedyenc' for 'obedience'), 'straing' does duty for 'strange', and 'how' for 'ho', 'deule' for 'devil', 'on' for 'one'. G. Blakemore Evans in *The Riverside Shakespeare* (1974) found traces of this spelling in the Folio ('on' for 'one' at 2.5.26, 'Angles' for 'angels' at 3.2.118, 'In' for 'E'en' at 3.2.15), and Shakespeare, said Dover Wilson, was consistent in this latter eccentricity, spelling 'England' with an 'I'. By and large, however, the Folio text does not exhibit what are called Shakespearean spellings, and this has prompted some scholars to suppose that a scribe whose spelling was less eccentric than Shakespeare's had made a transcript of the manuscript. Greg, who took this position, also argued paradoxically (in *The Shakespeare First Folio*, 1955) that the supposed transcript was not an improvement but a debasing, and that Jaggard's compositors would have done a better job had they had the manuscript before them. Hunter, for whom the evidence leaves 'little doubt that the copy for the Folio text was Shakespeare's foul papers', is willing to entertain the alternative that copy was furnished by a transcript. Evans follows suit. The alternative seems not worth invoking, however. Inconsistencies in the text are dramatic enough to point away from a scribe or book-keeper, whose labours would have been too servile to accomplish any useful purpose. The E/G designations, though singular, seem explicable only as they indicate an author writing with specific players in mind. And if characteristic Shakespearean spellings do not much survive the compositors, that is not necessarily surprising. As Dover Wilson pointed out, the compositors themselves might have normalised spelling routinely.

The view of most recent scholarship, beginning with R. B. McKerrow in 1935, is that the author's manuscript or 'foul papers' stands behind the Folio. Fredson Bowers defines these 'foul papers' as 'the author's last complete draft in a shape satisfactory to him for transfer to fair copy', and the supposition that they furnished copy for the printer is made more plausible by virtue of the inconsistency which marks the use of speech headings. The hero appears variously as *Ber.*, *Count.* and *Ros.*, while his mother the Countess is *Mo.*, *Cou.*, *Old Cou.* or *La.* The courtier Lafew is introduced as *Laf.*, *Ol. Laf.* and *Ol. Lord*. The interpreter of 4.1 is initially I. *Sol.*, subsequently *Inter*. Though the writer of the play might not be perplexed by these differing descriptions, actors would certainly find them confusing, and presumably the keeper of a prompt-copy would have made it his business to rationalise them all for performance. McKerrow's argument seems conclusive: 'a copy intended for use in the theatre would surely, of necessity, be accurate and unambiguous in the matter of character-names'.

In fact, the text as we have it is characterised by apparent errors and confusions that cannot be ascribed to the compositors and that suggest work in progress, Shakespeare clarifying or more fully realising his fiction in the course of writing. Not only are speech headings subject to change but stage directions are suspiciously permissive, as if the author had not made up his mind or didn't care to. 'Divers' attendants enter at 1.2, and 'divers' lords take leave at 2.1. At 2.3.45 'three or four' lords enter, and at 4.3 'some two or three soldiers'. As 4.1 begins, 'five or six' of these soldiers lie in ambush. A character called Violenta is named in 3.5 but makes no appearance; in any case she has nothing to say. Lafew at 4.5.66 refers to an unnamed intelligencer, and this may be the 'astringer' who enters at 5.1.6 and who (presumably) appears again at 5.3.127. An astringer is a falconer, but why his occupation is specified remains mysterious. In the course of the play, generic characters are particularised. The Widow is named Capilet and the Clown is named Lavatch. The anonymous French lords are displaced by the brothers Dumaine. A person hitherto called Steward is abruptly called Rinaldo. Shakespeare, said H. F. Brooks, 'was finding out, in the course of composition, what to call these characters'.

Loose ends or frayed ends are apparent. Lafew at 2.3.79 ff. seems not to know what is going on, and editors are unsuccessful in explaining away his confusion. Later in the same scene, he is given a son (216), otherwise unknown to the play. The Clown, who ought to leave the stage at 3.2.37, is left on stage but has nothing to do. At 4.3.136–8 we hear of characters called Sebastian, Jacques and Lodowick, familiar to us from other plays of Shakespeare's, and also of one Corambus, the name given to Polonius in the first quarto of *Hamlet*. These names which mean nothing for Shakespeare's play perhaps had some private and occult meaning for Shakespeare, and they seem to bring us close to the writer. The stage direction at 5.3.155 indicates an entrance for Parolles, who is summoned on stage more than 40 lines later. The confusion here and elsewhere suggests an original intention of Shakespeare's, preserved in his foul papers but not carried through.

Here and there, unlikely speech headings which most editors attribute to a compositor's error – as in the assigning of a speech to Bertram at 4.3.99 or to Parolles at 4.3.116 – may quite as tenably represent the author's aborted idea. Working through the text, I take the impression that the copy for the Folio is probably autograph and that its confusions are to be explained largely as authorial inconsistencies or changes of mind. I conclude that Shakespeare's manuscript lies behind the Folio text of the play.

READING LIST

Adams, J. F. '*All's Well That Ends Well*: the paradox of procreation', *SQ* 12 (1961), 261–70

Arthos, J. 'The comedy of generation', *EIC* 5 (1955), 97–117

Barnet, S. (ed.), *All's Well That Ends Well* (Signet Shakespeare), 1965

Bennett, J. W. 'New techniques of comedy in *All's Well That Ends Well*', *SQ* 18 (1967), 337–62

Bergeron, D. 'The mythical structure of *All's Well That Ends Well*', *TSLL* 14 (1972), 559–68

Bradbrook, M. C., *Shakespeare and Elizabethan Poetry*, 1951

Calderwood, J. L. 'The mingled yarn of *All's Well*', *JEGP* 62 (1963), 61–76
    'Styles of knowing in *All's Well*', *MLQ* 25 (1964), 272–94

Cole, H. C. *The 'All's Well' Story from Boccaccio to Shakespeare*, 1981

Donaldson, I. '*All's Well That Ends Well*: Shakespeare's play of endings', *EIC* 27 (1977), 34–55

Friedman, M. D. 'Male bonds and marriage in *All's Well* and *Much Ado*', *SEL* 35 (1995), 231–49
    ' "Service is no heritage": Bertram and the ideology of procreation', *SP* 92 (1995), 80–101

Haley, D. *Shakespeare's Courtly Mirror: Reflexivity and Prudence in All's Well That Ends Well*, 1993

Halio, J. L. '*All's Well That Ends Well*', *SQ* 15 (1964), 33–45

Hapgood, R. 'The life of shame: Parolles and *All's Well That Ends Well*', *EIC* 15 (1965), 269–78

Hodgdon, B. 'The making of virgins and mothers: sexual signs, substitute scenes and doubled presences in *All's Well That Ends Well*', *PQ* 66 (1987), 47–71

Hunter, G. K. (ed.), *All's Well That Ends Well* (Arden Shakespeare), 1959

Hunter, R. G. *Shakespeare and the Comedy of Forgiveness*, 1965

Houston, J. D. 'The function of Parolles', *SQ* 21 (1970), 431–8

King, W. N. 'Shakespeare's "mingled yard" ', *MLQ* 21 (1959), 33–44

Knight, G. W. *The Sovereign Flower*, 1958

Lawrence, W. W. *Shakespeare's Problem Comedies*, 1931

Leech, C. 'The theme of ambition in *All's Well*', *ELH* 21 (1954), 17–29

McCandless, D. *Gender and Performance in Shakespeare's Problem Comedies*, 1997.

Miola, R. S. 'New Comedy in *All's Well That Ends Well*', *RQ* 46 (1993), 23–43

Nagarajan, S. 'The structure of *All's Well That Ends Well*', *EIC* 10 (1960), 24–31

Parker, R. B. 'War and sex in *All's Well That Ends Well*', *S.Sur.* 37 (1984), 99–113

Price, J. G. *The Unfortunate Comedy*, 1968

Ranald, M. L. *Shakespeare and his Social Context*, 1987

Rossiter, A. P. *Angel with Horns*, 1960

Rothman, J. 'A vindication of Parolles', *SQ* 23 (1972), 183–96

Rutter, C. 'Helena's choosing: writing the couplets in a choreography of discontinuity (*All's Well That Ends Well* 2.3)', *EIT* 9 (1991), 121–39

Rutter, C. et al. *Clamorous Voices: Shakespeare's Women Today*, 1989

Salingar, L. *Shakespeare and the Traditions of Comedy*, 1974

Shaw, G. B. *Our Theatres in the Nineties*, I, 1932

Sisson, C. J. 'Shakespeare's Helena and Dr. William Harvey', *E&S* (1960), 1–20

Smallwood, R. L. '*All's Well That Ends Well* at the Royal Shakespeare Theatre', *CQ* 24.1 (1982), 25–51

 'The design of *All's Well That Ends Well*', *S.Sur.* 25 (1972), 45–61

Snyder, S. (ed.), *All's Well That Ends Well* (World's Classics), 1993

Styan, J. B. *Shakespeare in Performance: All's Well That Ends Well*, 1984

Sullivan, G. A. Jr., '"Be this sweet Helen's knell, and now forget her": forgetting, memory, and identity in *All's Well That Ends Well*', *SQ* 50 (1999), 51–69

Tillyard, E. M. W. *Shakespeare's Problem Plays*, 1950

Turner, R. Y. 'Dramatic conventions in *All's Well That Ends Well*', *PMLA* 75 (1960), 497–502

Vickers, B. *The Artistry of Shakespeare's Prose*, 1968

Warren, R. 'Why does it end well? Helena, Bertram, and the sonnets', *S.Sur.* 22 (1969), 79–92

Wheeler, R. P. *Shakespeare's Development and the Problem Comedies: Turn and Counter-Turn*, 1981

Wilson, H. S. 'Dramatic emphasis in *All's Well*', *HLQ* 13 (1949–50), 217–40

Zitner, S. P. *Twayne's [Harvester] New Critical Introductions to Shakespeare: All's Well That Ends Well*, 1989